Delivering Results

The Harvard Business Review Book Series

Delivering Results

A New Mandate for Human Resource Professionals

Edited with an Introduction by
Dave Ulrich

A Harvard Business Review Book

The *Harvard Business Review* articles in this collection are available as individual reprints. Discounts apply to quantity purchases. For information and ordering contact Customer Service, Harvard Business School Publishing, Boston, MA 02163. Telephone: (617) 496-1449, 8 A.M. to 6 P.M. Eastern Time, Monday through Friday. Fax: (617) 496-1029, 24 hours a day. E-mail: custserv@hbsp.harvard.edu.

Library of Congress Cataloging-in-Publication Data

Delivering results : a new mandate for human resource professionals /
    edited with an introduction by Dave Ulrich.
        p.   cm. — (A Harvard business review book)
    Includes bibliographical references and index.
    ISBN 0-87584-869-9 (alk. paper)
    1. Personnel management. I. Ulrich, David, 1953–   .
II. Series: Harvard business review book series.
HF5549.D4362   1998
658.3—dc21   98–26749
                                                                          CIP

The paper used in this publication meets the requirements of the American National Standard for Permanence of Paper for Printed Library Materials Z39.48-1984

Contents

Introduction

Dave Ulrich

This is a great time for those interested in human resources. Human resource issues have become central to business deliberations, surfacing in boardrooms where executives plan and in conference rooms where managers act. Discussions often seek answers to such questions as:

> How do we fight and win the war for talent,[1] both at the leadership level and throughout the firm? How do we invest in and receive a return on intellectual capital equal to or greater than economic capital?
>
> How do we create an organization with speed that adapts, changes, transforms, and reduces cycle time?
>
> How do we facilitate learning by both the individual and the organization?
>
> How do we create value as measured in the short term by investor and cash results and in the longer term by customer and employee value?
>
> How do we create a new culture that affects both employee and customer relationship?
>
> How do we profitably grow our business? How do we make sure that our aspirations lead to actions that create results?

In many ways, these are not new questions. Business leaders have always been challenged by them. The difference today lies in the approach taken to answer them: Increasingly, the spotlight is falling on human resource issues. To answer these questions, line managers and HR professionals must rethink and redefine human resources.

1

HR professionals have responded to this increased scrutiny with a major shift in thinking from their previous focus on *doables* to a new, more proactive focus on *deliverables*. Doables focus on improving HR practices, upgrading HR professionals, and reengineering HR departments. Doables emphasize actions, activities, and what happens. Deliverables refocus attention on outcomes, results, and value created from doing HR work. Traditional HR textbooks have been structured using the doables concept, with chapter headings such as staffing, training, compensation, teams, labor relations, and communications. These chapters summarize HR theory and action in the practice domain. Future HR textbooks will likely be organized around deliverables, with chapter headings such as intellectual capital, speed, cycle time, learning, value creation, growth, and culture. These chapters will focus on the results of doing HR practices.

While few disagree that HR practices, professionals, and departments should refocus on deliverables or results, discussions have just begun as to what constitutes HR results. Emerging questions for HR include the following:

- What are HR results?
- What capabilities may be defined as HR results?
- How does a results focus shift HR responsibility, practices, departments, and professionals?

This anthology provides readers with a clear point of view on HR results and offers specific definitions and examples of those results.

What Are HR Results?

Traditionally, HR results translate into HR "activities." Activities represent what people and organizations do. The president of a bank recently honored the bank's HR department for bringing more than 1,000 new employees on board during the previous year. Another HR department proudly announced that 90% of the managers in their firm had attended 40 hours of training in the preceding year. Another HR department rolled out an extensive communication program, measuring its success by the number of employees attending the communication sessions and by the quality of the videos produced.

In each of these cases, and in many others, HR results have been defined in terms of HR activities. This approach is seductive because activities are easy to observe and count. As an assessment of HR effectiveness, however, they are incomplete: Knowing *what* HR people do is not enough. Other professions measure results using accomplishments, not activities. Lawyers assess their performance more by whether they win their cases than by the number of words they use in their closing arguments; physicians assess success more by noting patients' improved health than by the number of office visits; pilots worry more about safety and on-time arrivals than about getting along with the crew.

For HR to become a profession, it must develop a deliverables focus that complements, not replaces, its traditional activity measures. Results alone are insufficient measures of effectiveness because the methods by which those results have been achieved also matter. Lawyers who place winning above consideration of financial or emotional cost to their clients may lose credibility with clients, peers, and judges and, over time, jeopardize their ability to solicit new business. A physician, however brilliant, with a too acrid bedside manner may find that patients quickly desert for other equally qualified but warmer physicians. HR professionals, too, must consider their activities as well as their results. The problem with the traditional approach has been its too exclusive focus on activities and the consequent neglect of results.

Typologies of what constitutes HR work that have emerged in the HR literature over the last few decades illustrate the effect of this imbalance. In the early 1980s, theories about HR work clustered its efforts into four categories: staffing, development, appraisal, and rewards.[2] This framework, as extended in the late 1980s and early 1990s, later included organization design and communication.[3] More recently, HR practices have been organized into nineteen categories.[4] These typologies, while becoming increasingly encompassing and elegant, continue to focus on activities more than on outcomes. Two parameters may be introduced to redistribute attention and accountability of HR professionals to results: firm performance and HR capabilities. Each defines the outcomes of HR activities.

HR RESULTS AS FIRM PERFORMANCE

To clarify HR results requires attention on what follows from investments in HR activity. The interest in quantifying the impact of HR practices on financial performance has led to a number of studies linking HR practices to specific firm outcomes. Turnover, for example, has been linked to job security, union presence, compensation, culture, and demographics.[5] Productivity has been linked to such HR practices as "transformational" labor relations (those emphasizing cooperation), quality of work life programs, quality circles, practices in training and recruiting, and incentive compensation systems.[6] Investments in various HR practices such as training,[7] selection and staffing,[8] appraisals,[9] and compensation,[10] have been linked to firm financial performance.

Other studies have focused on HR practices and financial performance in specific industries. Studies have shown relationships between progressive HR practices and firm performance in manufacturing, cooperative and innovative HR practices and organizational productivity in steel plants,[11] and bundles of integrated HR practices and higher productivity and quality in automotive plants.[12]

While this burgeoning research has demonstrated relationships between HR practices and firm results, the bulk of it looks only at individual HR practices or individual industries. Two more recent major studies have advanced the rigor of thought about links between HR and business results. The first, by the Society for Human Resource Management (SHRM) and CCH Incorporated,[13] under the direction of Dr. Cheri Ostroff, associate professor at the University of Minnesota's Industrial Relations Center, evaluated the financial impact of HR practices, based on data from 260 firms. The second such comprehensive study, undertaken by Mark Huselid, a professor at Rutgers University, used data he collected on 968 firms. Both studies demonstrated a clear linkage between HR and business performance.

The SHRM/CCH study correlated the quality of HR to four financial measures: market/book value (market value of the firm based on its stock price divided by those assets representing "value added" by management), productivity (dollar value of sales divided by number of employees), market value (stock price × outstanding shares), and sales. Analysis of the data on participating firms showed that all four financial measures increased dramatically with the quality of HR practices. A good fit between a firm's HR practices and its business strategy enhanced chances of success, proving that internal alignment of business strategy, HR practices, and management philosophy contribute to business results.

Huselid's study looked at the extent to which a given firm engaged in "high performance work practices," defined in terms of the firm's policies and procedures for employee selection, appraisal, and compensation; job design; handling grievances and labor-management relations; and information sharing, attitude assessment, training, and promotion.[14] Huselid examined the impact of higher work performance practices on three organizational performance measures: turnover, productivity, and financial results. For each he found a positive relation. For turnover, one standard deviation increase in work performance reduced turnover 7.05% on a per employee basis; for productivity, each standard deviation equaled a 16% increase in productivity (measured by sales per employee), or, in raw numbers, $27,044 sales per employee based on the $171,099 average sales per employee in the sample; for financial performance, one standard deviation increase yielded $27,044 in sales, $18,641 in market value, and $3,814 in profits.

These studies demonstrate a relationship between HR investment and business financial results. The questions of why this relationship exists and how it operates, however, remain unanswered. Unless and until the path or intermediate steps linking these two factors can be traced, such research may be more academic than useful.

HR RESULTS AS CAPABILITIES

An emerging view from the HR discipline itself and from the perspective of other disciplines has begun to reveal why and how HR practices affect firm performance.

In the strategy field, work traditionally falls into two parts: strategy formulation and strategy implementation. Strategy formulation focuses on positioning the firm in the market using competitive analysis, SWOT (*strengths, weaknesses, opportunities, treats*), five forces, or other analytic tools. Strategy implementation focuses on management and organizational actions, such as structure (for example, structure follows strategy) or systems analysis (for example, the 7-S McKinsey model). More recently, however, strategy theorists have sought a middle ground between formulation and implementation.

Theorists in other disciplines, as well, have been attempting to define a middle ground between strategy and action. Some, taking a quality perspective, focus on "processes" and the work needed to reengineer those processes. Others, viewing the issue from an organization development or change perspective, have termed the middle ground *culture*. Finally, those with an HR orientation have traditionally focused on high performing organizations or work teams.

Current definitions of the middle ground between strategy and ac-

Exhibit 1   Clarification of Competence or Capability

		Level of Analysis	
		Individual	Organizational
Organizational Perspective	Technical	1 Functional or technical competencies, such as individual abilities in finance, engineering, marketing, customer service, etc.	3 Core competence, such as organizational abilities in logistics, risk management, distribution, manufacturing, etc.
	Social/Cultural	2 Social competencies, such as individual leadership abilities in setting direction (vision, customer), mobilizing individual commitment (diversity), leveraging organizations (teamwork, change), personal credibility, etc.	4 Organizational capability, such as organizational abilities in speed, cycle time, leveraging intellectual capital, working across boundaries, etc.

tion remain somewhat murky. While most analysts agree on the existence of a middle ground between strategy and results or between HR investments and results, varying terms and frameworks help define this concept. The wide range of literatures and thinking on the middle ground indicates its pervasiveness and importance.

One way to bring clarity to the concept of the middle ground appears in Exhibit 1. This figure illustrates how organizational conceptions can proceed from a technical or a social perspective. Technical approaches emphasize functional orientation. Microsoft, Boeing, and Starbucks, for example, differ in their technical requirements: Microsoft must master computer science, Boeing must master aerospace physics, and Starbucks must master distribution and logistics. For each, a social dimension requires coping with how people and groups connect and collaborate. Thus, although Microsoft, Boeing, and Starbucks differ in their technology requirements, they may have similar or dissimilar social requirements.

As Exhibit 1 shows, social and technical perspectives apply at the individual as well as the organizational level. Individuals need certain technical or functional competencies to help their organizations meet business needs: Based on the functional requirements for employees hired, Boeing recruits differently than does Starbucks. Individuals in an organization also need social competencies, the ability to set direction, mobilize individual commitment, engender organizational capability, and demonstrate personal credibility.

Likewise, organizations can have technical know-how, an insight that gave rise to the original core competence argument, advanced by C.K. Prahalad and Gary Hamel in "The Core Competence of the Corporation." They show how technical competence enabled Honda, NEC, and other firms to build the technology platforms required by their businesses. Organizations may have social know-how as well, generally termed *organizational capability*.[15]

Organizational capabilities represent the missing link between strategy and action. Organizations, as distinct from the people who run them, may be said to possess capabilities if those capabilities meet the following criteria:

- Offer integration: Capabilities are not a matter of individual competence or management systems, but organizationally based.
- Add value to customers: Capabilities are defined by those outside the firm as important.
- Maintain continuity: Capabilities remain stable over time.
- Offer uniqueness: Capabilities cannot easily be copied by competitors.
- Engage employee commitment: Capabilities create meaning for employees.
- Establish identity: Capabilities delineate the organization's identity in the minds of customers, employees, and investors.

Capabilities represent the skills, abilities, and expertise of the organization. They describe what organizations can do and how they do it. They constitute collections of individual competencies transformed into organizational capabilities. By encapsulating the organization's identity, they complement its technical, core competencies. Capabilities represent the organization's ability to use resources, to get things done, and to reach goals.

Many theorists have seized on the organizational capabilities concept as a way to redefine the nature of organizations. George Stalk Jr., Philip Evans, and Lawrence E. Shulman examine this approach in "Competing on Capabilities: The New Rules of Corporate Strategy." HR practices integrate or bundle to form capabilities that help organizations succeed, and successful organizations are often imbued with

Exhibit 2   Strategy/Capability/Organization Assessment

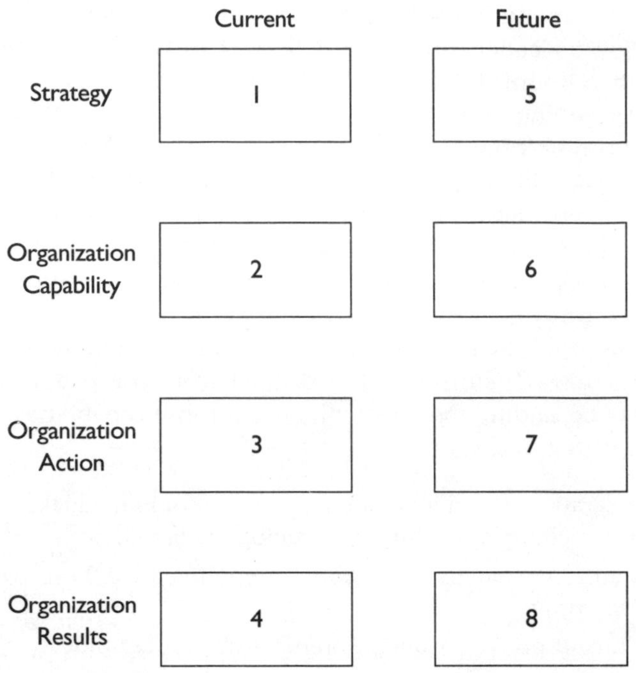

	Current	Future
Strategy	1	5
Organization Capability	2	6
Organization Action	3	7
Organization Results	4	8

and known for the capabilities they possess. Michael E. Porter's essay, "What Is Strategy?," provides an example of this process in action. Southwest Airlines has established the capabilities of productivity as they keep aircraft in the air by rapidly turning them around at the gate and a positive work environment as they encourage employees to be creative and have fun on their jobs. Additional work needs to be done, however, to uncover fully the operation of capabilities and to define them conclusively as the soul or core of an organization.

Following this logic, capabilities become HR results, filling the middle ground between HR investments and firm performance. They serve as the transition from mission, vision, strategies, and values to action, a process we can analyze using Exhibit 2. As leaders shift their organizations' strategies (moving from cell 1 to cell 5), they create visions, strategies, and missions that depict how to win in the future. Often, however, two mistakes are made once a future strategy represented by cell 5 is defined.

The first mistake leaders may make is to try to implement a new strategy with the old capabilities (cell 2) and actions (cell 3). When the Southern Company invested heavily in China by purchasing CEPA, for example, its leaders quickly learned that they had to manage their Chinese investment differently than they had their traditional utility investment in the southeastern United States: The capabilities required to win in China were substantially different. Chinese success depended on building and maintaining relationships of trust with key decision-makers and on adapting quickly to local markets; success in U.S. markets, in contrast, depended more on reducing cost and gaining economies of scale. As Southern's leaders recognized the required capabilities, they invested in new management actions (cell 7) to instill these capabilities within the company; these included partnering with local agencies to attract employees knowledgeable about the Chinese markets, holding training sessions to study doing business in China, and undertaking extensive communications programs to inform all Southern employees about the new organizational capabilities required to succeed in China.

The second common mistake among leaders attempting to implement a new strategy (cell 5) is investing in the latest management fads and initiatives (cell 7). Research by Mark Huselid and Brian Becker has shown that disconnected management actions do not lead to positive organization performance. When one set of competencies are used for staffing decisions, another for training, and another for compensation, for example, employees become more confused than focused, and organizational results languish. Huselid and Becker recommend bundling management actions so that congruent and aligned decision making occurs.[16] The integrated bundles of management actions represent the capabilities a firm needs to succeed.

HR professionals have the challenge and obligation of turning future strategies (cell 5) into future capabilities (cell 6) into future management actions (cell 7) to achieve organization results (cell 8). They do so by identifying the capabilities necessary to turn strategy into action.

Capabilities become HR results. Rather than measure the number of people hired, HR should assess the quality of those hires: How well do they help the organization innovate, change, and deliver other capabilities? Rather than measure training activity, HR should focus on the outcomes of training, such as speed to market, customer intimacy, or the level of knowledge of the work force. Rather than track the percent of employees on variable pay programs, HR should measure the productivity that results from those investments.

What Capabilities May Be Defined As HR Results?

If capabilities represent results from HR work, HR professionals must clarify which capabilities matter most. This anthology defines three critical generic capabilities as results of HR work: creating strategic clarity, making change happen, and creating intellectual capital. While these clearly are not the *only* capabilities that derive from HR work, they are indicative of HR results and delineate essential roles for HR professionals.

CREATING STRATEGIC CLARITY: BE A STRATEGIC PARTNER

An organization displays the capability of strategic clarity when its strategy focuses on both short- and long-term goals, creates meaning for those both inside and outside the company, translates into effective organizational practices, shapes employee behaviors, and differentiates the firm to customers and investors.

Successful firms possess the capability to create long- and short-term strategic clarity. Long-term strategies shape a vision through which companies are built to last. Research by James C. Collins and Jerry I. Porras, outlined in "Building Your Company's Vision," suggests that an effective long-term vision includes both ideology (vision combined with purpose) and an envisioned future defined as Big, Hairy, Audacious Goals (BHAGs). Executives who can create and inculcate these elements into their organizations will achieve more lasting structures and results. Christopher A. Bartlett and Sumantra Ghoshal, in "Changing the Role of Top Management: Beyond Strategy to Purpose," also stress purpose, which in their formulation represents an organization's identity, that is, what it stands for, which commits, engages, and motivates employees. Porter, in "What Is Strategy?" looks at short-term strategies, defining them in terms of fit among activity systems.

Firms with strategic clarity display focus; they have defined resource allocation processes that they use effectively; and they possess vision. Such firms also have strategic unity:[17] They engage employees and customers in both the end (the purpose) and the means (the processes) of work done by the firm. Strategic clarity may be tested by asking groups of employees to identify what the firm wants to be known for by its best customers. When answers to this question are similar, firms have strategic clarity.

HR professionals acting as strategic partners play a major role in creating strategic unity. As strategic partners, they design HR practices that can and should be used to both create and implement strategic clarity. Employees should be hired who embody the values and purposes of the firm; pay systems should be created that drive employee behaviors consistent with the strategy; training and development experiences should provide skills for delivering strategy; and governance systems (including, for example, team structures and decision-making processes) should ensure accountability for strategy. HR professionals as strategic partners serve as informed observers of how much clarity exists around a given strategy. Through their multiple contact points with employees (for example, in training courses, job interviews, employee surveys, and exit interviews), they collect current impressions and data on employees' perceptions about the firms' strategy. This information, regularly conveyed to the appropriate executives, provides guidance on how better to communicate the vision and make it real for employees.

To play the strategic partner role effectively, HR professionals must master the theory and practice of forming and implementing strategy. They must be able to engage managers in discussions of vision, values, purpose, and intent. They must help to define fit between organizational activities. They must understand who forms strategy, what form strategy statements should take, and how to turn strategy into action for both the organization and its employees.

MAKING CHANGE HAPPEN: BE A CHANGE AGENT

The environment for most organizations is unpredictable, uncontrollable, and unforeseeable. Rather than spend enormous amounts of resources creating strategies which may or may not succeed in such uncertain settings, organizations succeed by having the capacity to change quickly. Organizations with this capacity exhibit speed, agility, flexibility, and reduced cycle time. Both losers and winners will face uncertain futures. While losers form expensive and time-consuming task forces to study change, winners will have already adapted. Organizations act with varying degrees of speed. Some organizations, faced with uncertainty, become rigid and inflexible and resist change; others have a built-in capacity to shift, move, and adapt to keep on top of changing conditions.

Almost all firms find the capacity to make change happen to be a significant capability. They build it, however, in various ways. Richard Pascale and his colleagues note in "Changing the Way We Change," how organizations can begin to act with agility. His work lays out the ways in which Shell and the U.S. Army managed to move quickly by learning from their mistakes and by engaging all employees. In "Breaking the Functional Mind-Set in Process Organizations," Ann Majchrzak and Qianwei Wang cite reduction of cycle time and improvements to processes and show how, particularly in the U.S. Electronics industry, working across functional boundaries can be critical to making change happen. Harold Sirkin and George Stalk in "Fix the Process, Not the Problem" use a paper company to demonstrate how change can be made to happen through improved processes. Chris Argyris, in "Good Communication that Blocks Learning," points out the relationship between learning and change. Organizations that learn from change sustain change more productively than do organizations that make change an event. His work also shows that individual learning accumulates into organizational learning. Anthony J. Rucci, Steven P. Kirn, and Richard T. Quinn, in "The Employee-Customer-Profit Chain at Sears" offer an exceptional case study on Sears' transformation that brings together all of the change themes: the importance of agility, working across functional mindsets, improving processes, and focusing attention at the front-line employee through targeted communications.

Firms that undertake these practices have the capacity to make change happen. In a competitive world where speed replaces strategy, where reduced cycle time leads to customer commitment, and where agility increases market share; making change happen becomes a major part of business success.

Collectively, these essays lay out the minimum that HR professionals need to know to be effective change agents. HR professionals play four roles as change agents. First, HR professionals architect change by having a model, or theory, of change. A theory of change helps the HR professional know where to start, how to leverage the change, and how to turn events into patterns of behaviors. Second, HR professionals facilitate the change process by involving the right people at the right time. To do this, they must learn how to involve key decision-makers in a change project, how to run and to learn from experiments, and how to string together the events that will sustain a change. Third, HR professionals redesign HR systems to be congruent with change. Functions such as communications, training, hiring, and pay systems must be based on a total performance index with standards useful to and recognized by employees, customers, and investors. Finally, in their fourth aspect as change agents, HR professionals must first model in their departments and functions the practices they recommend to others: If an organization needs to decrease cycle time, the HR department, too, must reduce its cycle time for designing and delivering training, staffing, and compensation programs. Modeling what is preached becomes an important role for HR professionals as change agents.

Successful HR professionals help create organizations that act with speed. These leaders manage for the future, express discomfort with the status quo, act without complete knowledge, sense customers' future expectations, communicate directly with employees, and use their personal credibility to make change happen.[18]

CREATING INTELLECTUAL CAPITAL: ## BE AN EMPLOYEE CHAMPION

Every manager recognizes that intellectual capital matters. The challenge lies in figuring out what it is and how to increase it. Excellent new work on intellectual capital examines the concept in simple, measurable, and useful ways.[19] Much of this work can be synthesized in the following definition: intellectual capital = competence × commitment.[20]

This equation suggests that, within a given unit, overall employee competence may rise but that competence alone does not secure the unit's intellectual capital. Firms with high competence but low commitment may have talented employees who can't get things done. Firms with high commitment but low competence have dumb employees who get things done quickly. Both are dangerous. Intellectual capital requires both competence and commitment. Because the equation is a "×" not a "+," a low score on either competence or commitment significantly reduces overall intellectual capital.

Competence and commitment may be assessed at the firm, unit, or individual level. A restaurant chain with multiple establishments, for example, may measure the intellectual capital of each, using as measures the average skill level of employees (competence) times the average rate of employee retention (commitment). This intellectual capital index could reliably predict other positive outcomes at each restaurant, for example, customer loyalty, productivity, and profitability. An individual employee may document growth in intellectual capital by assessing increases in knowledge, skill, or abilities within a set time frame and by evaluating commitment to the goals and purposes of the organization. Such personal assessments may then be accumulated into a collective assessment of the intellectual capital within a unit.

James Brian Quinn, Philip Anderson, and Sydney Finkelstein, in "Managing Professional Intellect: Making the Most of the Best," define *professional intellect* as the cognitive knowledge, advanced skills, systems understanding, and self-motivated creativity that exists among key individuals in the firm. Developing, leveraging, and governing this intellect becomes a primary challenge for managers. Firms with the greatest ability to secure intellectual capital will be more productive as well as able to change, meet customer expectations, and be competitive than will rival firms.

THEORY AND TOOLS FOR COMPETENCE BUILDING.   Of the two aspects of intellectual capital, competence and commitment, more work has been done on developing tools for building competence. The five basic tools for increasing competence within a unit (whether a firm, site, business, or plant) are *buy, build, borrow, bounce,* and *bind.* Appropriately using all five tools ensures a more stable flow of competence.

Buy means managers go outside the unit to replace current talent with talent of higher quality. Buying new talent brings in new ideas, breaks old cultural roadblocks, and creates intellectual capital by shaking up the firm. A buy strategy works when available talent is available and accessible. The buy strategy carries risks. If external talent is not clearly better or more qualified than internal talent, long-time employees may be alienated, coming to resent management carpetbaggers who haven't paid their dues. Buy also risks integrating diverse talent into a smoothly functioning, knowledgeable team. In operations requiring teamwork, an investment in free agents may not win the championship.

Build means managers invest in finding new ways to think about and do work. Some such learning occurs in formal training programs and centers; but much more occurs in structured on-the-job development experiences. In either case, managers build intellectual capital by investing in employee learning that couples inquiry with action, that replaces old ideas with new, and that changes behaviors. The risk of a build strategy lies in spending enormous amounts of money and time on training that becomes an end in itself and fails to build the intellectual capital that creates business value.

Borrow means managers invest in outside vendors who bring ideas, frameworks, and tools to make the organization stronger, such as partners, consultants, or alliances. Using external help requires adapting, not adopting ideas, because each firm applies new concepts differently. It also requires transferring the outside knowledge inside, so that the vendor essentially works him or herself out of a job. It requires clients themselves who unravel the processes and tools offered by vendors so that they can be replicated, deployed, and incorporated internally. Risks of borrowing include unproductive expense of capital and time with little return, dependence on a consultant without knowledge transfer into the firm, and answers from another setting without appropriate adaptation. Appropriately used, however, borrowing competence can be a viable way to secure intellectual capital.

Bounce requires managers to remove individuals who fail to perform up to standards. Sometimes, this means that individuals who were qualified may have failed to keep up with skills required for current work practices. Other times, this means removing individuals who may be incapable of changing, learning, and adapting. This requires management courage so that difficult personnel decisions are made with decisiveness. It requires clear standards so that those who stay and those who leave know why and what is expected of them. It requires a fair and equitable process so that legal requirements are met. The practice of Bouncing comes with many risks: being seen as a panacea, losing the wrong individuals, demoralizing those who stay, making difficult personnel decisions based on perceptions not facts, and reducing management credibility.

Bind means retaining employees at all levels who are critical to the firm's success. A national bank's organization effectiveness unit risked losing a talented colleague because of a spouse career transition. Rather than lose this talent, the bank chose to let this OE consultant commute from out of state, working a fixed number of days at headquarters or in other bank operations. Deals were cut on salary, travel, benefits, and other items to make this a flexible, win/win arrangement. Binding works on the theory of customizing employee contracts, where maximum flexibility exists as a way to retain critical employees. Flexibility may be around compensation, benefits, work hours, work location, work projects, career expectations, or job duties—on anything, that is, that might make or keep a job attractive enough to hold a talented employee. Flexibility can exist only where clear outputs and standards exist and measures focus on the end more than on the means.

All managers use some version of one or more of the buy, build, borrow, bounce, or bind techniques for increasing competence. The more of them they use, and the greater the degree of integration, the greater and more lasting the effect on the organizations' level of competence, one of the two essential aspects of intellectual capital.

THEORY AND TOOLS FOR COMMITMENT.   One of the most serious mistakes managers make when seeking to increase intellectual capital is to focus only on competence. Having more competent employees who are not committed to doing good work is like trying to win a team sport with an all-star team. However talented the individual players, firm success derives from teamwork, from commitment and adherence to a commonly held goal and standard.

Securing employees' commitment involves engaging their emotional energy and attention. Commitment is reflected in how employees relate to each other and feel about the firm. In many cases, the competitive pressures firms place on employees reduce rather than build commitment. Firms today continually increase their demands on employees: Employees are asked to be more global, more responsive to customers, more flexible, more learning-oriented, more team driven, more productive, and so on. These very real competitive demands require increasing commitment from employees, who are being asked to give their emotional, intellectual, and physical energy to ensure firm success.

Unfortunately, many managers do not deal effectively with these increased demands on their employees. They continue to layer expectations and stretch goals on employees, creating not commitment but stress and burnout.

To replace burnout with commitment, HR professionals need to learn to share information. John Case, in "Opening the Books," discusses sharing information with all employees as a means of engendering not only an understanding of company identity and goals but the commitment required to make company goals personal. Dorothy Leonard and Susaan Straus suggest in "Putting Your Company's Whole Brain to Work" that managers do just that by incorporating different learning styles and approaches into an organization and by managing conflict in ways that allow everyone to feel involved. Robert H. Waterman, Judith A. Waterman, and Betsy A. Collard, writing in "Toward a Career-Resilient Workforce," discuss the new psychological contract between firms and employees, a contract based on employability rather than security and on the firm's commitment to create opportunities for employees to deploy skills.

HR professionals who increase competence and commitment build intellectual capital. By so doing, they become employee champions who are concerned about how employees' needs can be met by their company. These HR professionals strive to craft the practices for competence to assure the right mix of employees within a firm, they invest in HR practices for improving commitment, and they are sensitive to the ways in which organizational policies and practices help or hinder employee growth. When they find that a practice blocks employees from building either competence or commitment, they challenge and change it.

How Does a Results Focus Shift HR Responsibility, Practices, Departments, and Professionals?

HR RESPONSIBILITY

If capabilities such as strategic clarity, making change happen, and intellectual capital result from HR work, then responsibility for HR results shifts to line managers. Line managers bear ultimate responsibility for HR work, just as they must answer for finance, marketing, technology, and strategy. When HR professionals add value, however, the distinction between line and staff blurs. HR professionals who understand business and how HR issues create value act in ways that complement rather than compete with the roles of line managers. HR professionals with data, skills, and credibility do more than advise: They actually take positions and act to get business results. HR with a business and results attitude threatens only weak managers; capable managers endorse and even seek out strong staff to work *with* not *for* them to make things happen.

This results focus creates common measures of success for line managers and HR professionals. One senior HR executive, for example, has said that he would never draft another "HR Plan" because his HR initiatives were business initiatives, or he was focusing HR on the wrong things. He knew that once the operating committee had identified the capabilities necessary for success, his job was to bring about those capabilities. Just as line managers had the responsibility to deliver capabilities, so did he. This executive's comments and conclusions were right on target: When HR results focus on capabilities, line and HR share responsibility.

EMERGING HR PRACTICES

An HR results focus shifts HR work in two ways. First, HR begins to concentrate on diagnosing and assessing capabilities (cell 6 in Figure 2). This anthology presents three illustrative capabilities: strategic clarity, making change happen, and building intellectual capital. Other capabilities might include quality, customer relations, innovation, fast decision-making, accountability, learning, or building relationships. HR professionals should help their executive clients translate strategies into capabilities.[21]

Second, an HR results focus may lead to new HR practices. HR practices represent organizational processes and investments made in HR. They have evolved over the last 40 years, each decade bringing HR a new set of tools: labor relations and staffing in the 1940s; training in the 1950s; regulatory issues, compensation, benefits, and appraisal in the 1960s and 1970s; health care, cost containment, organization design, teamwork, and communication in the 1980s; and mergers, acquisitions, downsizing, and diversity in the 1990s. New HR tools will continue to develop as concern arises over such things as global HR (learning to manage HR issues to meet global competition), culture change (defining tools for crafting and changing a corporate culture), technology (adapting HR to the ever-changing information highway), leadership qualities of the future (defining the competencies required of the leader of the future, not the past), and knowledge transfer (understanding how to generate and generalize knowledge).

HR professionals in the next decade will be as informed and precise when discussing culture change as they now can be discussing successful training programs or hiring strategies. Since it is easier and more exciting to learn than to forget, mastering these new tools will require that old HR tools be more automated, done by others, and/or be discontinued.

EMERGING HR DEPARTMENTS

As HR departments focus on results, their structure and governance will change. Some theorists argue that HR should rediscover its past by dealing with employee unrest, unions, firm values, and administrative processes. Others argue that HR should become an elite strategic corps of business partners who create globally competitive organizations. Others argue that HR departments should disappear and their functions be outsourced. Other debate continues over naming the HR department—human relations, human resources, employee resources, or organizational capability.

Results-based HR departments have begun to automate transactional work and to innovate transformational work. Technology gradually replaces the bureaucratic and time-consuming paperwork found in traditional HR. Most standard, routine, and repetitive HR tasks (cutting pay checks, for example) have been automated. HR work requiring innovation and creativity, on the other hand, such as devising ways to attract and motivate Generation X employees, who may have different mental models of firm loyalty and commitment, consumes increasing amounts of HR time through involvement in task forces and project teams.

The HR community must expand. The present configuration of the HR community generally includes corporate, field, service center, and center of expertise HR professions—all of whom are within the HR function. In the future, HR will not just be provided by those within the HR function; the HR community will also include line managers, other staff managers, and strategic partnerships with outside vendors. Early outposts of HR communities exist today: General Electric uses line managers to teach executive programs; Fidelity teams finance and HR professionals to offer services to business units; and many firms have outsourced routine administrative and transaction HR work. The ultimate challenge facing HR as a community rather than as a function is the need to articulate the value added by each community member.

Traditionally, HR functions have been measured using a headcount of HR personnel per total employee population. These ratios have been popular as indices of the tightening of HR functions, with departments working to reduce ratios from 1:50 to 1:75 and even to 1:300+ in some cases. Clearly, HR functional accountability merits attention. Just as clearly, such generic indicators as HR to total employee headcount fail to fully define value created by HR; they focus internally on how HR spends resources not externally on how HR generates value by delivering capabilities.

EMERGING HR PROFESSIONALS

Just as a results focus changes HR responsibilities, practices, and departments, it also changes the competencies required of HR professionals. As HR comes increasingly to be recognized as a profession, with a body of knowledge, standards, and distinct competencies, various researchers, working collectively have generated numerous conclusions about what makes a good HR professional. I have synthesized these findings into the following list of five essential competencies based on our research at Michigan.[22]

- *Know the business.* Finance, strategy, marketing, technology, operations, service, and other business functions must become more than issues where HR professionals can glaze over in briefings. HR professionals must understand each functional area well enough to propose and debate the merits of an array of solutions to any issues or problems that arise. Knowing the business is the ticket of admission for HR professionals seeking to enter into business discussions.
- *Master HR practices.* HR practices increasingly rely on theory tested through research. HR professionals must draw on this information to make informed choices. Separating the wheat from the chaff in HR practices enables HR professionals to recommend and make wise investments in HR programs and initiatives.
- *Manage change processes.* HR professionals must learn how to make things happen. They must be able to design a change process for both HR initiatives (for example, implementation of a pay-for-performance program) and business initiatives (for example, implementation of an innovation strategy). Acting as catalyst for and architect of change enables HR professionals to deliver value as promises and hopes become realities and results.
- *Create cultures and workplaces that build individual capability and organizational commitment.* HR professionals must design organizations that ensure sustained capability and that grow intellectual capital. HR professionals are the guardians of old cultures and the craftsmen of new ones. They protect and nurture talent. Only through establishment and sustenance of a coherent culture can events turn into sustained patterns.

• *Demonstrate personal credibility.* HR professionals must be trustworthy. They embody the values of their organization and achieve credibility through their relationships of trust with key players. Personal credibility constitutes the relationship equity that allows HR professionals to make and follow through on tough decisions.

Having identified these competencies as basic requirements for HR professionals, it's about time HR professionals begin consistently demonstrating them. It's about time that entry-level screening for HR candidates attain the same level of rigor applied to other professions. No one would allow an attorney in court or a surgeon in the operating room without certification. Why let HR professionals make significant and life-changing decisions without ensuring that they are competent and prepared to make the right decisions. It's about time, too, that the rewards for HR professionals be based on standards of competence. Finally, it's about time to link promotions to senior HR positions to demonstrated competence.

Competence alone, however, does not guarantee professional status. Professionals must use their competencies to act boldly, decisively, and independently. Competent attorneys may at times act brashly in defense of their clients; talented surgeons do not mince words about what to do in an operation; airline pilots do not ask for team consensus when the plane is in trouble. Competence gives professionals license to act, but being a real professional requires acting with conviction.

The next step for HR professionals is to have "an attitude." HR professionals with an attitude comes when knowledge turns into action, when HR professionals have the mettle to challenge managers on uneducated choices.[23] HR professionals with an attitude make informed decisions about how to invest in HR practices to assure business results. HR professionals with an attitude act with confidence and a swagger with their peers, both HR and line managers. Such professionals know that they offer something of value. HR with an attitude but without competence is mere bravado. But attitude combined with competence makes an HR practitioner a full professional.

HR with an attitude implies confidence, not arrogance; decisiveness, not equivocality; risk-taking and action-oriented, not permission-seeking and glad-handing. An attitude follows mastery of the competencies required of HR professionals. HR professionals who demonstrate competence by acting with an attitude instill confidence in others.

Throughout the HR profession, increasing numbers of HR professionals have mastered competence and now possess the right to "an attitude." Because their actions follow theory, not instinct or whim, these HR professionals know why programs and practices they have instituted succeed or fail. They build relationships on trust because their clients respect their informed opinions. Other professionals have confidence in their recommendations because the underlying ideas are supported by research. These HR professionals deliver results and fulfill the new mandate for HR professionals.

Notes

1. The term *war for talent* is the title of a year-long study in 1988 sponsored by McKinsey Consulting Firm about large firms' next generation of leaders.

2. See M. A. Devanna, C. J. Fombrun, and N. M. Tichy, "Human Resource Management: A Strategic Perspective," *Organizational Dynamics* (Winter, 1981): 51–64; and M. A. Devanna, C. J. Fombrun, and N. M. Tichy, "A Framework for Strategic Human Resource Management," in *Strategic Human Resource Management*, ed. C. J. Fombrun, N. M. Tichy, and M. A. Devanna (New York: Wiley, 1984, 33–51.

3. See Dave Ulrich and Dale Lake, *Organizational Capability: Competing from the Inside Out* (New York: Wiley, 1990).

4. See J. Delaney and M. Huselid, "The Impact of Human Resource Practices on Perceptions of Organizational Performance," *Academy of Management Journal* 39 (1996): 949–969; Mark A. Huselid, "The Impact of Human Resource Management Practices on Turnover, Productivity, and Corporate Financial Performance," *Academy of Management Journal* 38, no. 3 (1995): 635–672; and S. Jackson and R. Schuler, "Understanding Human Resource Management in the Context of Organizations and Their Environments," *Annual Review of Psychology* 46 (1995): 237–264.

5. Studies of turnover have been summarized by Mark A. Huselid, "The Impact of Human Resource Management Practices on Turnover, Productivity, and Corporate Financial Performance," *Academy of Management Journal* 38, no. 3 (1995): 635–672.

    Specific turnover studies include those by H. J. Arnold and D. C. Feldman, "A Multivariate Analysis of the Determinants of Turnover," *Journal of Applied Psychology* 67 (1982): 350–360, B. D.

Baysinger and W. H. Mobley, "Employee Turnover: Individual and Organizational Analysis," in *Research in Personnel and Human Resource Management*, vol. 1, ed. K. W. Rowland and G. R. Ferris, (Greenwich, CT: JAI Press, 1983), 269–319; J. L. Cotton and J. M. Tuttle, "Employee Turnover: A Meta-Analysis and Review with Implications for Research," *Academy of Management Review* 11 (1986): 55–70; and J. E. Sheridan, "Organizational Culture and Employee Retention," *Academy of Management Review* 35 (1992): 1036–1056.

6. The summary of productivity research can be found in Mark A. Huselid, "The Impact of Human Resource Management Practices on Turnover, Productivity, and Corporate Financial Performance," *Academy of Management Journal* 38 (1995): 635–672. Specific research appears in J. Cutcher-Gershenfeld, "The Impact on Economic Performance of a (1991) Transformation in Labor Relations," *Industrial and Labor Relations Review* 44 (1991): 241–260; H. C. Katz, T. A. Kochan, and J. Keefe, *Industrial Relations and Productivity in the U.S. Automobile Industry* (Washington, D.C.: Brookings Institute, 1987); and M. L. Weitzman and D. L. Kruse, "Profit Sharing and Productivity," in Blinder (ed.), *Paying for Productivity*, ed. A. S. Binder (Washington, D.C.: Brookings Institute, 1990).

7. The training research comes from J. S. Russell, J. R. Terborg, and M. L. Powers, "Organizational Performances and Organizational Level Training and Support," *Personnel Psychology* 38 (1985): 849–863.

8. Staffing studies can be found in D. E. Terpstra and E. J. Rozell, "The Relationship of Staffing Practices to Organizational Level Measures of Performance," *Personnel Psychology* 46 (1993): 27–48.

9. Appraisal research linked to financial performance may be found in W. C. Borman, "Job Behavior, Performance, and Effectiveness," in *Handbook of Industrial and Organizational Psychology*, 2d ed., Vol. 2, ed. M. D. Dunnette and L. M. Hough (Palo Alto, CA: Consulting Psychologist Press, 1991).

10. Compensation and performance links can be found in B. Gerhart and G. T. Milkovich, "Employee Compensation: Research and Practice," in *Handbook of Industrial and Organizational Psychology*, Vol. 3, ed. M. D. Dunnette and L. M. Hough (Palo Alto, CA: Consulting Psychological Press, 1992).

11. Studies in the steel industry come from C. Ichniowski, K. Shaw, and G. Prennushi, "The Effects of Human Resource Management Practices on Productivity," working paper, Columbia University,

New York, N.Y., 1993; and J. B. Arthur, "Effects of Human Resource Management Systems on Manufacturing Performance and Turnover," *Academy of Management Journal* 37 (1994): 670–687.

12. See J. P. MacDuffie, "Human Resource Bundles and Manufacturing Performance: Organizational Logic and Flexible Production Systems in the World Auto Industry," *Industrial and Labor Relations Review* 48 (1995): 197–221.

13. The information on this study was obtained from *Human Resources Management: Ideas and Trends in Personnel,* issue number 356, June 21, 1995. This document is an internal publication of CCH Incorporated, 4025 W. Peterson Ave., Chicago, IL.

14. For a review of the practices used by Huselid, see work by J. T. Delaney, D. Lewin, and C. Ichniowski, *Human Resource Policies and Practices in American Firms* (Washington, D.C.: U.S. Government Printing Office, 1989); and U.S. Department of Labor, *High Performance Work Practices and Firm Performance* (Washington, D.C.: U.S. Government Printing Office, 1993).

15. The concept of organizational capability comes from work by Igor Ansoff, *Corporate Strategy: An Analytical Approach to Business Policy for Growth and Expansion* (New York: McGraw-Hill, 1965).

    This work was extended and focused as the bridge between strategy and results in Dave Ulrich, and Dale Lake, *Organizational Capability: Competing from the Inside Out* (New York: Wiley, 1990).

16. See B. E. Becker, M. A. Huselid, P. S. Pickus, and M. F. Spratt, "HR as a Source of Shareholder Value: Research and Recommendations, *Human Resource Management Journal* 36, no. 1 (1997): 39–48.

17. See J. Wayne Brockbank and D. Ulrich, "Avoiding SPOTS: Creating Strategic Unity," in *Handbook of Business Strategy 1990,* ed. H. Glass (New York: Gorham, Lambert, 1990).

18. This work on what leaders need to do to make things happen quickly comes from work on agility by R. Pascale, M. Millemann, and L. Gioja, "Changing the Way We Change," *Harvard Business Review* (November–December 1997): 126–139.

19. See J. B. Quinn, "Leveraging Intellect," *Academy of Management Executive* 10, no. 3 (1996): 7–27; H. Saint-Onge, "Tacit Knowledge: The Key to the Strategic Alignment of Intellectual Capital," *Strategy and Leadership* (March/April, 1996): 10–14; and T. Stewart, *Intellectual Capital* (New York: Doubleday, 1997).

20. See J. B. Quinn, "Leveraging Intellect," *Academy of Management Executive* 10, no. 3 (1996): 7–27; and D. Ulrich, "Intellectual Capital

= Competence × Commitment," *Sloan Management Review* 39, no. 2 (1998): 15–26.

21. Work with Lominger revealed 80 possible "cultributes" (or capabilities) that firms might require, which can be grouped into 16 clusters. Information on this analysis can be obtained from Lominger in Minneapolis, Minnesota.

22. Much of the competence work comes from work by W. W. Burke, "What Human Resource Practitioners Need to Know for the Twenty-First Century," *Human Resource Management Journal* 36, no. 1 (1997): 71–80; T. Lawson, *The Competency Initiative: Studies for Excellence in Human Resource Executives* (Minneapolis, MN: Golle & Holmes, Customer Education [in conjunction with the SHRM Foundation], 1990); and D. Ulrich, Wayne Brockbank, Arthur Yeung, and Dale Lake, "Human Resource Competencies: An Empirical Assessment," *Human Resource Management Journal* 34, no. 4 (1995): 473–496.

23. See Dave Ulrich and Robert Eichinger, "Delivering HR with an Attitude: Professional That Is," *HR Magazine*, June (1998): 54–61.

PART

I

Delivering
Core Capabilities

1
A New Mandate for Human Resources

Dave Ulrich

Should we do away with human resources (HR)? In recent years, a number of people who study and write about business—along with many who run businesses—have been debating that question. The debate arises out of serious and widespread doubts about HR's contribution to organizational performance. And as much as I like HR people—I have been working in the field as a researcher, professor, and consultant for 20 years—I must agree that there is good reason for HR's beleaguered reputation. It is often ineffective, incompetent, and costly; in a phrase, it is value sapping. Indeed, if HR were to remain configured as it is today in many companies, I would have to answer the question above with a resounding "Yes—abolish the thing!"

But the truth is, HR has never been more necessary. The competitive forces that managers face today and will continue to confront in the future demand organizational excellence. The efforts to achieve such excellence—through a focus on learning, quality, teamwork, and reengineering—are driven by the way organizations get things done and how they treat their people. Those are fundamental HR issues. To state it plainly: achieving organizational excellence must be the work of HR.

The question for senior managers, then, is not Should we do away with HR? but What should we do with HR? The answer is: create an entirely new role and agenda for the field that focuses it not on traditional HR activities, such as staffing and compensation, but on outcomes. HR should not be defined by what it does but by what it delivers—results that enrich the organization's value to customers, investors, and employees.

More specifically, HR can help deliver organizational excellence in the following four ways:

- First, HR should become a partner with senior and line managers in strategy execution, helping to move planning from the conference room to the marketplace.
- Second, it should become an expert in the way work is organized and executed, delivering administrative efficiency to ensure that costs are reduced while quality is maintained.
- Third, it should become a champion for employees, vigorously representing their concerns to senior management and at the same time working to increase employee contribution; that is, employees' commitment to the organization and their ability to deliver results.
- And finally, HR should become an agent of continuous transformation, shaping processes and a culture that together improve an organization's capacity for change.

Make no mistake: this new agenda for HR is a radical departure from the status quo. In most companies today, HR is sanctioned mainly to play policy police and regulatory watchdog. It handles the paperwork involved in hiring and firing, manages the bureaucratic aspects of benefits, and administers compensation decisions made by others. When it is more empowered by senior management, it might oversee recruiting, manage training and development programs, or design initiatives to increase workplace diversity. But the fact remains: the activities of HR appear to be—and often are—disconnected from the real work of the organization. The new agenda, however, would mean that every one of HR's activities would in some concrete way help the company better serve its customers or otherwise increase shareholder value.

Can HR transform itself alone? Absolutely not. In fact, the primary responsibility for transforming the role of HR belongs to the CEO and to every line manager who must achieve business goals. The reason? Line managers have ultimate responsibility for both the processes and the outcomes of the company. They are answerable to shareholders for creating economic value, to customers for creating product or service value, and to employees for creating workplace value. It follows that they should lead the way in fully integrating HR into the company's real work. Indeed, to do so, they must become HR champions themselves. They must acknowledge that competitive success is a function of organizational excellence. More important, they must hold HR accountable for delivering it.

Of course, the line should not *impose* the new agenda on the HR staff. Rather, operating managers and HR managers must form a partnership to quickly and completely reconceive and reconfigure the function—to overhaul it from one devoted to activities to one committed to outcomes. The process will be different in every organization, but the result will be the same: a business era in which the question Should we do away with HR? will be considered utterly ridiculous.

Why HR Matters Now More Than Ever

Regardless of their industry, size, or location, companies today face five critical business challenges. Collectively, these challenges require organizations to build new capabilities. Who is currently responsible for developing those capabilities? Everyone—and no one. That vacuum is HR's opportunity to play a leadership role in enabling organizations to meet the following competitive challenges:

Globalization. Gone are the days when companies created products at home and shipped them abroad "as is." With the rapid expansion of global markets, managers are struggling to balance the paradoxical demand to think globally and act locally. That imperative requires them to move people, ideas, products, and information around the world to meet local needs. They must add new and important ingredients to the mix when making strategy: volatile political situations, contentious global trade issues, fluctuating exchange rates, and unfamiliar cultures. They must be more literate in the ways of international customers, commerce, and competition than ever before. In short, globalization requires that organizations increase their ability to learn and collaborate and to manage diversity, complexity, and ambiguity.

Profitability Through Growth. During the past decade, most Western companies have been clearing debris, using downsizing, reengineering, delayering, and consolidation to increase efficiency and cut costs. The gains of such yard work, however, have largely been realized, and executives will now have to pay attention to the other part of the profitability equation: revenue growth.

The drive for revenue growth, needless to say, puts unique demands on an organization. Companies seeking to acquire new customers and develop new products must be creative and innovative, and must encourage the free flow of information and shared learning among employees. They must also become more market focused—more in touch with the fast changing and disparate needs of their customers. And companies seeking growth through mergers, acquisitions, or joint ventures require other capabilities, such as the finely honed skills needed to integrate different organizations' work processes and cultures.

Technology. From videoconferencing to the Internet, technology has made our world smaller and faster. Ideas and massive amounts of information are in constant movement. The challenge for managers is to make sense and good use of what technology offers. Not all technology adds value. But technology can and will affect how and where work gets done. In the coming years, managers will need to figure out how to make technology a viable, productive part of the work setting. They will need to stay ahead of the information curve and learn to leverage information for business results. Otherwise, they risk being swallowed by a tidal wave of data—not ideas.

Intellectual Capital. Knowledge has become a direct competitive advantage for companies selling ideas and relationships (think of professional service, software, and technology-driven companies) and an indirect competitive advantage for all companies attempting to differentiate themselves by how they serve customers. From now on, successful companies will be the ones that are the most adept at attracting, developing, and retaining individuals who can drive a global organization that is responsive to both its customers and the burgeoning opportunities of technology. Thus the challenge for organizations is making sure they have the capability to find, assimilate, develop, compensate, and retain such talented individuals.

Change, Change, and More Change. Perhaps the greatest competitive challenge companies face is adjusting to—indeed, embracing —nonstop change. They must be able to learn rapidly and continuously, innovate ceaselessly, and take on new strategic imperatives faster and more comfortably. Constant change means organizations must create a healthy discomfort with the status quo, an ability to detect emerging trends quicker than the competition, an ability to make rapid decisions, and the agility to seek new ways of doing business. To thrive, in other words, companies will need to be in a never-ending state of transformation, perpetually creating fundamental, enduring change.

HR's New Role

The five challenges described above have one overarching implication for business: the only competitive weapon left is organization.

Sooner or later, traditional forms of competitiveness—cost, technology, distribution, manufacturing, and product features—can be copied. They have become table stakes. You must have them to be a player, but they do not guarantee you will be a winner.

In the new economy, winning will spring from organizational capabilities such as speed, responsiveness, agility, learning capacity, and employee competence. Successful organizations will be those that are able to quickly turn strategy into action; to manage processes intelligently and efficiently; to maximize employee contribution and commitment; and to create the conditions for seamless change. The need to develop those capabilities brings us back to the mandate for HR set forth at the beginning of this article. Let's take a closer look at each HR imperative in turn.

Becoming a Partner in Strategy Execution. I'm not going to argue that HR should make strategy. Strategy is the responsibility of a company's executive team—of which HR is a member. To be full-fledged strategic partners with senior management, however, HR executives should impel and guide serious discussion of how the company should be organized to carry out its strategy. Creating the conditions for this discussion involves four steps.

First, HR should be held responsible for defining an organizational architecture. In other words, it should identify the underlying model of the company's way of doing business. Several well-established frameworks can be used in this process. Jay Galbraith's star model, for example, identifies five essential organizational components: strategy, structure, rewards, processes, and people. The well-known 7-S framework created by McKinsey & Company distinguishes seven components in a company's architecture: strategy, structure, systems, staff, style, skills, and shared values.

It's relatively unimportant which framework the HR staff uses to define the company's architecture, as long as it's robust. What matters more is that an architecture be articulated explicitly. Without such clarity, managers can become myopic about how the company runs—and thus about what drives strategy implementation and what stands in its way. They might think only of structure as the driving force behind actions and decisions, and neglect systems or skills. Or they might understand the company primarily in terms of its values and pay inadequate attention to the influence of systems on how work—that is, strategy execution—actually gets accomplished.

Senior management should ask HR to play the role of an architect called into an already-constructed building to draw up its plans. The architect makes measurements; calculates dimensions; notes windows, doors, and staircases; and examines the plumbing and heating infrastructures. The result is a comprehensive set of blueprints that contains all the building's parts and shows how they work together.

Next, HR must be accountable for conducting an organizational audit. Blueprints can illuminate the places in a house that require immediate improvement; organizational-architecture plans can be similarly useful. They are critical in helping managers identify which components of the company must change in order to facilitate strategy execution. Again, HR's role is to shepherd the dialogue about the company's blueprints.

Consider a company in which HR defined the organization's architecture in terms of its culture, competencies, rewards, governance, work processes, and leadership. The HR staff was able to use that model to guide management through a rigorous discussion of "fit"— did the company's culture fit its strategic goals, did its competencies, and so forth. When the answer was no, HR was able to guide a discussion of how to obtain or develop what was missing. (For an example of the questions asked in this discussion, see Table 1-1.)

The third role for HR as a strategic partner is to identify methods for renovating the parts of the organizational architecture that need it. In other words, HR managers should be assigned to take the lead in proposing, creating, and debating best practices in culture change programs, for example, or in appraisal and reward systems. Similarly, if strategy implementation requires, say, a team-based organizational structure, HR would be responsible for bringing state-of-the-art approaches for creating this structure to senior management's attention.

Fourth and finally, HR must take stock of its own work and set clear priorities. At any given moment, the HR staff might have a dozen initiatives in its sights, such as pay-for-performance, global teamwork, and action-learning development experiences. But to be truly tied to business outcomes, HR needs to join forces with operating managers to systematically assess the impact and importance of each one of these initiatives. Which ones are really aligned with strategy implementation? Which ones should receive attention immediately, and which can wait? Which ones, in short, are truly linked to business results?

Because becoming a strategic partner means an entirely new role for HR, it may have to acquire new skills and capabilities. Its staff may need more education in order to perform the kind of in-depth analysis an organizational audit involves, for example. Ultimately, such new

Table 1-1   From Architecture to Audit

After HR has determined the company's underlying architecture, it can use a framework like the one below to guide the organization through the discussion and debate of the audit process.

	Question	Rating (1-10)	Description of best practice	Gap between company's current practice and best practice
Shared mind-set	To what extent does our company have the right culture to reach its goals?			
Competence	To what extent does our company have the required knowledge, skills, and abilities?			
Consequence	To what extent does our company have the appropriate measures, rewards, and incentives?			
Governance	To what extent does our company have the right organizational structure, communications systems, and policies?			
Capacity for change	To what extent does our company have the ability to improve work processes, to change, and to learn?			
Leadership	To what extent does our company have the leadership to achieve its goals?			

knowledge will allow HR to add value to the executive team with confidence. In time, the concept of HR as a strategic partner will make business sense.

Becoming an Administrative Expert. For decades, HR professionals have been tagged as administrators. In their new role as administrative experts, however, they will need to shed their traditional image of rule-making policy police, while still making sure that all the required routine work in companies is done well. In order to move from their old role as administrators into their new role, HR staff will have to improve the efficiency of both their own function and the entire organization.

Within the HR function are dozens of processes that can be done better, faster, and cheaper. Finding and fixing those processes is part of the work of the new HR. Some companies have already embraced these tasks, and the results are impressive. One company has created a fully automated and flexible benefits program that employees can manage without paperwork; another has used technology to screen résumés and reduce the cycle time for hiring new candidates; and a third has created an electronic bulletin board that allows employees to communicate with senior executives. In all three cases, the quality of HR work improved and costs were lowered, generally by removing steps or leveraging technology.

But decreased costs aren't the only benefit of HR's becoming the organization's administrative expert. Improving efficiency will build HR's credibility, which, in turn, will open the door for it to become a partner in executing strategy. Consider the case of a CEO who held a very low opinion of the company's HR staff after they sent a letter to a job candidate offering a salary figure with the decimal point in the wrong place. (The candidate called the CEO and joked that she didn't realize the job would make her a millionaire.) It was only after the HR staff proved they could streamline the organization's systems and procedures and deliver flawless administrative service that the CEO finally felt comfortable giving HR a seat at the strategy table.

HR executives can also prove their value as administrative experts by rethinking how work is done throughout the organization. For example, they can design and implement a system that allows departments to share administrative services. At Amoco, for instance, HR helped create a shared-service organization that encompassed 14 business units. HR can also create centers of expertise that gather, coordinate, and disseminate vital information about market trends, for instance, or organizational processes. Such groups can act as internal consultants, not only saving the company money but also improving its competitive situation.

Becoming an Employee Champion. Work today is more demanding than ever—employees are continually being asked to do more with less. And as companies withdraw the old employment contract, which was based on security and predictable promotions, and replace it with faint promises of trust, employees respond in kind. Their relationship with the organization becomes transactional. They give their time but not much more.

That kind of curtailed contribution is a recipe for organizational failure. Companies cannot thrive unless their employees are engaged fully. Engaged employees—that is, employees who believe they are valued—share ideas, work harder than the necessary minimum, and relate better to customers, to name just three benefits.

In their new role, HR professionals must be held accountable for ensuring that employees are engaged—that they feel committed to the organization and contribute fully. In the past, HR sought that commitment by attending to the social needs of employees—picnics, parties, United Way campaigns, and so on. While those activities must still be organized, HR's new agenda supersedes them. HR must now take responsibility for orienting and training line management about the importance of high employee morale and how to achieve it. In addition, the new HR should be the employees' voice in management discussions; offer employees opportunities for personal and professional growth; and provide resources that help employees meet the demands put on them.

Orienting and training line management about how to achieve high employee morale can be accomplished using several tools, such as workshops, written reports, and employee surveys. Such tools can help managers understand the sources of low morale within the organization—not just specifically, but conceptually. For instance, HR might inform the line that 82% of employees feel demoralized because of a recent downsizing. That's useful. But more than that, HR should be responsible for educating the line about the *causes* of low employee morale. For instance, it is generally agreed by organizational behavior experts that employee morale decreases when people believe the demands put upon them exceed the resources available to meet those demands. Morale also drops when goals are unclear, priorities are unfocused, or performance measurement is ambiguous. HR serves an important role in holding a mirror in front of senior executives.

HR can play a critical role in recommending ways to ameliorate morale problems. Recommendations can be as simple as urging the hiring of additional support staff or as complex as suggesting that reengineering be considered for certain tasks. The new role for HR might also involve suggesting that more teams be used on some projects or that employees be given more control over their own work schedules. It may mean suggesting that line executives pay attention to the possibility that some employees are being asked to do boring or repetitive work. HR at Baxter Healthcare, for example, identified boring work as a problem and then helped to solve it by redesigning work processes to connect employees more directly with customers.

Along with educating operating managers about morale, HR staff must also be an advocate for employees—they must represent the employees to management and be their voice in management discussions. Employees should have confidence that when decisions are made that affect them (such as a plant closing), HR's involvement in the decision-making process clearly represents employees' views and supports their rights. Such advocacy cannot be invisible. Employees must know that HR is their voice before they will communicate their opinions to HR managers.

Becoming a Change Agent. To adapt a phrase, "Change happens." And the pace of change today, because of globalization, technological innovation, and information access, is both dizzying and dazzling. That said, the primary difference between winners and losers in business will be the ability to respond to the pace of change. Winners will be able to adapt, learn, and act quickly. Losers will spend time trying to control and master change.

The new HR has as its fourth responsibility the job of building the organization's capacity to embrace and capitalize on change. It will make sure that change initiatives that are focused on creating high-performing teams, reducing cycle time for innovation, or implementing new technology are defined, developed, and delivered in a timely way. The new HR can also make sure that broad vision statements (such as, We will be the global leader in our markets) get transformed into specific behaviors by helping employees figure out what work they can stop, start, and keep doing to make the vision real. At Hewlett-Packard, HR has helped make sure that the company's value of treating employees with trust, dignity, and respect translates into practices that, for example, give employees more control over when and where they work.

Change has a way of scaring people—scaring them into inaction.

HR's role as a change agent is to replace resistance with resolve, planning with results, and fear of change with excitement about its possibilities. How? The answer lies in the creation and use of a change model. (For an example of a very effective change model, developed with and used extensively by GE, see Table 1-2.) HR professionals must introduce such a model to their organizations and guide executive teams through it—that is, steer the conversation and debate that answers the multitude of questions it raises. The model, in short, must be a managerial tool championed by HR. It helps an organization identify the key success factors for change and assess the organization's strengths and weaknesses regarding each factor. The process can be arduous, but it is one of the most valuable roles HR can play. As change agents, HR professionals do not themselves execute change—but they make sure that it is carried out.

Consider the case of a company whose senior management team announced that "valuing diversity" was a top priority in 1996. Six months into the year, the team acknowledged that the diversity initiative had received more rhetoric than action. The company's HR professionals asked the team to spend several hours profiling the diversity initiative using a change model. (See Exhibit 1-1.) The resulting analysis revealed that the diversity initiative would fail unless the senior management team explored several critical questions, among them: Why are we seeking diversity? What will be the benefit to the business and its customers? What is the ideal form of diversity for this organization? Who needs to be supportive and involved to make the initiative come to life?

HR leaders spent several more hours with the management team guiding a conversation that answered those questions. Shortly afterward, they were able to present the team with an action plan for moving the diversity initiative forward. Thus HR did not decide what changes the organization was going to embrace, but it did lead the process to make them explicit.

Perhaps the hardest and most important challenge facing many companies in this era of flux is changing their culture. In helping to bring about a new culture, HR must follow a four-step process:

- First, it must define and clarify the concept of culture change.
- Second, it must articulate why culture change is central to business success.
- Third, it must define a process for assessing the current culture and the desired new culture, as well as for measuring the gap between the two.

Table 1-2   *Change Begins by Asking Who, Why, What, and How*

HR staff at GE used this change model to guide a transformation process at the company.

Key Success Factors for Change	Questions to Assess and Accomplish The Key Success Factors for Change
Leading change (Who is responsible?)	Do we have a leader . . . who owns and champions the change? who publicly commits to making it happen? who will garner the resources necessary to sustain it? who will put in the personal time and attention needed to follow through?
Creating a shared need (Why do it?)	Do employees . . . see the reason for the change? understand why it is important? see how it will help them and the business in the short term and long term?
Shaping a vision (What will it look like when we are done?)	Do employees . . . see the outcomes of the change in behavioral terms (that is, in terms of what they will do differently as a result of the change)? get excited about the results of accomplishing the change? understand how it will benefit customers and other stakeholders?

- And fourth, it must identify alternative approaches to creating culture change.

    HR played an important part in changing the culture at Sears, which underwent a transformation of its business beginning in 1994. In facilitating that change, HR first took on the task of getting the organization to define and clarify the concept of culture. It helped lead the top 100 managers through discussions and debates of the questions, What are the top three things we want to be known for by our customers? and What do we do that is world class in those things? Ultimately,

Table 1-2 (continued)

Mobilizing commitment (Who else needs to be involved?)	Do the sponsors of the change . . . recognize who else needs to be committed to the change to make it happen? know how to build a coalition of support for the change? have the ability to enlist support of key individuals in the organization? have the ability to build a responsibility matrix to make the change happen?
Modifying systems and structures (How will it be institutionalized?)	Do the sponsors of the change . . . understand how to link it to other HR systems such as staffing, training, appraisal, rewards, structure, and communication? recognize the systems implications of the change?
Monitoring progress (How will it be measured?)	Do the sponsors of the change . . . have a means of measuring its success? plan to benchmark progress against both the results of the change and the process of implementing it?
Making it last (How will it get started and last?)	Do the sponsors of the change . . . recognize the first steps in getting started? have a short-term and long-term plan to keep attention focused on the change? have a plan to adapt the change over time?

those conversations led to a consensus that Sears would define its culture as "the identity of the company in the minds of the best customers." In addition, HR at Sears took on the responsibility of making the business case for a transformation of the company's culture. It compiled data showing that even a small increase in employee commitment led to a measurable increase in customer commitment and store profitability. The data illustrate conclusively that Sears's transformation affected employees, customers, and investors.

HR at Sears guided the company's culture change in numerous other ways.[1] The specific details, however, are not nearly as important

Exhibit 1-1   *Profile of a Change Initiative in Distress*

One company's HR professionals used this chart to help senior management understand why a high-profile diversity initiative was going nowhere.

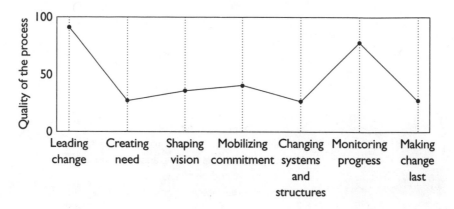

as their implications. HR can be the architect of new cultures, but to do so, its purpose must be redefined. Virtually every imperative of the new mandate for HR requires such a redefinition. And for it to happen, senior managers must lead the way.

Four Changes for the Line

The new mandate for HR requires dramatic changes in how HR professionals think and behave. But perhaps more important, it also requires that senior executives change what they expect from HR and how they behave toward the HR staff. The following are four ways senior operating managers can create an era in which HR is focused on outcomes instead of activities:

Communicate to the organization that the "soft stuff" matters. At Hewlett-Packard, managing people was one of the two *hoshin* (major objectives) of the CEO for 1997. At General Electric, CEO Jack Welch claims he spends 40% of this time on people issues. At Southern Company, senior managers are working to create an empowered organization to ensure faster and better decision making. The point? For HR to be taken seriously, senior managers must demonstrate that they believe typical HR issues—the soft stuff like culture change and intellectual capital—are critical to business success.

Operating managers can signal this belief in several ways. They can talk seriously about how organizational capabilities create value for investors, customers, and employees. They can invest the time needed to make sure organizational changes are debated and implemented. They can include HR professionals in strategy discussions and state explicitly that without the collaboration of HR, strategies are more hopes than realities, promises than acts, and concepts than results.

Explicitly define the deliverables from HR, and hold HR accountable for results. It is one thing to tell HR that it is responsible for employee contribution and quite another to set a specific goal—say, a 10% increase in employee morale as measured by a survey. And once such specific goals are set, consequences must follow if they are missed.

The new mandate for HR is like any other business initiative in this way. A company has a much better chance of achieving its goals if senior managers state specifically what they expect from HR and then track, measure, and reward performance.

Invest in innovative HR practices. Like every other area of business, HR gets its share of new technologies and practices, and senior line executives should be always on the lookout for such practices. Conferences and management literature are always good places to hear of new ways of approaching HR, but senior managers should also be aware of innovative HR practices going on at other companies and of new practices that are being advocated by respected consultants.

Investing in new HR practices is another way to signal to the organization that HR is worthy of the company's money and attention. It is also a way to make sure that HR has the tools, information, and processes that it needs to execute its new mandate.

As new practices are identified, line managers should expect HR to adapt to them, not adopt them. Too often, after learning about an innovative idea, HR immediately tries to copy it wholesale. Such efforts often fail, and at a high emotional cost. Instead, investment in new HR practices should focus on learning not only what works elsewhere but also how a new practice should work in the company's unique competitive situation.

Upgrade HR professionals. Finally, the hardest but perhaps most important thing senior managers can do to drive forward the new mandate for HR is to improve the quality of the HR staff itself. Too often, HR departments are like computers made up of used parts. While the individual parts may work, they don't work well together. When more is expected of HR, a higher quality of HR professional must be found. Companies need people who know the business, understand the theory and practice of HR, can manage culture and make change happen, and have personal credibility. Sometimes, such individuals already exist within the HR function but need additional training. Other times, they have to be brought in from other parts of the company. In still other cases, they must be hired from outside.

Regardless, HR cannot expand its role in an organization without the requisite expertise. Becoming a strategic partner demands a degree of knowledge about strategy, markets, and the economy. Becoming an administrative expert demands some knowledge of reengineering, as well as the intricacies of what the line actually does. If HR is to effect real change, it must be made up of people who have the skills they need to work from a base of confidence and earn what too often it lacks—respect.

Hard Work Ahead

To meet the increased expectations of their organizations, HR professionals must begin to act professionally. They must focus more on the deliverables of their work and less on just getting their work done. They must articulate their role in terms of the value they create. They must create mechanisms so that business results quickly follow. They must measure their effectiveness in terms of business competitiveness rather than employee comfort and lead cultural transformation rather than consolidate, reengineer, or downsize in order to turn a company around.

Senior executives who recognize the economic value and the benefit to their customers of intellectual capital and organizational capability need to demand more of the HR function. They need to invest in HR as if it were a business. And they must get beyond the stereotype of HR professionals as incompetent value-sapping support staff. It's time to destroy that stereotype and unleash HR's full potential.

Note

1. For more on the transformation of Sears, see *The Employee-Customer-Profit Chain at Sears,* by Anthony J. Rucci, Steven P. Kirn, and Richard T. Quinn, *Harvard Business Review* 76, no. 1 (1998): 82–97.

2

The Core Competence of the Corporation

C.K. Prahalad and Gary Hamel

The most powerful way to prevail in global competition is still invisible to many companies. During the 1980s, top executives were judged on their ability to restructure, declutter, and delayer their corporations. In the 1990s, they'll be judged on their ability to identify, cultivate, and exploit the core competencies that make growth possible—indeed, they'll have to rethink the concept of the corporation itself.

Consider the last ten years of GTE and NEC. In the early 1980s, GTE was well positioned to become a major player in the evolving information technology industry. It was active in telecommunications. Its operations spanned a variety of businesses including telephones, switching and transmission systems, digital PABX, semiconductors, packet switching, satellites, defense systems, and lighting products. And GTE's Entertainment Products Group, which produced Sylvania color TVs, had a position in related display technologies. In 1980, GTE's sales were $9.98 billion, and net cash flow was $1.73 billion. NEC, in contrast, was much smaller, at $3.8 billion in sales. It had a comparable technological base and computer businesses, but it had no experience as an operating telecommunications company.

Yet look at the positions of GTE and NEC in 1988. GTE's 1988 sales were $16.46 billion, and NEC's sales were considerably higher at $21.89 billion. GTE has, in effect, become a telephone operating company with a position in defense and lighting products. GTE's other businesses are small in global terms. GTE has divested Sylvania TV and Telenet, put switching, transmission, and digital PABX into joint ventures, and closed down semiconductors. As a result, the international position of GTE has eroded. Non-U.S. revenue as a percent of total revenue dropped from 20% to 15% between 1980 and 1988.

NEC has emerged as the world leader in semiconductors and as a first-tier player in telecommunications products and computers. It has consolidated its position in mainframe computers. It has moved beyond public switching and transmission to include such lifestyle products as mobile telephones, facsimile machines, and laptop computers—bridging the gap between telecommunications and office automation. NEC is the only company in the world to be in the top five in revenue in telecommunications, semiconductors, and mainframes. Why did these two companies, starting with comparable business portfolios, perform so differently? Largely because NEC conceived of itself in terms of "core competencies," and GTE did not.

Rethinking the Corporation

Once, the diversified corporation could simply point its business units at particular end product markets and admonish them to become world leaders. But with market boundaries changing ever more quickly, targets are elusive and capture is at best temporary. A few companies have proven themselves adept at inventing new markets, quickly entering emerging markets, and dramatically shifting patterns of customer choice in established markets. These are the ones to emulate. The critical task for management is to create an organization capable of infusing products with irresistible functionality or, better yet, creating products that customers need but have not yet even imagined.

This is a deceptively difficult task. Ultimately, it requires radical change in the management of major companies. It means, first of all, that top managements of Western companies must assume responsibility for competitive decline. Everyone knows about high interest rates, Japanese protectionism, outdated antitrust laws, obstreperous unions, and impatient investors. What is harder to see, or harder to acknowledge, is how little added momentum companies actually get from political or macroeconomic "relief." Both the theory and practice of Western management have created a drag on our forward motion. It is the principles of management that are in need of reform.

NEC versus GTE, again, is instructive and only one of many such comparative cases we analyzed to understand the changing basis for global leadership. Early in the 1970s, NEC articulated a strategic intent to exploit the convergence of computing and communications, what it called "C&C."[1] Success, top management reckoned, would hinge on acquiring *competencies,* particularly in semiconductors. Management adopted an appropriate "strategic architecture," summarized by C&C, and then communicated its intent to the whole organization and the outside world during the mid-1970s.

NEC constituted a "C&C Committee" of top managers to oversee the development of core products and core competencies. NEC put in place coordination groups and committees that cut across the interests of individual businesses. Consistent with its strategic architecture, NEC shifted enormous resources to strengthen its position in components and central processors. By using collaborative arrangements to multiply internal resources, NEC was able to accumulate a broad array of core competencies.

NEC carefully identified three interrelated streams of technological and market evolution. Top management determined that computing would evolve from large mainframes to distributed processing, components from simple ICs to VLSI, and communications from mechanical cross-bar exchange to complex digital systems we now call ISDN. As things evolved further, NEC reasoned, the computing, communications, and components businesses would so overlap that it would be very hard to distinguish among them, and that there would be enormous opportunities for any company that had built the competencies needed to serve all three markets.

NEC top management determined that semiconductors would be the company's most important "core product." It entered into myriad strategic alliances—over 100 as of 1987—aimed at building competencies rapidly and at low cost. In mainframe computers, its most noted relationship was with Honeywell and Bull. Almost all the collaborative arrangements in the semiconductor-component field were oriented toward technology access. As they entered collaborative arrangements, NEC's operating managers understood the rationale for these alliances and the goal of internalizing partner skills. NEC's director of research summed up its competence acquisition during the 1970s and 1980s this way: "From an investment standpoint, it was much quicker and cheaper to use foreign technology. There wasn't a need for us to develop new ideas."

No such clarity of strategic intent and strategic architecture appeared to exist at GTE. Although senior executives discussed the implications of the evolving information technology industry, no commonly accepted view of which competencies would be required to compete in that industry were communicated widely. While significant staff work was done to identify key technologies, senior line managers continued to act as if they were managing independent business units. Decentralization made it difficult to focus on core competencies. Instead, individual businesses became increasingly dependent on outsiders for critical skills, and collaboration became a route to staged exits. Today, with a new management team in place, GTE has repositioned itself to apply its competencies to emerging markets in telecommunications services.

The Roots of Competitive Advantage

The distinction we observed in the way NEC and GTE conceived of themselves—a portfolio of competencies versus a portfolio of businesses—was repeated across many industries. From 1980 to 1988, Canon grew by 264%, Honda by 200%. Compare that with Xerox and Chrysler. And if Western managers were once anxious about the low cost and high quality of Japanese imports, they are now overwhelmed by the pace at which Japanese rivals are inventing new markets, creating new products, and enhancing them. Canon has given us personal copiers; Honda has moved from motorcycles to four-wheel off-road buggies. Sony developed the 8mm camcorder; Yamaha, the digital piano. Komatsu developed an underwater remote-controlled bulldozer, while Casio's latest gambit is a smallscreen color LCD television. Who would have anticipated the evolution of these vanguard markets?

In more established markets, the Japanese challenge has been just as disquieting. Japanese companies are generating a blizzard of features and functional enhancements that bring technological sophistication to everyday products. Japanese car producers have been pioneering four-wheel steering, four-valve-per-cylinder engines, in-car navigation systems, and sophisticated electronic engine-management systems. On the strength of its product features, Canon is now a player in facsimile transmission machines, desktop laser printers, even semiconductor manufacturing equipment.

In the short run, a company's competitiveness derives from the price/performance attributes of current products. But the survivors of the first wave of global competition, Western and Japanese alike, are all converging on similar and formidable standards for product cost and quality—minimum hurdles for continued competition, but less and less important as sources of differential advantage. In the long run, competitiveness derives from an ability to build, at lower cost and more speedily than competitors, the core competencies that spawn unanticipated products. The real sources of advantage are to be found in management's ability to consolidate corporatewide technologies and production skills into competencies that empower individual businesses to adapt quickly to changing opportunities.

Senior executives who claim that they cannot build core competencies either because they feel the autonomy of business units is sacrosanct or because their feet are held to the quarterly budget fire should think again. The problem in many Western companies is not that their senior executives are any less capable than those in Japan nor that Japanese companies possess greater technical capabilities. Instead, it is their adherence to a concept of the corporation that unnecessarily limits the ability of individual businesses to fully exploit the deep reservoir of technological capability that many American and European companies possess.

The diversified corporation is a large tree. The trunk and major limbs are core products, the smaller branches are business units; the leaves, flowers, and fruit are end products. The root system that provides nourishment, sustenance, and stability is the core competence. You can miss the strength of competitors by looking only at their end products, in the same way you miss the strength of a tree if you look only at its leaves. (See Exhibit 2-1.)

Core competencies are the collective learning in the organization, especially how to coordinate diverse production skills and integrate multiple streams of technologies. Consider Sony's capacity to miniaturize or Philips's optical-media expertise. The theoretical knowledge of how to put a radio on a chip does not in itself assure a company the skill to produce a miniature radio no bigger than a business card. To bring off this feat, Casio must harmonize know-how in miniaturization, microprocessor design, material science, and ultrathin precision casing—the same skills it applies in its miniature card calculators, pocket TVs, and digital watches.

If core competence is about harmonizing streams of technology, it is also about the organization of work and the delivery of value. Among Sony's competencies is miniaturization. To bring miniaturization to its products, Sony must ensure that technologists, engineers, and marketers have a shared understanding of customer needs and of technological possibilities. The force of core competence is felt as decisively in services as in manufacturing. Citicorp was ahead of others investing in

Exhibit 2-1   Competencies: The Roots of Competitiveness

The corporation, like a tree, grows from its roots. Core products are nourished by competencies and engender business units, whose fruit are end products.

End Products

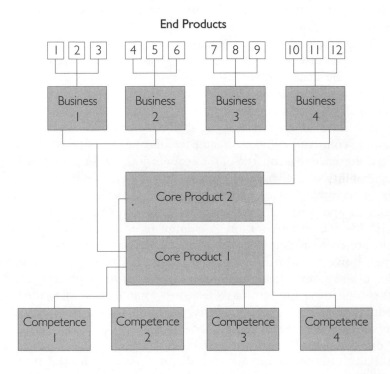

an operating system that allowed it to participate in world markets 24 hours a day. Its competence in systems has provided the company the means to differentiate itself from many financial service institutions.

Core competence is communication, involvement, and a deep commitment to working across organizational boundaries. It involves many levels of people and all functions. World-class research in, for example, lasers or ceramics can take place in corporate laboratories without having an impact on any of the businesses of the company. The skills that together constitute core competence must coalesce around individuals whose efforts are not so narrowly focused that they cannot recognize the opportunities for blending their functional expertise with those of others in new and interesting ways.

Core competence does not diminish with use. Unlike physical assets, which do deteriorate over time, competencies are enhanced as they are applied and shared. But competencies still need to be nurtured and protected; knowledge fades if it is not used. Competencies are the glue that binds existing businesses. They are also the engine for new business development. Patterns of diversification and market entry may be guided by them, not just by the attractiveness of markets.

Consider 3M's competence with sticky tape. In dreaming up businesses as diverse as "Post-it" notes, magnetic tape, photographic film, pressure-sensitive tapes, and coated abrasives, the company has brought to bear widely shared competencies in substrates, coatings, and adhesives and devised various ways to combine them. Indeed, 3M has invested consistently in them. What seems to be an extremely diversified portfolio of businesses belies a few shared core competencies.

In contrast, there are major companies that have had the potential to build core competencies but failed to do so because top management was unable to conceive of the company as anything other than a collection of discrete businesses. GE sold much of its consumer electronics business to Thomson of France, arguing that it was becoming increasingly difficult to maintain its competitiveness in this sector. That was undoubtedly so, but it is ironic that it sold several key businesses to competitors who were already competence leaders—Black & Decker in small electrical motors, and Thomson, which was eager to build its competence in microelectronics and had learned from the Japanese that a position in consumer electronics was vital to this challenge.

Management trapped in the strategic business unit (SBU) mind-set almost inevitably finds its individual businesses dependent on external sources for critical components, such as motors or compressors. But these are not just components. They are core products that contribute to the competitiveness of a wide range of end products. They are the physical embodiments of core competencies.

How Not to Think of Competence

Since companies are in a race to build the competencies that determine global leadership, successful companies have stopped imagining themselves as bundles of businesses making products. Canon, Honda, Casio, or NEC may seem to preside over portfolios of businesses unrelated in terms of customers, distribution channels, and merchandising strategy. Indeed, they have portfolios that may seem idiosyncratic at times: NEC is the only global company to be among leaders in computing, telecommunications, and semiconductors *and* to have a thriving consumer electronics business.

But looks are deceiving. In NEC, digital technology, especially VLSI and systems integration skills, is fundamental. In the core competencies underlying them, disparate businesses become coherent. It is Honda's core competence in engines and power trains that gives it a distinctive advantage in car, motorcycle, lawn mower, and generator businesses. Canon's core competencies in optics, imaging, and microprocessor controls have enabled it to enter, even dominate, markets as seemingly diverse as copiers, laser printers, cameras, and image scanners. Philips worked for more than 15 years to perfect its optical-media (laser disc) competence, as did JVC in building a leading position in video recording. Other examples of core competencies might include mechantronics (the ability to marry mechanical and electronic engineering), video displays, bioengineering, and microelectronics. In the early stages of its competence building, Philips could not have imagined all the products that would be spawned by its optical-media competence, nor could JVC have anticipated miniature camcorders when it first began exploring videotape technologies.

Unlike the battle for global brand dominance, which is visible in the world's broadcast and print media and is aimed at building global "share of mind," the battle to build world-class competencies is invisible to people who aren't deliberately looking for it. Top management often tracks the cost and quality of competitors' products, yet how many managers untangle the web of alliances their Japanese competitors have constructed to acquire competencies at low cost? In how many Western boardrooms is there an explicit, shared understanding of the competencies the company must build for world leadership? Indeed, how many senior executives discuss the crucial distinction between competitive strategy at the level of a business and competitive strategy at the level of an entire company?

Let us be clear. Cultivating core competence does *not* mean outspending rivals on research and development. In 1983, when Canon surpassed Xerox in worldwide unit market share in the copier business, its R&D budget in reprographics was but a small fraction of Xerox's. Over the past 20 years, NEC has spent less on R&D as a percentage of sales than almost all of its American and European competitors.

Nor does core competence mean shared costs, as when two or more SBUs use a common facility—a plant, service facility, or sales force—or share a common component. The gains of sharing may be substantial, but the search for shared costs is typically a post hoc effort to rationalize production across existing businesses, not a premeditated effort to build the competencies out of which the businesses themselves grow.

Building core competencies is more ambitious and different than integrating vertically, moreover. Managers deciding whether to make or buy will start with end products and look upstream to the efficiencies of the supply chain and downstream toward distribution and customers. They do not take inventory of skills and look forward to applying them in nontraditional ways. (Of course, decisions about competencies *do* provide a logic for vertical integration. Canon is not particularly integrated in its copier business, except in those aspects of the vertical chain that support the competencies it regards as critical.)

Identifying Core Competencies—And Losing Them

At least three tests can be applied to identify core competencies in a company. First, a core competence provides potential access to a wide variety of markets. Competence in display systems, for example, enables a company to participate in such diverse businesses as calculators, miniature TV sets, monitors for laptop computers, and automotive dash-boards—which is why Casio's entry into the handheld TV market was predictable. Second, a core competence should make a significant contribution to the perceived customer benefits of the end product. Clearly, Honda's engine expertise fills this bill.

Finally, a core competence should be difficult for competitors to imitate. And it *will* be difficult if it is a complex harmonization of individual technologies and production skills. A rival might acquire some of the technologies that comprise the core competence, but it will find it more difficult to duplicate the more or less comprehensive pattern of internal coordination and learning. JVC's decision in the early 1960s to pursue the development of a videotape competence passed the three tests outlined here. RCA's decision in the late 1970s to develop a stylus-based video turntable system did not.

Few companies are likely to build world leadership in more than five or six fundamental competencies. A company that compiles a list of 20 to 30 capabilities has probably not produced a list of core competencies. Still, it is probably a good discipline to generate a list of this sort and to see aggregate capabilities as building blocks. This tends to prompt the search for licensing deals and alliances through which the company may acquire, at low cost, the missing pieces.

Most Western companies hardly think about competitiveness in these terms at all. It is time to take a tough-minded look at the risks they are running. Companies that judge competitiveness, their own and their competitors', primarily in terms of the price/performance of end products are courting the erosion of core competencies—or making too little effort to enhance them. The embedded skills that give rise to the next generation of competitive products cannot be "rented in" by outsourcing and OEM-supply relationships. In our view, too many companies have unwittingly surrendered core competencies when they cut internal investment in what they mistakenly thought were just "cost centers" in favor of outside suppliers.

Consider Chrysler. Unlike Honda, it has tended to view engines and power trains as simply one more component. Chrysler is becoming increasingly dependent on Mitsubishi and Hyundai: between 1985 and 1987, the number of outsourced engines went from 252,000 to 382,000. It is difficult to imagine Honda yielding manufacturing responsibility, much less design, of so critical a part of a car's function to an outside company—which is why Honda has made such an enormous commitment to Formula One auto racing. Honda has been able to pool its engine-related technologies; it has parlayed these into a corporatewide competency from which it develops world-beating products, despite R&D budgets smaller than those of GM and Toyota.

Of course, it is perfectly possible for a company to have a competitive product line up but be a laggard in developing core competencies—at least for a while. If a company wanted to enter the copier business today, it would find a dozen Japanese companies more than willing to supply copiers on the basis of an OEM private label. But when fundamental technologies changed or if its supplier decided to enter the market directly and become a competitor, that company's product line, along with all of its investments in marketing and distribution, could be vulnerable. Outsourcing can provide a shortcut to a more competitive product, but it typically contributes little to building the people-embodied skills that are needed to sustain product leadership.

Nor is it possible for a company to have an intelligent alliance or sourcing strategy if it has not made a choice about where it will build competence leadership. Clearly, Japanese companies have benefited from alliances. They've used them to learn from Western partners who were not fully committed to preserving core competencies of their own. As we've argued in these pages before, learning within an alliance takes a positive commitment of resources—travel, a pool of dedicated people, test-bed facilities, time to internalize and test what has been learned.[2] A company may not make this effort if it doesn't have clear goals for competence building.

Another way of losing is forgoing opportunities to establish competencies that are evolving in existing businesses. In the 1970s and 1980s, many American and European companies—like GE, Motorola, GTE, Thorn, and GEC—chose to exit the color television business, which they regarded as mature. If by "mature" they meant that they had run out of new product ideas at precisely the moment global rivals had targeted the TV business for entry, then yes, the industry was mature. But it certainly wasn't mature in the sense that all opportunities to enhance and apply video-based competencies had been exhausted.

In ridding themselves of their television businesses, these companies failed to distinguish between divesting the business and destroying their video media-based competencies. They not only got out of the TV business but they also closed the door on a whole stream of future opportunities reliant on video-based competencies. The television industry, considered by many U.S. companies in the 1970s to be unattractive, is today the focus of a fierce public policy debate about the inability of U.S. corporations to benefit from the $20-billion-a-year opportunity that HDTV will represent in the mid- to late 1990s. Ironically, the U.S. government is being asked to fund a massive research project—in effect, to compensate U.S. companies for their failure to preserve critical core competencies when they had the chance.

In contrast, one can see a company like Sony reducing its emphasis on VCRs (where it has not been very successful and where Korean companies now threaten), without reducing its commitment to video-related competencies. Sony's Betamax led to a debacle. But it emerged with its videotape recording competencies intact and is currently challenging Matsushita in the 8mm camcorder market.

There are two clear lessons here. First, the costs of losing a core competence can be only partly calculated in advance. The baby may be thrown out with the bathwater in divestment decisions. Second, since core competencies are built through a process of continuous improvement and enhancement that may span a decade or longer, a company that has failed to invest in core competence building will find it very difficult to enter an emerging market, unless, of course, it will be content simply to serve as a distribution channel.

American semiconductor companies like Motorola learned this

painful lesson when they elected to forgo direct participation in the 256k generation of DRAM chips. Having skipped this round, Motorola, like most of its American competitors, needed a large infusion of technical help from Japanese partners to rejoin the battle in the 1-megabyte generation. When it comes to core competencies, it is difficult to get off the train, walk to the next station, and then reboard.

From Core Competencies to Core Products

The tangible link between identified core competencies and end products is what we call the core products—the physical embodiments of one or more core competency. Honda's engines, for example, are core products, linchpins between design and development skills that ultimately lead to a proliferation of end products. Core products are the components or subassemblies that actually contribute to the value of the end products. Thinking in terms of core products forces a company to distinguish between the brand share it achieves in end product markets (for example, 40% of the U.S. refrigerator market) and the manufacturing share it achieves in any particular core product (for example, 5% of the world share of compressor output).

Canon is reputed to have an 84% world manufacturing share in desktop laser printer "engines," even though its brand share in the laser printer business is minuscule. Similarly, Matsushita has a world manufacturing share of about 45% in key VCR components, far in excess of its brand share (Panasonic, JVC, and others) of 20%. And Matsushita has a commanding core product share in compressors worldwide, estimated at 40%, even though its brand share in both the air-conditioning and refrigerator businesses is quite small.

It is essential to make this distinction between core competencies, core products, and end products because global competition is played out by different rules and for different stakes at each level. To build or defend leadership over the long term, a corporation will probably be a winner at each level. At the level of core competence, the goal is to build world leadership in the design and development of a particular class of product functionality—be it compact data storage and retrieval, as with Philips's optical-media competence, or compactness and ease of use, as with Sony's micromotors and microprocessor controls.

To sustain leadership in their chosen core competence areas, these companies *seek to maximize their world manufacturing share in core products*. The manufacture of core products for a wide variety of external (and internal) customers yields the revenue and market feedback that, at least partly, determines the pace at which core competencies can be enhanced and extended. This thinking was behind JVC's decision in the mid-1970s to establish VCR supply relationships with leading national consumer electronics companies in Europe and the United States. In supplying Thomson, Thorn, and Telefunken (all independent companies at that time) as well as U.S. partners, JVC was able to gain the cash and the diversity of market experience that ultimately enabled it to outpace Philips and Sony. (Philips developed videotape competencies in parallel with JVC, but it failed to build a worldwide network of OEM relationships that would have allowed it to accelerate the refinement of its videotape competence through the sale of core products.)

JVC's success has not been lost on Korean companies like Goldstar, Sam Sung, Kia, and Daewoo, who are building core product leadership in areas as diverse as displays, semiconductors, and automotive engines through their OEM-supply contracts with Western companies. Their avowed goal is to capture investment initiative away from potential competitors, often U.S. companies. In doing so, they accelerate their competence-building efforts while "hollowing out" their competitors. By focusing on competence and embedding it in core products, Asian competitors have built up advantages in component markets first and have then leveraged off their superior products to move downstream to build brand share. And they are not likely to remain the low-cost suppliers forever. As their reputation for brand leadership is consolidated, they may well gain price leadership. Honda has proven this with its Acura line, and other Japanese car makers are following suit.

Control over core products is critical for other reasons. A dominant position in core products allows a company to shape the evolution of applications and end markets. Such compact audio disc-related core products as data drives and lasers have enabled Sony and Philips to influence the evolution of the computer-peripheral business in optical-media storage. As a company multiplies the number of application arenas for its core products, it can consistently reduce the cost, time, and risk in new product development. In short, well-targeted core products can lead to economies of scale *and* scope.

The Tyranny of the SBU

The new terms of competitive engagement cannot be understood using analytical tools devised to manage the diversified corporation of 20 years ago, when competition was primarily domestic (GE versus Westinghouse, General Motors versus Ford) and all the key players were speaking the language of the same business schools and consultancies. Old prescriptions have potentially toxic side effects. The need for new principles is most obvious in companies organized exclusively according to the logic of SBUs. The implications of the two alternate concepts of the corporation are summarized in Table 2-1.

Obviously, diversified corporations have a portfolio of products and a portfolio of businesses. But we believe in a view of the company as a portfolio of competencies as well. U.S. companies do not lack the technical resources to build competencies, but their top management often lacks the vision to build them and the administrative means for assembling resources spread across multiple businesses. A shift in commitment will inevitably influence patterns of diversification, skill deployment, resource allocation priorities, and approaches to alliances and outsourcing.

We have described the three different planes on which battles for global leadership are waged: core competence, core products, and end products. A corporation has to know whether it is winning or losing on each plane. By sheer weight of investment, a company might be able to beat its rivals to blue-sky technologies yet still lose the race to build core competence leadership. If a company is winning the race to build core competencies (as opposed to building leadership in a few technologies), it will almost certainly outpace rivals in new business development. If a company is winning the race to capture world manufacturing share in core products, it will probably outpace rivals in improving product features and the price/performance ratio.

Determining whether one is winning or losing end product battles is more difficult because measures of product market share do not necessarily reflect various companies' underlying competitiveness. Indeed, companies that attempt to build market share by relying on the competitiveness of others, rather than investing in core competencies and world core-product leadership, may be treading on quicksand. In the race for global brand dominance, companies like 3M, Black & Decker, Canon, Honda, NEC, and Citicorp have built global brand umbrellas by proliferating products out of their core competencies. This

Table 2-1   *Two Concepts of the Corporation: SBU or Core Competence*

	SBU	Core Competence
Basis for competition	Competitiveness of today's products	Interfirm competition to build competencies
Corporate structure	Portfolio of businesses related in product-market terms	Portfolio of competencies, core products, and businesses
Status of the business unit	Autonomy is sacrosanct; the SBU "owns" all resources other than cash	SBU is a potential reservoir of core competencies
Resource allocation	Discrete businesses are the unit of analysis; capital is allocated business by business	Businesses and competencies are the unit of analysis: top management allocates capital and talent
Value added of top management	Optimizing corporate returns through capital allocation trade-offs among businesses	Enunciating strategic architecture and building competencies to secure the future

has allowed their individual businesses to build image, customer loyalty, and access to distribution channels.

When you think about this reconceptualization of the corporation, the primacy of the SBU—an organizational dogma for a generation—is now clearly an anachronism. Where the SBU is an article of faith, resistance to the seductions of decentralization can seem heretical. In many companies, the SBU prism means that only one plane of the global competitive battle, the battle to put competitive products on the shelf *today,* is visible to top management. What are the costs of this distortion?

UNDERINVESTMENT IN DEVELOPING CORE COMPETENCIES AND CORE PRODUCTS. When the organization is conceived of as a multiplicity of SBUs, no single business may feel responsible for maintaining a viable position in core products nor be able to justify the investment required to build world leadership in some core competence. In the absence of a more comprehensive view imposed by corporate management, SBU managers will tend to underinvest. Recently, companies such as Kodak and Philips have recognized this as a potential problem and have begun searching for new organizational forms that will allow them to develop and manufacture core products for both internal and external customers.

SBU managers have traditionally conceived of competitors in the same way they've seen themselves. On the whole, they've failed to note the emphasis Asian competitors were placing on building leadership in core products or to understand the critical linkage between world manufacturing leadership and the ability to sustain development pace in core competence. They've failed to pursue OEM-supply opportunities or to look across their various product divisions in an attempt to identify opportunities for coordinated initiatives.

IMPRISONED RESOURCES.   As an SBU evolves, it often develops unique competencies. Typically, the people who embody this competence are seen as the sole property of the business in which they grew up. The manager of another SBU who asks to borrow talented people is likely to get a cold rebuff. SBU managers are not only unwilling to lend their competence carriers but they may actually hide talent to prevent its redeployment in the pursuit of new opportunities. This may be compared to residents of an underdeveloped country hiding most of their cash under their mattresses. The benefits of competencies, like the benefits of the money supply, depend on the velocity of their circulation as well as on the size of the stock the company holds.

Western companies have traditionally had an advantage in the stock of skills they possess. But have they been able to reconfigure them quickly to respond to new opportunities? Canon, NEC, and Honda have had a lesser stock of the people and technologies that compose core competencies but could move them much quicker from one business unit to another. Corporate R&D spending at Canon is not fully indicative of the size of Canon's core competence stock and tells the casual observer nothing about the velocity with which Canon is able to move core competencies to exploit opportunities.

When competencies become imprisoned, the people who carry the competencies do not get assigned to the most exciting opportunities, and their skills begin to atrophy. Only by fully leveraging core competencies can small companies like Canon afford to compete with industry giants like Xerox. How strange that SBU managers, who are perfectly willing to compete for cash in the capital budgeting process, are unwilling to compete for people—the company's most precious asset. We find it ironic that top management devotes so much attention to the capital budgeting process yet typically has no comparable mechanism for allocating the human skills that embody core competencies. Top managers are seldom able to look four or five levels down into the organization, identify the people who embody critical competencies, and move them across organizational boundaries.

BOUNDED INNOVATION. If core competencies are not recognized, individual SBUs will pursue only those innovation opportunities that are close at hand—marginal product-line extensions or geographic expansions. Hybrid opportunities like fax machines, laptop computers, hand-held televisions, or portable music keyboards will emerge only when managers take off their SBU blinkers. Remember, Canon appeared to be in the camera business at the time it was preparing to become a world leader in copiers. Conceiving of the corporation in terms of core competencies widens the domain of innovation.

Developing Strategic Architecture

The fragmentation of core competencies becomes inevitable when a diversified company's information systems, patterns of communication, career paths, managerial rewards, and processes of strategy development do not transcend SBU lines. We believe that senior management should spend a significant amount of its time developing a corporatewide strategic architecture that establishes objectives for competence building. A strategic architecture is a road map of the future that identifies which core competencies to build and their constituent technologies.

By providing an impetus for learning from alliances and a focus for internal development efforts, a strategic architecture like NEC's C&C can dramatically reduce the investment needed to secure future market leadership. How can a company make partnerships intelligently without a clear understanding of the core competencies it is trying to build and those it is attempting to prevent from being unintentionally transferred?

Of course, all of this begs the question of what a strategic architecture should look like. The answer will be different for every company.

But it is helpful to think again of that tree, of the corporation organized around core products and, ultimately, core competencies. To sink sufficiently strong roots, a company must answer some fundamental questions: How long could we preserve our competitiveness in this business if we did not control this particular core competence? How central is this core competence to perceived customer benefits? What future opportunities would be foreclosed if we were to lose this particular competence?

The architecture provides a logic for product and market diversification, moreover. An SBU manager would be asked: Does the new market opportunity add to the overall goal of becoming the best player in the world? Does it exploit or add to the core competence? At Vickers, for example, diversification options have been judged in the context of becoming the best power and motion control company in the world (see "Vickers Learns the Value of Strategic Architecture").

Vickers Learns the Value of Strategic Architecture

The idea that top management should develop a corporate strategy for acquiring and deploying core competencies is relatively new in most U.S. companies. There are a few exceptions. An early convert was Trinova (previously Libbey Owens Ford), a Toledo-based corporation, which enjoys a worldwide position in power and motion controls and engineered plastics. One of its major divisions is Vickers, a premier supplier of hydraulics components like valves, pumps, actuators, and filtration devices to aerospace, marine, defense, automotive, earth-moving, and industrial markets.

Vickers saw the potential for a transformation of its traditional business with the application of electronics disciplines in combination with its traditional technologies. The goal was "to ensure that change in technology does not displace Vickers from its customers." This, to be sure, was initially a defensive move: Vickers recognized that unless it acquired new skills, it could not protect existing markets or capitalize on new growth opportunities. Managers at Vickers attempted to conceptualize the likely evolution of (a) technologies relevant to the power and motion control business, (b) functionalities that would satisfy emerging customer needs, and (c) new competencies needed to creatively manage the marriage of technology and customer needs.

Despite pressure for short-term earnings, top management looked to a 10- to 15-year time horizon in developing a map of emerging customer

Exhibit 2-2 Vickers Map of Competencies

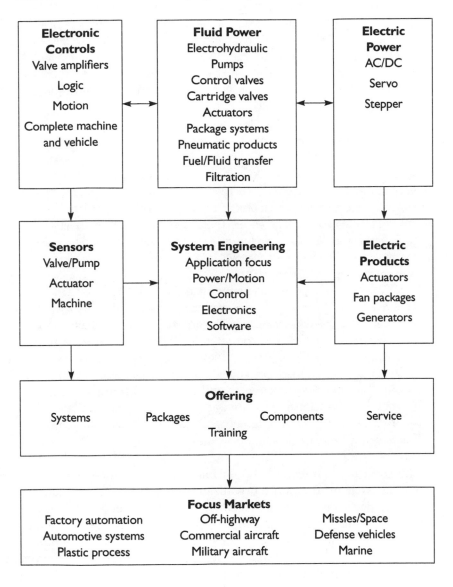

Electronic Controls
Valve amplifiers
Logic
Motion
Complete machine and vehicle

Fluid Power
Electrohydraulic
Pumps
Control valves
Cartridge valves
Actuators
Package systems
Pneumatic products
Fuel/Fluid transfer
Filtration

Electric Power
AC/DC
Servo
Stepper

Sensors
Valve/Pump
Actuator
Machine

System Engineering
Application focus
Power/Motion
Control
Electronics
Software

Electric Products
Actuators
Fan packages
Generators

Offering
Systems   Packages   Components   Service
Training

Focus Markets
Factory automation   Off-highway   Missles/Space
Automotive systems   Commercial aircraft   Defense vehicles
Plastic process   Military aircraft   Marine

needs, changing technologies, and the core competencies that would be necessary to bridge the gap between the two. Its slogan was "Into the 21st Century." (A simplified version of the overall architecture developed is shown in "Vickers Map of Competencies.") Vickers is currently in fluid-power components. The architecture identifies two additional competencies, electric-power components and electronic controls. A systems integration capability that would unite hardware, software, and service was also targeted for development.

The strategic architecture, as illustrated by the Vickers example, is not a forecast of specific products or specific technologies but a broad map of the evolving linkages between customer functionality requirements, potential technologies, and core competencies. It assumes that products and systems cannot be defined with certainty for the future but that preempting competitors in the development of new markets requires an early start to building core competencies. The strategic architecture developed by Vickers, while describing the future in competence terms, also provides the basis for making "here and now" decisions about product priorities, acquisitions, alliances, and recruitment.

Since 1986, Vickers has made more than ten clearly targeted acquisitions, each one focused on a specific component or technology gap identified in the overall architecture. The architecture is also the basis for internal development of new competencies. Vickers has undertaken, in parallel, a reorganization to enable the integration of electronics and electrical capabilities with mechanical-based competencies. We believe that it will take another two to three years before Vickers reaps the total benefits from developing the strategic architecture, communicating it widely to all its employees, customers, and investors, and building administrative systems consistent with the architecture.

The strategic architecture should make resource allocation priorities transparent to the entire organization. It provides a template for allocation decisions by top management. It helps lower level managers understand the logic of allocation priorities and disciplines senior management to maintain consistency. In short, it yields a definition of the company and the markets it serves. 3M, Vickers, NEC, Canon, and Honda all qualify on this score. Honda *knew* it was exploiting what it had learned from motorcycles—how to make high-revving, smooth-running, lightweight engines—when it entered the car business. The task of creating a strategic architecture forces the organization to identify and commit to the technical and production linkages across SBUs that will provide a distinct competitive advantage.

It is consistency of resource allocation and the development of an administrative infrastructure appropriate to it that breathes life into a strategic architecture and creates a managerial culture, teamwork, a capacity to change, and a willingness to share resources, to protect proprietary skills, and to think long term. That is also the reason the specific architecture cannot be copied easily or overnight by competitors. Strategic architecture is a tool for communicating with customers and other external constituents. It reveals the broad direction without giving away every step.

Redeploying to Exploit Competencies

If the company's core competencies are its critical resource and if top management must ensure that competence carriers are not held hostage by some particular business, then it follows that SBUs should bid for core competencies in the same way they bid for capital. We've made this point glancingly. It is important enough to consider more deeply.

Once top management (with the help of divisional and SBU managers) has identified overarching competencies, it must ask businesses to identify the projects and people closely connected with them. Corporate officers should direct an audit of the location, number, and quality of the people who embody competence.

This sends an important signal to middle managers: core competencies are *corporate* resources and may be reallocated by corporate management. An individual business doesn't own anybody. SBUs are entitled to the services of individual employees so long as SBU management can demonstrate that the opportunity it is pursuing yields the highest possible pay-off on the investment in their skills. This message is further underlined if each year in the strategic planning or budgeting process, unit managers must justify their hold on the people who carry the company's core competencies.

Elements of Canon's core competence in optics are spread across businesses as diverse as cameras, copiers, and semiconductor lithographic equipment and are shown in Exhibit 2-3. When Canon identified an opportunity in digital laser printers, it gave SBU managers the right to raid other SBUs to pull together the required pool of talent. When Canon's reprographics products division undertook to develop microprocessor-controlled copiers, it turned to the photo products group, which had developed the world's first microprocessor-controlled camera.

Also, reward systems that focus only on product-line results and

Exhibit 2-3   Core Competencies at Canon

Every Canon product is the result of at least one core competency.

	Precision Mechanics	Fine Optics	Micro-electronics
Basic camera	■	■	
Compact fashion camera	■	■	
Electronic camera	■	■	
EOS autofocus camera	■	■	■
Video still camera	■	■	■
Laser beam printer	■	■	■
Color video printer	■		■
Bubble jet printer	■		■
Basic fax	■		■
Laser fax	■		■
Calculator			■
Plain paper copier	■	■	■
Battery PPC	■	■	■
Color copier	■	■	■
Laser copier	■	■	■
Color laser copier	■	■	■
NAVI	■	■	■
Still video system	■	■	■
Laser imager	■	■	■
Cell analyzer	■	■	■
Mask aligners	■		■
Stepper aligners	■		■
Excimer laser aligners	■	■	■

career paths that seldom cross SBU boundaries engender patterns of behavior among unit managers that are destructively competitive. At NEC, divisional managers come together to identify next-generation competencies. Together they decide how much investment needs to be made to build up each future competency and the contribution in capital and staff support that each division will need to make. There is also a sense of equitable exchange. One division may make a disproportionate contribution or may benefit less from the progress made, but such short-term inequalities will balance out over the long term.

Incidentally, the positive contribution of the SBU manager should be made visible across the company. An SBU manager is unlikely to surrender key people if only the other business (or the general manager of that business who may be a competitor for promotion) is going to benefit from the redeployment. Cooperative SBU managers should be celebrated as team players. Where priorities are clear, transfers are less likely to be seen as idiosyncratic and politically motivated.

Transfers for the sake of building core competence must be recorded and appreciated in the corporate memory. It is reasonable to expect a business that has surrendered core skills on behalf of corporate opportunities in other areas to lose, for a time, some of its competitiveness. If these losses in performance bring immediate censure, SBUs will be unlikely to assent to skills transfers next time.

Finally, there are ways to wean key employees off the idea that they belong in perpetuity to any particular business. Early in their careers, people may be exposed to a variety of businesses through a carefully planned rotation program. At Canon, critical people move regularly between the camera business and the copier business and between the copier business and the professional optical-products business. In mid-career, periodic assignments to cross-divisional project teams may be necessary, both for diffusing core competencies and for loosening the bonds that might tie an individual to one business even when brighter opportunities beckon elsewhere. Those who embody critical core competencies should know that their careers are tracked and guided by corporate human resource professionals. In the early 1980s at Canon, all engineers under 30 were invited to apply for membership on a seven-person committee that was to spend two years plotting Canon's future direction, including its strategic architecture.

Competence carriers should be regularly brought together from across the corporation to trade notes and ideas. The goal is to build a strong feeling of community among these people. To a great extent, their loyalty should be to the integrity of the core competence area they represent and not just to particular businesses. In traveling regularly, talking frequently to customers, and meeting with peers, competence carriers may be encouraged to discover new market opportunities.

Core competencies are the wellspring of new business development. They should constitute the focus for strategy at the corporate level. Managers have to win manufacturing leadership in core products and capture global share through brand-building programs aimed at exploiting economies of scope. Only if the company is conceived of as a hierarchy of core competencies, core products, and market-focused business units will it be fit to fight.

Nor can top management be just another layer of accounting consolidation, which it often is in a regime of radical decentralization. Top management must add value by enunciating the strategic architecture that guides the competence acquisition process. We believe an obsession with competence building will characterize the global winners of the 1990s. With the decade underway, the time for rethinking the concept of the corporation is already overdue.

Notes

1. For a fuller discussion, see our article, "Strategic Intent," *Harvard Business Review* 67, no. 3 (1989): 63.
2. G. Hamel, Y.L. Doz, and C.K. Prahalad, "Collaborate with Your Competitors—and Win," *Harvard Business Review* 67, no. 3 (1989): 133.

3

Competing on Capabilities: The New Rules of Corporate Strategy

George Stalk Jr., Philip Evans, and Lawrence E. Shulman

In the 1980s, companies discovered time as a new source of competitive advantage. In the 1990s, they will learn that time is just one piece of a more far-reaching transformation in the logic of competition.

Companies that compete effectively on time—speeding new products to market, manufacturing just in time, or responding promptly to customer complaints—tend to be good at other things as well: for instance, the consistency of their product quality, the acuity of their insight into evolving customer needs, the ability to exploit emerging markets, enter new businesses, or generate new ideas and incorporate them in innovations. But all these qualities are mere reflections of a more fundamental characteristic: a new conception of corporate strategy that we call "capabilities-based competition."

For a glimpse of the new world of capabilities-based competition, consider the astonishing reversal of fortunes represented by Kmart and Wal-Mart.

In 1979, Kmart was king of the discount retailing industry, an industry it had virtually created. With 1,891 stores and average revenues per store of $7.25 million, Kmart enjoyed enormous size advantages. This allowed economies of scale in purchasing, distribution, and marketing that, according to just about any management textbook, are crucial to competitive success in a mature and low-growth industry. By contrast, Wal-Mart was a small niche retailer in the South with only 229 stores and average revenues about half of those of Kmart stores—hardly a serious competitor.

And yet, only ten years later, Wal-Mart had transformed itself and the discount retailing industry. Growing nearly 25% a year, the company achieved the highest sales per square foot, inventory turns, and operating profit of any discount retailer. Its 1989 pretax return on sales was 8%, nearly double that of Kmart.

Today Wal-Mart is the largest and highest profit retailer in the world—a performance that has translated into a 32% return on equity and a market valuation more than ten times book value. What's more, Wal-Mart's growth has been concentrated in half the United States, leaving ample room for further expansion. If Wal-Mart continues to gain market share at just one-half its historical rate, by 1995 the company will have eliminated all competitors from discount retailing with the exception of Kmart and Target.

The Secret of Wal-Mart's Success

What accounts for Wal-Mart's remarkable success? Most explanations focus on a few familiar and highly visible factors: the genius of founder Sam Walton, who inspires his employees and has molded a culture of service excellence; the "greeters" who welcome customers at the door; the motivational power of allowing employees to own part of the business; the strategy of "everyday low prices" that offers the customer a better deal and saves on merchandising and advertising costs. Economists also point to Wal-Mart's big stores, which offer economies of scale and a wider choice of merchandise.

But such explanations only redefine the question. *Why* is Wal-Mart able to justify building bigger stores? Why does Wal-Mart alone have a cost structure low enough to accommodate everyday low prices and greeters? And what has enabled the company to continue to grow far beyond the direct reach of Sam Walton's magnetic personality? The real secret of Wal-Mart's success lies deeper, in a set of strategic business decisions that transformed the company into a capabilities-based competitor.

The starting point was a relentless focus on satisfying customer needs. Wal-Mart's goals were simple to define but hard to execute: to provide customers access to quality goods, to make these goods available when and where customers want them, to develop a cost structure that enables competitive pricing, and to build and maintain a reputation for absolute trustworthiness. The key to achieving these goals was to make the way the company replenished inventory the centerpiece of its competitive strategy.

This strategic vision reached its fullest expression in a largely invisible logistics technique known as "cross-docking." In this system, goods are continuously delivered to Wal-Mart's warehouses, where they are selected, repacked, and then dispatched to stores, often without ever sitting in inventory. Instead of spending valuable time in the warehouse, goods just cross from one loading dock to another in 48 hours or less.

Cross-docking enables Wal-Mart to achieve the economies that come with purchasing full truck-loads of goods while avoiding the usual inventory and handling costs. Wal-Mart runs a full 85% of its goods through its warehouse system—as opposed to only 50% for Kmart. This reduces Wal-Mart's costs of sales by 2% to 3% compared with the industry average. That cost difference makes possible the everyday low prices.

But that's not all. Low prices in turn mean that Wal-Mart can save even more by eliminating the expense of frequent promotions. Stable prices also make sales more predictable, thus reducing stock-outs and excess inventory. Finally, everyday low prices bring in the customers, which translates into higher sales per retail square foot. These advantages in basic economics make the greeters and the profit sharing easy to afford.

With such obvious benefits, why don't all retailers use cross-docking? The reason: it is extremely difficult to manage. To make cross-docking work, Wal-Mart has had to make strategic investments in a variety of interlocking support systems far beyond what could be justified by conventional ROI criteria.

For example, cross-docking requires continuous contact among Wal-Mart's distribution centers, suppliers, and every point of sale in every store to ensure that orders can flow in and be consolidated and executed within a matter of hours. So Wal-Mart operates a private satellite-communication system that daily sends point-of-sale data directly to Wal-Mart's 4,000 vendors.

Another key component of Wal-Mart's logistics infrastructure is the company's fast and responsive transportation system. The company's 19 distribution centers are serviced by nearly 2,000 company owned trucks. This dedicated truck fleet permits Wal-Mart to ship goods from warehouse to store in less than 48 hours and to replenish its store shelves twice a week on average. By contrast, the industry norm is once every two weeks.

To gain the full benefits of cross-docking, Wal-Mart has also had to make fundamental changes in its approach to managerial control. Traditionally in the retail industry, decisions about merchandising, pricing, and promotions have been highly centralized and made at the corporate level. Cross-docking, however, turns this command-and-control logic on its head. Instead of the retailer pushing products into the system, customers "pull" products when and where they need them. This approach places a premium on frequent, informal cooperation among stores, distribution centers, and suppliers—with far less centralized control.

The job of senior management at Wal-Mart, then, is not to tell individual store managers what to do but to create an environment where they can learn from the market—and from each other. The company's information systems, for example, provide store managers with detailed information about customer behavior, while a fleet of airplanes regularly ferries store managers to the Bentonville, Arkansas, headquarters for meetings on market trends and merchandising.

As the company has grown and its stores have multiplied, even Wal-Mart's own private air force hasn't been enough to maintain the necessary contacts among store managers. So Wal-Mart has installed a video link connecting all its stores to corporate headquarters and to each other. Store managers frequently hold videoconferences to exchange information on what's happening in the field, like which products are selling and which ones aren't, which promotions work and which don't.

The final piece of this capabilities mosaic is Wal-Mart's human resources system. The company realizes that its frontline employees play a significant role in satisfying customer needs. So it set out to enhance its organizational capability with programs like stock ownership and profit sharing geared toward making its personnel more responsive to customers. Even the way Wal-Mart stores are organized contributes to this goal. Where Kmart has 5 separate merchandise departments in each store, Wal-Mart has 36. This means that training can be more focused and more effective, and employees can be more attuned to customers.

Kmart did not see its business this way. While Wal-Mart was fine-tuning its business processes and organizational practices, Kmart was following the classic textbook approach that had accounted for its original success. Kmart managed its business by focusing on a few product-centered strategic business units, each a profit center under strong centralized line management. Each SBU made strategy—selecting merchandise, setting prices, and deciding which products to promote. Senior management spent most of its time and resources making line decisions rather than investing in a support infrastructure.

Similarly, Kmart evaluated its competitive advantage at each stage along a value chain and subcontracted activities that managers concluded others could do better. While Wal-Mart was building its ground transportation fleet, Kmart was moving out of trucking because a subcontracted fleet was cheaper. While Wal-Mart was building close relationships with its suppliers, Kmart was constantly switching suppliers in search of price improvements. While Wal-Mart was controlling all the departments in its stores, Kmart was leasing out many of its departments to other companies on the theory that it could make more per square foot in rent than through its own efforts.

This is not to say that Kmart managers do not care about their business processes. After all, they have quality programs too. Nor is it that Wal-Mart managers ignore the structural dimension of strategy: they focus on the same consumer segments as Kmart and still have to make traditional strategic decisions like where to open new stores. The difference is that Wal-Mart emphasizes behavior—the organizational practices and business processes in which capabilities rooted—as the primary object of strategy and therefore focuses its managerial attention on the infrastructure that supports capabilities. This subtle distinction has made all the difference between exceptional and average performance.

Four Principles of Capabilities-Based Competition

The story of Kmart and Wal-Mart illustrates the new paradigm of competition in the 1990s. In industry after industry, established competitors are being outmaneuvered and overtaken by more dynamic rivals.

- In the years after World War II, Honda was a modest manufacturer of a 50 cc. engine designed to be attached to a bicycle. Today it is challenging General Motors and Ford for dominance of the global automobile industry.

- Xerox invented xerography and the office copier market. But between 1976 and 1982, Canon introduced more than 90 new models, cutting Xerox's share of the mid-range copier market in half.[1] Today Canon is a key competitor not only in mid-range copiers but also in high-end color copiers.

- The greatest challenge to department store giants like Macy's comes neither from other large department stores nor from small boutiques but from The Limited, a $5.25 billion design, procurement, delivery, and re-tailing machine that exploits dozens of consumer segments with the agility of many small boutiques.

- Citicorp may still be the largest U.S. bank in terms of assets, but Banc One has consistently enjoyed the highest return on assets in the U.S. banking industry and now enjoys a market capitalization greater than Citicorp's.

These examples represent more than just the triumph of individual companies. They signal a fundamental shift in the logic of competition, a shift that is revolutionizing corporate strategy.

When the economy was relatively static, strategy could afford to be static. In a world characterized by durable products, stable customer needs, well-defined national and regional markets, and clearly identified competitors, competition was a "war of position" in which companies occupied competitive space like squares on a chessboard, building and defending market share in clearly defined product or market segments. The key to competitive advantage was *where* a company chose to compete. *How* it chose to compete was also important but secondary, a matter of execution.

Few managers need reminding of the changes that have made this traditional approach obsolete. As markets fragment and proliferate, "owning" any particular market segment becomes simultaneously more difficult and less valuable. As product life cycles accelerate, dominating existing product segments becomes less important than being able to create new products and exploit them quickly. Meanwhile, as globalization breaks down barriers between national and regional markets, competitors are multiplying and reducing the value of national market share.

In this more dynamic business environment, strategy has to become correspondingly more dynamic. Competition is now a "war of movement" in which success depends on anticipation of market trends and quick response to changing customer needs. Successful competitors move quickly in and out of products, markets, and sometimes even entire businesses—a process more akin to an interactive video game than to chess. In such an environment, the essence of strategy is *not* the structure of a company's products and markets but the dynamics of its behavior. And the goal is to identify and develop the hard-to-imitate organizational capabilities that distinguish a company from its competitors in the eyes of customers.

Companies like Wal-Mart, Honda, Canon, The Limited, or Banc One have learned this lesson. Their experience and that of other successful companies suggest four basic principles of capabilities-based competition:

1. The building blocks of corporate strategy are not products and markets but business processes.
2. Competitive success depends on transforming a company's key processes into strategic capabilities that consistently provide superior value to the customer.
3. Companies create these capabilities by making strategic investments in a support infrastructure that links together and transcends traditional SBUs and functions.
4. Because capabilities necessarily cross functions, the champion of a capabilities-based strategy is the CEO.

A capability is a set of business processes strategically understood. Every company has business processes that deliver value to the customer. But few think of them as the primary object of strategy. Capabilities-based competitors identify their key business processes, manage them centrally, and invest in them heavily, looking for a long-term payback. (See Exhibit 3-1.)

Take the example of cross-docking at Wal-Mart. Cross-docking is not the cheapest or the easiest way to run a warehouse. But seen in the broader context of Wal-Mart's inventory-replenishment capability, it is an essential part of the overall process of keeping retail shelves filled while also minimizing inventory and purchasing in truckload quantities.

What transforms a set of individual business processes like cross-docking into a strategic capability? The key is to connect them to real customer needs. A capability is strategic only when it begins and ends with the customer.

Of course, just about every company these days claims to be "close to the customer." But there is a qualitative difference in the customer focus of capabilities-driven competitors. These companies conceive of the organization as a giant feedback loop that begins with identifying the needs of the customer and ends with satisfying them.

As managers have grasped the importance of time-based competition, for example, they have increasingly focused on the speed of new product development. But as a unit of analysis, new product *development* is too narrow. It is only part of what is necessary to satisfy a customer and, therefore, to build an organizational capability. Better to

Exhibit 3-1   Capabilities Help Wal-Mart Outperform Its Industry

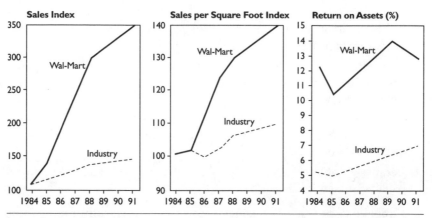

Source: The Boston Consulting Group

think in terms of new product *realization,* a capability that includes the way a product is not only developed but also marketed and serviced. The longer and more complex the string of business processes, the harder it is to transform them into a capability—but the greater the value of that capability once built because competitors have more difficulty imitating it.

Weaving business processes together into organizational capabilities in this way also mandates a new logic of vertical integration. At a time when cost pressures are pushing many companies to outsource more and more activities, capabilities-based competitors are integrating vertically to ensure that they, not a supplier or distributor, control the performance of key business processes. Remember Wal-Mart's decision to own its transportation fleet in contrast to Kmart's decision to subcontract.

Even when a company doesn't actually own every link of the capability chain, the capabilities-based competitor works to tie these parts into its own business systems. Consider WalMart's relationships with its suppliers. In order for Wal-Mart's inventory-replenishment capability to work, vendors have to change their own business processes to be more responsive to the Wal-Mart system. In exchange, they get far better payment terms from Wal-Mart than they do from other discount retailers. At Wal-Mart, the average "days payable," the time between the receipt of an invoice from a supplier and its payment, is 29 days. At Kmart, it is 45.

Another attribute of capabilities is that they are collective and cross-functional—a small part of many people's jobs, not a large part of a few. This helps explain why most companies underexploit capabilities-based competition. Because a capability is "everywhere and no-where," no one executive controls it entirely. Moreover, leveraging capabilities requires a panoply of strategic investments across SBUs and functions far beyond what traditional cost-benefit metrics can justify. Traditional internal accounting and control systems often miss the strategic nature of such investments. For these reasons, building strategic capabilities cannot be treated as an operating matter and left to operating managers, to corporate staff, or still less to SBU heads. It is the primary agenda of the CEO.

Only the CEO can focus the entire company's attention on creating capabilities that serve customers. Only the CEO can identify and authorize the infrastructure investments on which strategic capabilities depend. Only the CEO can insulate individual managers from any short-term penalties to the P&Ls of their operating units that such investments might bring about.

Indeed, a CEO's success in building and managing capabilities will be the chief test of management skill in the 1990s. The prize will be companies that combine scale and flexibility to outperform the competition along five dimensions:

- *Speed.* The ability to respond quickly to customer or market demands and to incorporate new ideas and technologies quickly into products.
- *Consistency.* The ability to produce a product that unfailingly satisfies customers' expectations.
- *Acuity.* The ability to see the competitive environment clearly and thus to anticipate and respond to customers' evolving needs and wants.
- *Agility.* The ability to adapt simultaneously to many different business environments.
- *Innovativeness.* The ability to generate new ideas and to combine existing elements to create new sources of value.

Becoming a Capabilities-Based Competitor

Few companies are fortunate enough to begin as capabilities-based competitors. For most, the challenge is to become one.

The starting point is for senior managers to undergo the fundamental shift in perception that allows them to see their business in terms of strategic capabilities. Then they can begin to identify and link together essential business processes to serve customer needs. Finally, they can reshape the organization—including managerial roles and responsiblities—to encourage the new kind of behavior necessary to make capabilities-based competition work.

The experience of a medical-equipment company we'll call Medequip illustrates this change process. An established competitor, Medequip recently found itself struggling to regain market share it had lost to a new competitor. The rival had introduced a lower priced, lower performance version of the company's most popular product. Medequip had developed a similar product in response, but senior managers were hesitant to launch it.

Their reasoning made perfect sense according to the traditional competitive logic. As managers saw it, the company faced a classic no-win situation. The new product was lower priced but also lower profit. If the company promoted it aggressively to regain market share, overall profitability would suffer.

But when Medequip managers began to investigate their competitive situation more carefully, they stopped defining the problem in terms of static products and markets. Increasingly, they saw it in terms of the organization's business processes.

Traditionally, the company's functions had operated autonomously. Manufacturing was separate from sales, which was separate from field service. What's more, the company managed field service the way most companies do—as a classic profit center whose resources were deployed to reduce costs and maximize profitability. For instance, Medequip assigned full-time service personnel only to those customers who bought enough equipment to justify the additional cost.

However, a closer look at the company's experience with these steady customers led to a fresh insight: at accounts where Medequip had placed one or more full-time service representatives on-site, the company renewed its highly profitable service contracts at three times the rate of its other accounts. When these accounts needed new equipment, they chose Medequip twice as often as other accounts did and tended to buy the broadest mix of Medequip products as well.

The reason was simple. Medequip's on-site service representatives had become expert in the operations of their customers. They knew what equipment mix best suited the customer and what additional equipment the customer needed. So they had teamed up informally with Medequip's salespeople to become part of the selling process. Because the service reps were on-site full-time, they were also able to respond quickly to equipment problems. And of course, whenever a competitor's equipment broke down, the Medequip reps were on hand to point out the product's shortcomings.

This new knowledge about the dynamics of service delivery inspired top managers to rethink how their company should compete. Specifically, they redefined field service from a stand-alone function to one part of an integrated sales and service capability. They crystallized this new approach in three key business decisions.

First, Medequip decided to use its service personnel *not* to keep costs low but to maximize the life-cycle profitability of a set of targeted accounts. This decision took the form of a dramatic commitment to place at least one service rep on-site with selected customers—no matter how little business each account currently represented.

The decision to guarantee on-site service was expensive, so choosing which customers to target was crucial; there had to be potential for considerable additional business. The company divided its accounts into three categories: those it dominated, those where a single competitor dominated, and those where several competitors were present. Medequip protected the accounts it dominated by maintaining the already high level of service and by offering attractive terms for renewing service contracts. The company ignored those customers dominated by a single competitor—unless the competitor was having serious problems. All the remaining resources were focused on those accounts where no single competitor had the upper hand.

Next Medequip combined its sales, service, and order-entry organizations into cross-functional teams that concentrated almost exclusively on the needs of the targeted accounts. The company trained service reps in sales techniques so they could take full responsibility for generating new sales leads. This freed up the sales staff to focus on the more strategic role of understanding the long-term needs of the customer's business. Finally, to emphasize Medequip's new commitment to total service, the company even taught its service reps how to fix competitors' equipment.

Once this new organizational structure was in place, Medequip finally introduced its new low-price product. The result: the company has not only stopped its decline in market share but also *increased* share by almost 50%. The addition of the lower priced product has reduced profit margins, but the overall mix still includes many higher priced products. And absolute profits are much higher than before.

This story suggests four steps by which any company can transform itself into a capabilities-based competitor:

Shift the strategic framework to achieve aggressive goals. At Medequip, managers transformed what looked like a no-win situation—either lose share or lose profits—into an opportunity for a major competitive victory. They did so by abandoning the company's traditional function, cost, and profit-center orientation and by identifying and managing the capabilities that link customer need to customer satisfaction. The chief expression of this new capabilities-based strategy was the decision to provide on-site service reps to targeted accounts and to create cross-functional sales and service teams.

Organize around the chosen capability and make sure employees have the necessary skills and resources to achieve it. Having set this ambitious competitive goal, Medequip managers next set about reshaping the company in terms of it. Rather than retaining the existing functional structure and trying to encourage coordination through some kind of matrix, they created a brand new organization—Customer Sales and Service—and divided it into "cells" with overall responsibility for specific customers. The company also provided the necessary training so that employees could understand how their new roles would help achieve new business goals. Finally, Medequip created systems to support employees in their new roles. For example, one information system uses CD-ROMs to give field-service personnel quick access to information about Medequip's product line as well as those of competitors.

Make progress visible and bring measurements and reward into alignment. Medequip also made sure that the company's measurement and reward systems reflected the new competitive strategy. Like most companies, the company had never known the profitability of individual customers. Traditionally, field-service employees were measured on overall service profitability. With the shift to the new approach, however, the company had to develop a whole new set of measures—for example, Medequip's "share-by-customer-by-product," the amount of money the company invested in servicing a particular customer, and the customer's current and estimated lifetime profitability. Team members' compensation was calculated according to these new measures.

Do not delegate the leadership of the transformation. Becoming a capabilities-based competitor requires an enormous amount of change. For that reason, it is a process extremely difficult to delegate. Because capabilities are cross-functional, the change process can't be left to middle managers. It requires the hands-on guidance of the CEO and the active involvement of top line managers. At Medequip, the heads of sales, service, and order entry led the sub-teams that made the actual recommendations, but it was the CEO who oversaw the change process, evaluated their proposals, and made the final decision. His leading role ensured senior management's commitment to the recommended changes.

This top-down change process has the paradoxical result of driving business decision making down to those directly participating in key processes—for example, Medequip's sales and service staff. This leads to a high measure of operational flexibility and an almost reflex-like responsiveness to external change.

A New Logic of Growth: The Capabilities Predator

Once managers reshape the company in terms of its underlying capabilities, they can use these capabilities to define a growth path for the corporation. At the center of capabilities-based competition is a new logic of growth.

In the 1960s, most managers assumed that when growth in a company's basic business slowed, the company should turn to diversification. This was the age of the multibusiness conglomerate. In the 1970s and 1980s, however, it became clear that growth through diversification was difficult. And so, the pendulum of management thinking swung once again. Companies were urged to "stick to their knitting"— that is, to focus on their core business, identify where the profit was, and get rid of everything else. The idea of the corporation became increasingly narrow.

Competing on capabilities provides a way for companies to gain the benefits of both focus and diversification. Put another way, a company that focuses on its strategic capabilities can compete in a remarkable diversity of regions, products, and businesses and do it far more coherently than the typical conglomerate can. Such a company is a "capabilities predator"—able to come out of nowhere and move rapidly from nonparticipant to major player and even to industry leader.

Capabilities-based companies grow by transferring their essential business processes—first to new geographic areas and then to new businesses. Wal-Mart CEO David Glass alludes to this method of growth when he characterizes Wal-Mart as "always pushing from the inside out; we never jump and backfill."

Strategic advantages built on capabilities are easier to transfer geographically than more traditional competitive advantages. Honda, for example, has become a manufacturer in Europe and the United States with relatively few problems. The quality of its cars made in the United States is so good that the company is exporting some of them back to Japan.

In many respects, Wal-Mart's move from small towns in the South to large, urban, northern cities spans as great a cultural gap as Honda's move beyond Japan. And yet, Wal-Mart has done it with barely a hiccup. While the stores are much bigger and the product lines different, the capabilities are exactly the same. Wal-Mart simply replicates its system as soon as the required people are trained. The company estimates that it can train enough new employees to grow about 25% a year.

But the big payoff for capabilities-led growth comes not through geographical expansion but through rapid entry into whole new businesses. Capabilities-based companies do this in at least two ways. The first is by "cloning" their key business processes. Again, Honda is a typical example.

Most people attribute Honda's success to the innovative design of its products or the way the company manufactures them. These factors are certainly important. But the company's growth has been spearheaded by less visible capabilities.

For example, a big part of Honda's original success in motorcycles was due to the company's distinctive capability in "dealer management," which departed from the traditional relationship between motorcycle manufacturers and dealers. Typically, local dealers were motorcycle enthusiasts who were more concerned with finding a way to support their hobby than with building a strong business. They were not particularly interested in marketing, parts-inventory management, or other business systems.

Honda, by contrast, managed its dealers to ensure that they would become successful businesspeople. The company provided operating procedures and policies for merchandising, selling, floor planning, and service management. It trained all its dealers and their entire staffs in these new management systems and supported them with a computerized dealer-management information system. The part-time dealers of competitors were no match for the better prepared and better financed Honda dealers.

Honda's move into new businesses, including lawn mowers, outboard motors, and automobiles, has depended on re-creating this same dealer-management capability in each new sector. Even in segments like luxury cars, where local dealers are generally more service-oriented than those in the motorcycle business, Honda's skill at managing its dealers is transforming service standards. Honda dealers consistently receive the highest ratings for customer satisfaction among auto companies selling in the United States. One reason is that Honda gives its dealers far more autonomy to decide on the spot whether a needed repair is covered by warranty. (See "How Capabilities Differ from Core Competencies: The Case of Honda.")

How Capabilities Differ from Core Competencies: The Case of Honda

In their influential 1990 HBR article, "The Core Competence of the Corporation," Gary Hamel and C.K. Prahalad mount an attack on traditional notions of strategy that is not so dissimilar from what we are arguing here.* For Hamel and Prahalad, however, the central building block of corporate strategy is "core competence." How is a competence different from a capability, and how do the two concepts relate to each other?

Hamel and Prahalad define core competence as the combination of individual technologies and production skills that underlie a company's myriad product lines. Sony's core competence in miniaturization, for example, allows the company to make everything from the Sony Walkman to videocameras to notebook computers. Canon's core competencies in optics, imaging, and microprocessor controls have enabled it to enter markets as seemingly diverse as copiers, laser printers, cameras, and image scanners.

As the above examples suggest, Hamel and Prahalad use core competence to explain the ease with which successful competitors are able to enter new and seemingly unrelated businesses. But a closer look reveals that competencies are not the whole story.

Consider Honda's move from motorcycles into other businesses, including lawn mowers, outboard motors, and automobiles. Hamel and Prahalad attribute Honda's success to its underlying competence in engines and power trains. While Honda's engine competence is certainly important, it alone cannot explain the speed with which the company has successfully moved into a wide range of businesses over the past 20 years. After all, General Motors (to take just one example) is also an accomplished designer and manufacturer of engines. What distinguishes Honda from its competitors is its focus on capabilities.

One important but largely invisible capability is Honda's expertise in "dealer management"—its ability to train and support its dealer network with operating procedures and policies for merchandising, selling, floor planning, and service management. First developed for its motorcycle business, this set of business processes has since been replicated in each new business the company has entered.

Another capability central to Honda's success has been its skill at "product realization." Traditional product development separates planning, proving, and executing into three sequential activities: assessing the market's needs and whether existing products are meeting those needs; testing the proposed product; then building a prototype. The end result of this process is a new factory or organization to introduce the new product. This traditional approach takes a long time—and with time goes money.

Honda has arranged these activities differently. First, planning and proving go on continuously and in parallel. Second, these activities are clearly separated from execution. At Honda, the highly disciplined execution cycle schedules major product revisions every four years and minor revisions every two years. The 1990 Honda Accord, for example, which is the first major redesign of that model since 1986, incorporates a power train developed two years earlier and first used in the 1988 Accord. Finally, when a new product is ready, it is released to *existing* factories and organizations, which dramatically shortens the amount of time needed to launch it. As time is reduced, so are cost and risk.

Consider the following comparison between Honda and GM. In 1984, Honda launched its Acura division; one year later, GM created Saturn. Honda chose to integrate Acura into its existing organization and facilities. In Europe, for example, the Acura Legend is sold through the same sales force as the Honda Legend. The Acura division now makes three models—the Legend, Integra, and Vigor—and is turning out 300,000 cars a year. At the end of 1991, seven years after it was launched, the division had produced a total of 800,000 vehicles. More important, it had already introduced eight variations of its product line.

By contrast, GM created a separate organization and a separate facility for Saturn. Production began in late 1990, and 1991 will be its first full model year. If GM is lucky, it will be producing 240,000 vehicles in the next year or two and will have two models out.

As the Honda example suggests, competencies and capabilities represent two different but complementary dimensions of an emerging paradigm for corporate strategy. Both concepts emphasize "behavioral" aspects of strategy in contrast to the traditional structural model. But whereas core competence emphasizes technological and production expertise at specific points along the value chain, capabilities are more broadly based, encompassing the entire value chain. In this respect, capabilities are visible to the customer in a way that core competencies rarely are.

Like the "grand unified theory" that modern-day physicists are searching for to explain physical behavior at both the subatomic level and that of the entire cosmos, the combination of core competence and capabilities may define the universal model for corporate strategy in the 1990s and beyond.

Harvard Business Review 68, no. 3 (1990): 79–91.

But the ultimate form of growth in the capabilities-based company may not be cloning business processes so much as creating processes so flexible and robust that the same set can serve many different businesses. This is the case with Wal-Mart. The company uses the same inventory-replenishment system that makes its discount stores so successful to propel itself into new and traditionally distinct retail sectors.

Take the example of warehouse clubs, no-frills stores that sell products in bulk at a deep discount. In 1983, Wal-Mart created Sam's Club to compete with industry founder Price Club and Kmart's own PACE Membership Warehouse. Within four years, Sam's Club sales had passed those of both Price and PACE, making it the largest wholesale club in the country. Sam's 1990 sales were $5.3 billion, compared with $4.9 billion for Price and $1.6 billion for PACE. What's more, Wal-Mart has repeated this rapid penetration strategy in other retail sectors, including pharmacies, European-style hypermarkets, and large, no-frills grocery stores known as superstores.

While Wal-Mart has been growing by quickly entering these new businesses, Kmart has tried to grow by acquisition, with mixed success. In the past decade, Kmart has bought and sold a number of companies in unrelated businesses such as restaurants and insurance—an indication the company has had difficulty adding value.

This is not to suggest that growth by acquisition is necessarily doomed to failure. Indeed, the company that is focused on its capabilities is often better able to target sensible acquisitions and then integrate them successfully. For example, Wal-Mart has recently begun to supplement its growth "from the inside out" by acquiring companies—for example, other small warehouse clubs and a retail and grocery distributor—whose operations can be folded into the Wal-Mart system. (See Exhibit 3-2.)

It is interesting to speculate where Wal-Mart will strike next. The company's inventory-replenishment capability could prove to be a strong competitive advantage in a wide variety of retail businesses. In the past decade, Wal-Mart came out of nowhere to challenge Kmart. In the next decade, companies such as Toys "R" Us (Wal-Mart already controls as much as 10% of the $13 billion toy market) and Circuit City (consumer electronics) may find themselves in the sights of this capabilities predator.

The Future of Capabilities-Based Competition

For the moment, capabilities-based companies have the advantage of competing against rivals still locked into the old way of seeing the competitive environment. But such a situation won't last forever. As more and more companies make the transition to capabilities-based competition, the simple fact of competing on capabilities will become less important than the specific capabilities a company has chosen to build. Given the necessary long-term investments, the strategic choices managers make will end up determining a company's fate.

If Wal-Mart and Kmart are a good example of the present state of capabilities-based competition, the story of two fast-growing regional banks suggests its future. Wachovia Corporation, with dual headquarters in Winston-Salem, North Carolina and Atlanta, Georgia, has superior returns and growing market share throughout its core markets in both states. Banc One, based in Columbus, Ohio, has consistently enjoyed the highest return on assets in the U.S. banking industry. Both banks compete on capabilities, but they do it in very different ways.

Wachovia competes on its ability to understand and serve the needs of individual customers, a skill that manifests itself in probably the highest "cross-sell ratio"—the average number of products per customer—of any bank in the country. The linchpin of this capability is the company's roughly 600 "personal bankers," frontline employees who provide Wachovia's mass-market customers with a degree of personalized service approaching what has traditionally been available

Exhibit 3-2   Portrait of a Capabilities Predator

By applying capabilities developed in its core business, Wal-Mart was able to penetrate the wholesale club market quickly. Its unit, Sam's Club, overtook industry leader Price Club in a mere four years.

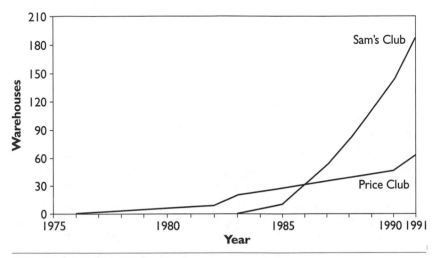

Source: The Boston Consulting Group

only to private banking clients. The company's specialized support systems allow each personal banker to serve about 1,200 customers. Among those systems: an integrated customer-information file, simplified work processes that allow the bank to respond to almost all customer requests by the end of business that day, and a five-year personal banker training program.

Where Wachovia focuses on meeting the needs of individual customers, Banc One's distinctive ability is to understand and respond to the needs of entire *communities*. To do community banking effectively, a bank has to have deep roots in the local community. But traditionally, local banks have not been able to muster the professional expertise, state-of-the-art products, and highly competitive cost structure of large national banks like Citicorp. Banc One competes by offering its customers the best of both these worlds. Or in the words of one company slogan, Banc One "out-locals the national banks and out-nationals the local banks."

Striking this balance depends on two factors. One is local autonomy.

The central organizational role in the Banc One business system is played not by frontline employees but by the presidents of the 51 affiliate banks in the Banc One network. Affiliate presidents have exceptional power within their own region. They select products, establish prices and marketing strategy, make credit decisions, and set internal management policies. They can even over-rule the activities of Banc One's centralized direct-marketing businesses. But while Banc One's affiliate system is highly decentralized, its success also depends on an elaborate, and highly centralized, process of continuous organizational learning. Affiliate presidents have the authority to mold bank products and services to local conditions, but they are also expected to learn from best practice throughout the Banc One system and to adapt it to their own operations.

Banc One collects an extraordinary amount of detailed and current information on each affiliate bank's internal and external performance. For example, the bank regularly publishes "league tables" on numerous measures of operating performance, with the worst performers listed first. This encourages collaboration to improve the weakest affiliates rather than competition to be the best. The bank also continuously engages in workflow re-engineering and process simplification. The 100 most successful projects, known as the "Best of the Best," are documented and circulated among affiliates.

Wachovia and Banc One both compete on capabilities. Both banks focus on key business processes and place critical decision-making authority with the people directly responsible for them. Both manage these processes through a support system that spans the traditional functional structure, and senior managers concentrate on managing this system rather than controlling decisions. Both are decentralized but focused, single-minded but flexible.

But there the similarities end. Wachovia responds to individual customers en masse with personalization akin to that of a private banker. Banc One responds to local markets en masse with the flexibility and canniness of the traditional community bank. As a result, they focus on different business processes: Wachovia on the transfer of customer-specific information across numerous points of customer contact; Banc One on the transfer of best practices across affiliate banks. They also empower different levels in the organization: the personal banker at Wachovia, the affiliate president at Banc One.

Most important, they grow differently. Because so much of Wachovia's capability is embedded in the training of the personal bankers, the bank has made few acquisitions and can integrate them only very slowly. Banc One's capabilities, by contrast, are especially easy to transfer to new acquisitions. All the company needs to do is install its corporate MIS and intensively train the acquired bank's senior officers, a process that can be done in a few months, as opposed to the much longer period it takes Wachovia to train a new cadre of frontline bankers. Banc One has therefore made acquisitions almost a separate line of business.

If Banc One and Wachovia were to compete against each other, it is not clear who would win. Each would have strengths that the other could not match. Wachovia's capability to serve individual customers by cross-selling a wide range of banking products will in the long term probably allow the company to extract more profit per customer than Banc One. On the other hand, Wachovia cannot adapt its products, pricing, and promotion to local market conditions the way Banc One can. And Wachovia's growth rate is limited by the amount of time it takes to train new personal bankers.

Moreover, these differences are deep-seated. They define each of the two companies in ways that are not easy to change. Capabilities are often mutually exclusive. Choosing the right ones is the essence of strategy.

Note

1. See T. Michael Nevens, Gregory L. Summe, and Bro Uttal, "Commercializing Technology: What the Best Companies Do," *Harvard Business Review* 68, no. 3 (1990): 154.

PART

II

Creating Strategic Clarity: Become a Strategic Partner

1
What Is Strategy?

Michael E. Porter

Operational Effectiveness Is Not Strategy

For almost two decades, managers have been learning to play by a new set of rules. Companies must be flexible to respond rapidly to competitive and market changes. They must benchmark continuously to achieve best practice. They must outsource aggressively to gain efficiencies. And they must nurture a few core competencies in the race to stay ahead of rivals.

Positioning—once the heart of strategy—is rejected as too static for today's dynamic markets and changing technologies. According to the new dogma, rivals can quickly copy any market position, and competitive advantage is, at best, temporary.

But those beliefs are dangerous half-truths, and they are leading more and more companies down the path of mutually destructive competition. True, some barriers to competition are falling as regulation eases and markets become global. True, companies have properly invested energy in becoming leaner and more nimble. In many industries, however, what some call *hypercompetition* is a self-inflicted wound, not the inevitable outcome of a changing paradigm of competition.

The root of the problem is the failure to distinguish between

This chapter has benefited greatly from the assistance of many individuals and companies. The author gives special thanks to Jan Rivkin, the coauthor of a related paper. Substantial research contributions have been made by Nicolaj Siggelkow, Dawn Sylvester, and Lucia Marshall. Tarun Khanna, Roger Martin, and Anita McGahan have provided especially extensive comments.

operational effectiveness and strategy. The quest for productivity, quality, and speed has spawned a remarkable number of management tools and techniques: total quality management, benchmarking, time-based competition, outsourcing, partnering, reengineering, change management. Although the resulting operational improvements have often been dramatic, many companies have been frustrated by their inability to translate those gains into sustainable profitability. And bit by bit, almost imperceptibly, management tools have taken the place of strategy. As managers push to improve on all fronts, they move farther away from viable competitive positions.

OPERATIONAL EFFECTIVENESS: NECESSARY BUT NOT SUFFICIENT

Operational effectiveness and strategy are both essential to superior performance, which, after all, is the primary goal of any enterprise. But they work in very different ways.

A company can outperform rivals only if it can establish a difference that it can preserve. It must deliver greater value to customers or create comparable value at a lower cost, or do both. The arithmetic of superior profitability then follows: delivering greater value allows a company to charge higher average unit prices; greater efficiency results in lower average unit costs.

Ultimately, all differences between companies in cost or price derive from the hundreds of activities required to create, produce, sell, and deliver their products or services, such as calling on customers, assembling final products, and training employees. Cost is generated by performing activities, and cost advantage arises from performing particular activities more efficiently than competitors. Similarly, differentiation arises from both the choice of activities and how they are performed. Activities, then, are the basic units of competitive advantage. Overall advantage or disadvantage results from all of a company's activities, not only a few.[1]

Operational effectiveness (OE) means performing similar activities *better* than rivals perform them. Operational effectiveness includes but is not limited to efficiency. It refers to any number of practices that allow a company to better utilize its inputs by, for example, reducing defects in products or developing better products faster. In contrast, stra-

Exhibit 1-1   *Operational Effectiveness Versus Strategic Positioning*

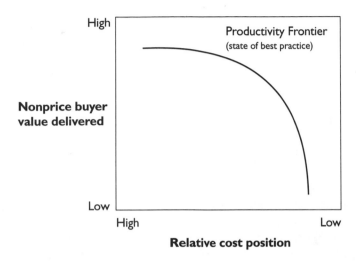

tegic positioning means performing *different* activities from rivals' or performing similar activities in *different ways*. (See Exhibit 1-1.)

Differences in operational effectiveness among companies are pervasive. Some companies are able to get more out of their inputs than others because they eliminate wasted effort, employ more advanced technology, motivate employees better, or have greater insight into managing particular activities or sets of activities. Such differences in operational effectiveness are an important source of differences in profitability among competitors because they directly affect relative cost positions and levels of differentiation.

Differences in operational effectiveness were at the heart of the Japanese challenge to Western companies in the 1980s. The Japanese were so far ahead of rivals in operational effectiveness that they could offer lower cost and superior quality at the same time. It is worth dwelling on this point, because so much recent thinking about competition depends on it. Imagine for a moment a *productivity frontier* that constitutes the sum of all existing best practices at any given time. Think of it as the maximum value that a company delivering a particular product or service can create at a given cost, using the best available technologies, skills, management techniques, and purchased inputs. The productivity frontier can apply to individual activities, to groups of linked activities such as order processing and manufacturing, and to an entire company's activities. When a company improves its operational effectiveness, it moves toward the frontier. Doing so may require capital investment, different personnel, or simply new ways of managing.

The productivity frontier is constantly shifting outward as new technologies and management approaches are developed and as new inputs become available. Laptop computers, mobile communications, the Internet, and software such as Lotus Notes, for example, have redefined the productivity frontier for sales-force operations and created rich possibilities for linking sales with such activities as order processing and after-sales support. Similarly, lean production, which involves a family of activities, has allowed substantial improvements in manufacturing productivity and asset utilization.

For at least the past decade, managers have been preoccupied with improving operational effectiveness. Through programs such as TQM, time-based competition, and benchmarking, they have changed how they perform activities in order to eliminate inefficiencies, improve customer satisfaction, and achieve best practice. Hoping to keep up with shifts in the productivity frontier, managers have embraced continuous improvement, empowerment, change management, and the so-called learning organization. The popularity of outsourcing and the virtual corporation reflect the growing recognition that it is difficult to perform all activities as productively as specialists.

As companies move to the frontier, they can often improve on multiple dimensions of performance at the same time. For example, manufacturers that adopted the Japanese practice of rapid changeovers in the 1980s were able to lower cost and improve differentiation simultaneously. What were once believed to be real trade-offs—between defects and costs, for example—turned out to be illusions created by poor operational effectiveness. Managers have learned to reject such false trade-offs.

Constant improvement in operational effectiveness is necessary to achieve superior profitability. However, it is not usually sufficient. Few companies have competed successfully on the basis of operational effectiveness over an extended period, and staying ahead of rivals gets harder every day. The most obvious reason for that is the rapid diffusion of best practices. Competitors can quickly imitate management techniques, new technologies, input improvements, and superior ways of meeting customers' needs. The most generic solutions—those that can be used in multiple settings—diffuse the fastest. Witness the proliferation of OE techniques accelerated by support from consultants.

OE competition shifts the productivity frontier outward, effectively raising the bar for everyone. But although such competition produces absolute improvement in operational effectiveness, it leads to relative improvement for no one. Consider the $5 billion-plus U.S. commercial-printing industry. The major players—R.R. Donnelley & Sons Company, Quebecor, World Color Press, and Big Flower Press—are competing head to head, serving all types of customers, offering the same array of printing technologies (gravure and web offset), investing heavily in the same new equipment, running their presses faster, and reducing crew sizes. But the resulting major productivity gains are being captured by customers and equipment suppliers, not retained in superior profitability. Even industry-leader Donnelley's profit margin, consistently higher than 7% in the 1980s, fell to less than 4.6% in 1995. This pattern is playing itself out in industry after industry. Even the Japanese, pioneers of the new competition, suffer from persistently low profits. (See "Japanese Companies Rarely Have Strategies.")

Japanese Companies Rarely Have Strategies

The Japanese triggered a global revolution in operational effectiveness in the 1970s and 1980s, pioneering practices such as total quality management and continuous improvement. As a result, Japanese manufacturers enjoyed substantial cost and quality advantages for many years.

But Japanese companies rarely developed distinct strategic positions of the kind discussed in this article. Those that did—Sony, Canon, and Sega, for example—were the exception rather than the rule. Most Japanese companies imitate and emulate one another. All rivals offer most if not all product varieties, features, and services; they employ all channels and match one anothers' plant configurations.

The dangers of Japanese-style competition are now becoming easier to recognize. In the 1980s, with rivals operating far from the productivity frontier, it seemed possible to win on both cost and quality indefinitely. Japanese companies were all able to grow in an expanding domestic economy and by penetrating global markets. They appeared unstoppable. But as the gap in operational effectiveness narrows, Japanese companies are increasingly caught in a trap of their own making. If they are to escape the mutually destructive battles now ravaging their performance, Japanese companies will have to learn strategy.

To do so, they may have to overcome strong cultural barriers. Japan is notoriously consensus oriented, and companies have a strong tendency to mediate differences among individuals rather than accentuate them. Strategy, on the other hand, requires hard choices. The Japanese also have a deeply ingrained service tradition that predisposes them to go to great lengths to satisfy any need a customer expresses. Companies that compete in that way end up blurring their distinct positioning, becoming all things to all customers.

This discussion of Japan is drawn from the author's research with Hirotaka Takeuchi, with help from Mariko Sakakibara.

The second reason that improved operational effectiveness is insufficient—competitive convergence—is more subtle and insidious. The more benchmarking companies do, the more they look alike. The more that rivals outsource activities to efficient third parties, often the same ones, the more generic those activities become. As rivals imitate one another's improvements in quality, cycle times, or supplier partnerships, strategies converge and competition becomes a series of races down identical paths that no one can win. Competition based on operational effectiveness alone is mutually destructive, leading to wars of attrition that can be arrested only by limiting competition.

The recent wave of industry consolidation through mergers makes sense in the context of OE competition. Driven by performance pressures but lacking strategic vision, company after company has had no better idea than to buy up its rivals. The competitors left standing are often those that outlasted others, not companies with real advantage.

After a decade of impressive gains in operational effectiveness, many companies are facing diminishing returns. Continuous improvement has been etched on managers' brains. But its tools unwittingly draw companies toward imitation and homogeneity. Gradually, managers have let operational effectiveness supplant strategy. The result is zero-sum competition, static or declining prices, and pressures on costs that compromise companies' ability to invest in the business for the long term.

Strategy Rests on Unique Activities

Competitive strategy is about being different. It means deliberately choosing a different set of activities to deliver a unique mix of value. (See "Finding New Positions: The Entrepreneurial Edge.")

Finding New Positions: The Entrepreneurial Edge

Strategic competition can be thought of as the process of perceiving new positions that woo customers from established positions or draw new customers into the market. For example, superstores offering depth of merchandise in a single product category take market share from broad-line department stores offering a more limited selection in many categories. Mail-order catalogs pick off customers who crave convenience. In principle, incumbents and entrepreneurs face the same challenges in finding new strategic positions. In practice, new entrants often have the edge.

Strategic positionings are often not obvious, and finding them requires creativity and insight. New entrants often discover unique positions that have been available but simply overlooked by established competitors. Ikea, for example, recognized a customer group that had been ignored or served poorly. Circuit City Stores' entry into used cars, CarMax, is based on a new way of performing activities—extensive refurbishing of cars, product guarantees, no-haggle pricing, sophisticated use of in-house customer financing—that has long been open to incumbents.

New entrants can prosper by occupying a position that a competitor once held but has ceded through years of imitation and straddling. And entrants coming from other industries can create new positions because of distinctive activities drawn from their other businesses. CarMax borrows heavily from Circuit City's expertise in inventory management, credit, and other activities in consumer electronics retailing.

Most commonly, however, new positions open up because of change. New customer groups or purchase occasions arise; new needs emerge as societies evolve; new distribution channels appear; new technologies are developed; new machinery or information systems become available. When such changes happen, new entrants, unencumbered by a long history in the industry, can often more easily perceive the potential for a new way of competing. Unlike incumbents, newcomers can be more flexible because they face no trade-offs with their existing activities.

Southwest Airlines Company, for example, offers short-haul, low-cost, point-to-point service between midsize cities and secondary airports in large cities. Southwest avoids large airports and does not fly great distances. Its customers include business travelers, families, and students. Southwest's frequent departures and low fares attract price-sensitive customers who otherwise would travel by bus or car, and convenience-oriented travelers who would choose a full-service airline on other routes.

Most managers describe strategic positioning in terms of their customers: "Southwest Airlines serves price- and convenience-sensitive travelers," for example. But the essence of strategy is in the activities—choosing to perform activities differently or to perform different activities than rivals. Otherwise, a strategy is nothing more than a marketing slogan that will not withstand competition.

A full-service airline is configured to get passengers from almost any point A to any point B. To reach a large number of destinations and serve passengers with connecting flights, full-service airlines employ a hub-and-spoke system centered on major airports. To attract passengers who desire more comfort, they offer first-class or business-class service. To accommodate passengers who must change planes, they coordinate schedules and check and transfer baggage. Because some passengers will be traveling for many hours, full-service airlines serve meals.

Southwest, in contrast, tailors all its activities to deliver low-cost, convenient service on its particular type of route. Through fast turn-arounds at the gate of only 15 minutes, Southwest is able to keep planes flying longer hours than rivals and provide frequent departures with fewer aircraft. Southwest does not offer meals, assigned seats, interline baggage checking, or premium classes of service. Automated ticketing at the gate encourages customers to bypass travel agents, allowing Southwest to avoid their commissions. A standardized fleet of 737 aircraft boosts the efficiency of maintenance.

Southwest has staked out a unique and valuable strategic position based on a tailored set of activities. On the routes served by Southwest, a full-service airline could never be as convenient or as low cost. (See Exhibit 1-2.)

IKEA, the global furniture retailer based in Sweden, also has a clear strategic positioning. IKEA targets young furniture buyers who want style at low cost. What turns this marketing concept into a strategic positioning is the tailored set of activities that make it work. Like Southwest, IKEA has chosen to perform activities differently from its rivals.

Exhibit 1-2   Southwest Airlines' Activity System

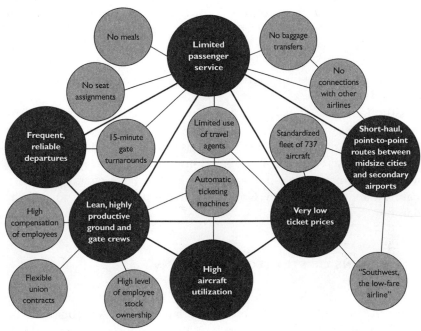

Consider the typical furniture store. Showrooms display samples of the merchandise. One area might contain 25 sofas; another will display five dining tables. But those items represent only a fraction of the choices available to customers. Dozens of books displaying fabric swatches or wood samples or alternate styles offer customers thousands of product varieties to choose from. Salespeople often escort customers through the store, answering questions and helping them navigate this maze of choices. Once a customer makes a selection, the order is relayed to a third-party manufacturer. With luck, the furniture will be delivered to the customer's home within six to eight weeks. This is a value chain that maximizes customization and service but does so at high cost.

In contrast, IKEA serves customers who are happy to trade off service for cost. Instead of having a sales associate trail customers around the store, IKEA uses a self-service model based on clear, in-store displays. Rather than rely solely on third-party manufacturers, IKEA designs its own low-cost, modular, ready-to-assemble furniture to fit its positioning. In huge stores, IKEA displays every product it sells in room-like settings, so customers don't need a decorator to help them imagine how to put the pieces together. Adjacent to the furnished showrooms is a warehouse section with the products in boxes on pallets. Customers are expected to do their own pickup and delivery, and IKEA will even sell you a roof rack for your car that you can return for a refund on your next visit.

Although much of its low-cost position comes from having customers "do it themselves," IKEA offers a number of extra services that its competitors do not. In-store child care is one. Extended hours are another. Those services are uniquely aligned with the needs of its customers, who are young, not wealthy, likely to have children (but no nanny), and, because they work for a living, have a need to shop at odd hours. (See Exhibit 1-3.)

THE ORIGINS OF STRATEGIC POSITIONS

Strategic positions emerge from three distinct sources, which are not mutually exclusive and often overlap. First, positioning can be based on producing a subset of an industry's products or services. I call this *variety-based positioning* because it is based on the choice of product or service varieties rather than customer segments. Variety-based positioning makes economic sense when a company can best produce particular products or services using distinctive sets of activities.

Jiffy Lube International, for instance, specializes in automotive lubricants and does not offer other car repair or maintenance services. Its value chain produces faster service at a lower cost than broader line repair shops, a combination so attractive that many customers subdivide their purchases, buying oil changes from the focused competitor, Jiffy Lube, and going to rivals for other services.

The Vanguard Group, a leader in the mutual fund industry, is another example of variety-based positioning. Vanguard provides an array of common stock, bond, and money market funds that offer predictable performance and rock-bottom expenses. The company's investment approach deliberately sacrifices the possibility of extraordinary performance in any one year for good relative performance in every year. Vanguard is known, for example, for its index funds. It avoids making bets on interest rates and steers clear of narrow stock groups. Fund managers keep trading levels low, which holds expenses

Exhibit 1-3   Mapping Activity Systems

Activity-system maps, such as this one for IKEA, show how a company's strategic position is contained in a set of tailored activities designed to deliver it. In companies with a clear strategic position, a number of higher-order strategic themes (in light grey) can be identified and implemented through clusters of tightly linked activities (in black).

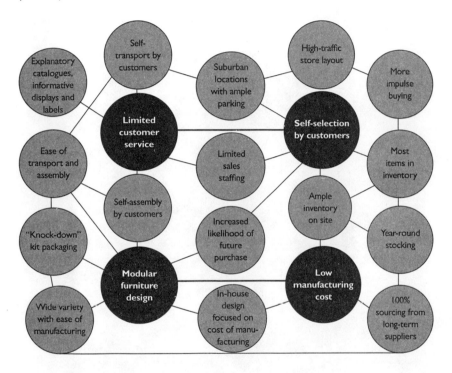

down; in addition, the company discourages customers from rapid buying and selling because doing so drives up costs and can force a fund manager to trade in order to deploy new capital and raise cash for redemptions. Vanguard also takes a consistent low-cost approach to managing distribution, customer service, and marketing. Many investors include one or more Vanguard funds in their portfolio, while buying aggressively managed or specialized funds from competitors.

The people who use Vanguard or Jiffy Lube are responding to a superior value chain for a particular type of service. A variety-based positioning can serve a wide array of customers, but for most it will meet only a subset of their needs. (See Exhibit 1-4.)

Exhibit 1-4 Vanguard's Activity System

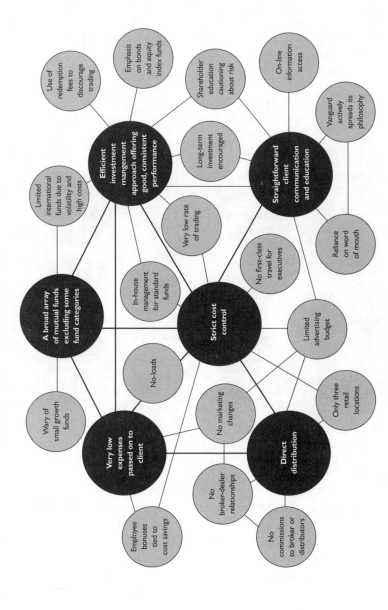

A second basis for positioning is that of serving most or all the needs of a particular group of customers. I call this *needs-based positioning,* which comes closer to traditional thinking about targeting a segment of customers. It arises when there are groups of customers with differing needs, and when a tailored set of activities can serve those needs best. Some groups of customers are more price sensitive than others, demand different product features, and need varying amounts of information, support, and services. IKEA's customers are a good example of such a group. IKEA seeks to meet all the home furnishing needs of its target customers, not just a subset of them.

A variant of needs-based positioning arises when the same customer has different needs on different occasions or for different types of transactions. The same person, for example, may have different needs when traveling on business than when traveling for pleasure with the family. Buyers of cans—beverage companies, for example—will likely have different needs from their primary supplier than from their secondary source.

It is intuitive for most managers to conceive of their business in terms of the customers' needs they are meeting. But a critical element of needs-based positioning is not at all intuitive and is often overlooked. Differences in needs will not translate into meaningful positions unless the best set of activities to satisfy them *also* differs. If that were not the case, every competitor could meet those same needs, and there would be nothing unique or valuable about the positioning.

In private banking, for example, Bessemer Trust Company targets families with a minimum of $5 million in investable assets who want capital preservation combined with wealth accumulation. By assigning one sophisticated account officer for every 14 families, Bessemer has configured its activities for personalized service. Meetings, for example, are more likely to be held at a client's ranch or yacht than in the office. Bessemer offers a wide array of customized services, including investment management and estate administration, oversight of oil and gas investments, and accounting for racehorses and aircraft. Loans, a staple of most private banks, are rarely needed by Bessemer's clients and make up a tiny fraction of its client balances and income. Despite the most generous compensation of account officers and the highest personnel cost as a percentage of operating expenses, Bessemer's differentiation with its target families produces a return on equity estimated to be the highest of any private banking competitor.

Citibank's private bank, on the other hand, serves clients with minimum assets of about $250,000 who, in contrast to Bessemer's clients, want convenient access to loans—from jumbo mortgages to deal financing. Citibank's account managers are primarily lenders. When clients need other services, their account manager refers them to other Citibank specialists, each of whom handles prepackaged products. Citibank's system is less customized than Bessemer's and allows it to have a lower manager-to-client ratio of 1:125. Biannual office meetings are offered only for the largest clients. Both Bessemer and Citibank have tailored their activities to meet the needs of a different group of private banking customers. The same value chain cannot profitably meet the needs of both groups.

The third basis for positioning is that of segmenting customers who are accessible in different ways. Although their needs are similar to those of other customers, the best configuration of activities to reach them is different. I call this *access-based positioning*. Access can be a function of customer geography or customer scale—or of anything that requires a different set of activities to reach customers in the best way.

Segmenting by access is less common and less well understood than the other two bases. Carmike Cinemas, for example, operates movie theaters exclusively in cities and towns with populations under 200,000. How does Carmike make money in markets that are not only small but also won't support big-city ticket prices? It does so through a set of activities that result in a lean cost structure. Carmike's small-town customers can be served through standardized, low-cost theater complexes requiring fewer screens and less sophisticated projection technology than big-city theaters. The company's proprietary information system and management process eliminate the need for local administrative staff beyond a single theater manager. Carmike also reaps advantages from centralized purchasing, lower rent and payroll costs (because of its locations), and rock-bottom corporate overhead of 2% (the industry average is 5%). Operating in small communities also allows Carmike to practice a highly personal form of marketing in which the theater manager knows patrons and promotes attendance through personal contacts. By being the dominant if not the only theater in its markets—the main competition is often the high school football team—Carmike is also able to get its pick of films and negotiate better terms with distributors.

Rural versus urban-based customers are one example of access driving differences in activities. Serving small rather than large customers or densely rather than sparsely situated customers are other examples in which the best way to configure marketing, order processing, logistics, and after-sale service activities to meet the similar needs of distinct groups will often differ.

Positioning is not only about carving out a niche. A position emerging from any of the sources can be broad or narrow. A focused competitor, such as IKEA, targets the special needs of a subset of customers and designs its activities accordingly. Focused competitors thrive on groups of customers who are overserved (and hence overpriced) by more broadly targeted competitors, or underserved (and hence underpriced). A broadly targeted competitor—for example, Vanguard or Delta Air Lines—serves a wide array of customers, performing a set of activities designed to meet their common needs. It ignores or meets only partially the more idiosyncratic needs of particular customer groups. (See "The Connection with Generic Strategies.")

Whatever the basis—variety, needs, access, or some combination of the three—positioning requires a tailored set of activities because it is always a function of differences on the supply side; that is, of differences in activities. However, positioning is not always a function of differences on the demand, or customer, side. Variety and access positionings, in particular, do not rely on *any* customer differences. In practice, however, variety or access differences often accompany needs differences. The tastes—that is, the needs—of Carmike's small-town customers, for instance, run more toward comedies, Westerns, action films, and family entertainment. Carmike does not run any films rated NC-17.

The Connection with Generic Strategies

In *Competitive Strategy* (The Free Press, 1985), I introduced the concept of generic strategies—cost leadership, differentiation, and focus—to represent the alternative strategic positions in an industry. The generic strategies remain useful to characterize strategic positions at the simplest and broadest level. Vanguard, for instance, is an example of a cost leadership strategy, whereas IKEA, with its narrow customer group, is an example of cost-based focus. Neutrogena is a focused differentiator. The bases for positioning—varieties, needs, and access—carry the understanding of those generic strategies to a greater level of specificity. IKEA and Southwest are both cost-based focusers, for example, but Ikea's focus is based on the needs of a customer group, and Southwest's is based on offering a particular service variety.

The generic strategies framework introduced the need to choose in order to avoid becoming caught between what I then described as the inherent contradictions of different strategies. Trade-offs between the activities of incompatible positions explain those contradictions. Witness Continental Lite, which tried and failed to compete in two ways at once.

Having defined positioning, we can now begin to answer the question, "What is strategy?" Strategy is the creation of a unique and valuable position, involving a different set of activities. If there were only one ideal position, there would be no need for strategy. Companies would face a simple imperative—win the race to discover and preempt it. The essence of strategic positioning is to choose activities that are different from rivals'. If the same set of activities were best to produce all varieties, meet all needs, and access all customers, companies could easily shift among them and operational effectiveness would determine performance.

A Sustainable Strategic Position Requires Trade-offs

Choosing a unique position, however, is not enough to guarantee a sustainable advantage. A valuable position will attract imitation by incumbents, who are likely to copy it in one of two ways.

First, a competitor can reposition itself to match the superior performer. J.C. Penney, for instance, has been repositioning itself from a Sears clone to a more upscale, fashion-oriented, soft-goods retailer. A second and far more common type of imitation is straddling. The straddler seeks to match the benefits of a successful position while maintaining its existing position. It grafts new features, services, or technologies onto the activities it already performs.

For those who argue that competitors can copy any market position, the airline industry is a perfect test case. It would seem that nearly any competitor could imitate any other airline's activities. Any airline can buy the same planes, lease the gates, and match the menus and ticketing and baggage handling services offered by other airlines.

Continental Airlines saw how well Southwest was doing and decided to straddle. While maintaining its position as a full-service airline, Continental also set out to match Southwest on a number of point-to-point routes. The airline dubbed the new service Continental Lite. It eliminated meals and first-class service, increased departure frequency, lowered fares, and shortened turnaround time at the gate. Because Continental remained a full-service airline on other routes, it continued to use travel agents and its mixed fleet of planes and to provide baggage checking and seat assignments.

But a strategic position is not sustainable unless there are trade-offs with other positions. Trade-offs occur when activities are incompatible. Simply put, a trade-off means that more of one thing necessitates less of another. An airline can choose to serve meals—adding cost and slowing turnaround time at the gate—or it can choose not to, but it cannot do both without bearing major inefficiencies.

Trade-offs create the need for choice and protect against repositioners and straddlers. Consider Neutrogena soap. Neutrogena Corporation's variety-based positioning is built on a "kind to the skin," residue-free soap formulated for pH balance. With a large detail force calling on dermatologists, Neutrogena's marketing strategy looks more like a drug company's than a soap maker's. It advertises in medical journals, sends direct mail to doctors, attends medical conferences, and performs research at its own Skincare Institute. To reinforce its positioning, Neutrogena originally focused its distribution on drugstores and avoided price promotions. Neutrogena uses a slow, more expensive manufacturing process to mold its fragile soap.

In choosing this position, Neutrogena said no to the deodorants and skin softeners that many customers desire in their soap. It gave up the large-volume potential of selling through supermarkets and using price promotions. It sacrificed manufacturing efficiencies to achieve the soap's desired attributes. In its original positioning, Neutrogena made a whole raft of trade-offs like those, trade-offs that protected the company from imitators.

Trade-offs arise for three reasons. The first is inconsistencies in image or reputation. A company known for delivering one kind of value may lack credibility and confuse customers—or even undermine its reputation—if it delivers another kind of value or attempts to deliver two inconsistent things at the same time. For example, Ivory soap, with its position as a basic, inexpensive everyday soap would have a hard time reshaping its image to match Neutrogena's premium "medical" reputation. Efforts to create a new image typically cost tens or even hundreds of millions of dollars in a major industry—a powerful barrier to imitation.

Second, and more important, trade-offs arise from activities themselves. Different positions (with their tailored activities) require different product configurations, different equipment, different employee behavior, different skills, and different management systems. Many trade-offs reflect inflexibilities in machinery, people, or systems. The more IKEA has configured its activities to lower costs by having its customers do their own assembly and delivery, the less able it is to satisfy customers who require higher levels of service.

However, trade-offs can be even more basic. In general, value is destroyed if an activity is overdesigned or underdesigned for its use. For example, even if a given salesperson were capable of providing a high level of assistance to one customer and none to another, the salesperson's talent (and some of his or her cost) would be wasted on the second customer. Moreover, productivity can improve when variation of an activity is limited. By providing a high level of assistance all the time, the salesperson and the entire sales activity can often achieve efficiencies of learning and scale.

Finally, trade-offs arise from limits on internal coordination and control. By clearly choosing to compete in one way and not another, senior management makes organizational priorities clear. Companies that try to be all things to all customers, in contrast, risk confusion in the trenches as employees attempt to make day-to-day operating decisions without a clear framework.

Positioning trade-offs are pervasive in competition and essential to strategy. They create the need for choice and purposefully limit what a company offers. They deter straddling or repositioning, because competitors that engage in those approaches undermine their strategies and degrade the value of their existing activities.

Trade-offs ultimately grounded Continental Lite. The airline lost hundreds of millions of dollars, and the CEO lost his job. Its planes were delayed leaving congested hub cities or slowed at the gate by baggage transfers. Late flights and cancellations generated a thousand complaints a day. Continental Lite could not afford to compete on price and still pay standard travel-agent commissions, but neither could it do without agents for its full-service business. The airline compromised by cutting commissions for all Continental flights across the board. Similarly, it could not afford to offer the same frequent-flier benefits to travelers paying the much lower ticket prices for Lite service. It compromised again by lowering the rewards of Continental's entire frequent-flier program. The results: angry travel agents and full-service customers.

Continental tried to compete in two ways at once. In trying to be low cost on some routes and full service on others, Continental paid an enormous straddling penalty. If there were no trade-offs between the two positions, Continental could have succeeded. But the absence of trade-offs is a dangerous half-truth that managers must unlearn. Quality is not always free. Southwest's convenience, one kind of high quality, happens to be consistent with low costs because its frequent departures are facilitated by a number of low-cost practices—fast gate turnarounds and automated ticketing, for example. However, other dimensions of airline quality—an assigned seat, a meal, or baggage transfer—require costs to provide.

In general, false trade-offs between cost and quality occur primarily when there is redundant or wasted effort, poor control or accuracy, or weak coordination. Simultaneous improvement of cost and differentiation is possible only when a company begins far behind the productivity frontier or when the frontier shifts outward. At the frontier, where companies have achieved current best practice, the trade-off between cost and differentiation is very real indeed.

After a decade of enjoying productivity advantages, Honda Motor Company and Toyota Motor Corporation recently bumped up against the frontier. In 1995, faced with increasing customer resistance to higher automobile prices, Honda found that the only way to produce a less-expensive car was to skimp on features. In the United States, it replaced the rear disk brakes on the Civic with lower-cost drum brakes and used cheaper fabric for the back seat, hoping customers would not notice. Toyota tried to sell a version of its best-selling Corolla in Japan with unpainted bumpers and cheaper seats. In Toyota's case, customers rebelled, and the company quickly dropped the new model.

For the past decade, as managers have improved operational effectiveness greatly, they have internalized the idea that eliminating trade-offs is a good thing. But if there are no trade-offs companies will never achieve a sustainable advantage. They will have to run faster and faster just to stay in place.

As we return to the question, What is strategy? we see that trade-offs add a new dimension to the answer. Strategy is making trade-offs in competing. The essence of strategy is choosing what *not* to do. Without trade-offs, there would be no need for choice and thus no need for strategy. Any good idea could and would be quickly imitated. Again, performance would once again depend wholly on operational effectiveness.

Fit Drives Both Competitive Advantage and Sustainability

Positioning choices determine not only which activities a company will perform and how it will configure individual activities but also how activities relate to one another. While operational effectiveness is about achieving excellence in individual activities, or functions, strategy is about *combining* activities.

Southwest's rapid gate turnaround, which allows frequent departures and greater use of aircraft, is essential to its high-convenience, low-cost positioning. But how does Southwest achieve it? Part of the answer lies in the company's well-paid gate and ground crews, whose productivity in turn-arounds is enhanced by flexible union rules. But the bigger part of the answer lies in how Southwest performs other activities. With no meals, no seat assignment, and no interline baggage transfers, Southwest avoids having to perform activities that slow down other airlines. It selects airports and routes to avoid congestion that introduces delays. Southwest's strict limits on the type and length of routes make standardized aircraft possible: every aircraft Southwest turns is a Boeing 737.

What is Southwest's core competence? Its key success factors? The correct answer is that everything matters. Southwest's strategy involves a whole system of activities, not a collection of parts. Its competitive advantage comes from the way its activities fit and reinforce one another.

Fit locks out imitators by creating a chain that is as strong as its *strongest* link. As in most companies with good strategies, Southwest's activities complement one another in ways that create real economic value. One activity's cost, for example, is lowered because of the way other activities are performed. Similarly, one activity's value to customers can be enhanced by a company's other activities. That is the way strategic fit creates competitive advantage and superior profitability.

TYPES OF FIT

The importance of fit among functional policies is one of the oldest ideas in strategy. Gradually, however, it has been supplanted on the management agenda. Rather than seeing the company as a whole, managers have turned to "core" competencies, "critical" resources, and "key" success factors. In fact, fit is a far more central component of competitive advantage than most realize.

Fit is important because discrete activities often affect one another. A sophisticated sales force, for example, confers a greater advantage when the company's product embodies premium technology and its marketing approach emphasizes customer assistance and support. A production line with high levels of model variety is more valuable when combined with an inventory and order processing system that minimizes the need for stocking finished goods, a sales process equipped to explain and encourage customization, and an advertising theme that stresses the benefits of product variations that meet a customer's special needs. Such complementarities are pervasive in strategy. Although some fit among activities is generic and applies to many companies, the most valuable fit is strategy-specific because it enhances a position's uniqueness and amplifies trade-offs.[2]

There are three types of fit, although they are not mutually exclusive. First-order fit is *simple consistency* between each activity (function) and the overall strategy. Vanguard, for example, aligns all activities with its low-cost strategy. It minimizes portfolio turnover and does not need highly compensated money managers. The company distributes its funds directly, avoiding commissions to brokers. It also limits advertising, relying instead on public relations and word-of-mouth recommendations. Vanguard ties its employees' bonuses to cost savings.

Consistency ensures that the competitive advantages of activities cumulate and do not erode or cancel themselves out. It makes the strategy easier to communicate to customers, employees, and shareholders, and improves implementation through single-mindedness in the corporation.

Second-order fit occurs when *activities are reinforcing.* Neutrogena, for example, markets to upscale hotels eager to offer their guests a soap recommended by dermatologists. Hotels grant Neutrogena the privilege of using its customary packaging while requiring other soaps to feature the hotel's name. Once guests have tried Neutrogena in a luxury hotel, they are more likely to purchase it at the drugstore or ask their doctor about it. Thus Neutrogena's medical and hotel marketing activities reinforce one another, lowering total marketing costs.

In another example, Bic Corporation sells a narrow line of standard, low-priced pens to virtually all major customer markets (retail, commercial, promotional, and giveaway) through virtually all available channels. As with any variety-based positioning serving a broad group of customers, Bic emphasizes a common need (low price for an acceptable pen) and uses marketing approaches with a broad reach (a large sales force and heavy television advertising). Bic gains the benefits of consistency across nearly all activities, including product design that emphasizes ease of manufacturing, plants configured for low cost, aggressive purchasing to minimize material costs, and in-house parts production whenever the economics dictate.

Yet Bic goes beyond simple consistency because its activities are reinforcing. For example, the company uses point-of-sale displays and frequent packaging changes to stimulate impulse buying. To handle point-of-sale tasks, a company needs a large sales force. Bic's is the largest in its industry, and it handles point-of-sale activities better than its rivals do. Moreover, the combination of point-of-sale activity, heavy television advertising, and packaging changes yields far more impulse buying than any activity in isolation could.

Third-order fit goes beyond activity reinforcement to what I call *optimization of effort*. The Gap, a retailer of casual clothes, considers product availability in its stores a critical element of its strategy. The Gap could keep products either by holding store inventory or by restocking from warehouses. The Gap has optimized its effort across these activities by restocking its selection of basic clothing almost daily out of three warehouses, thereby minimizing the need to carry large in-store inventories. The emphasis is on restocking because The Gap's merchandising strategy sticks to basic items in relatively few colors. While comparable retailers achieve turns of three to four times per year, The Gap turns its inventory seven and a half times per year. Rapid restocking, moreover, reduces the cost of implementing The Gap's short model cycle, which is six to eight weeks long.[3]

Coordination and information exchange across activities to eliminate redundancy and minimize wasted effort are the most basic types of effort optimization. But there are higher levels as well. Product design choices, for example, can eliminate the need for after-sale service or make it possible for customers to perform service activities themselves. Similarly, coordination with suppliers or distribution channels can eliminate the need for some in-house activities, such as end-user training.

In all three types of fit, the whole matters more than any individual part. Competitive advantage grows out of the *entire system* of activities. The fit among activities substantially reduces cost or increases differentiation. Beyond that, the competitive value of individual activities— or the associated skills, competencies, or resources—cannot be decoupled from the system or the strategy. Thus in competitive companies it can be misleading to explain success by specifying individual strengths, core competencies, or critical resources. The list of strengths cuts across many functions, and one strength blends into others. It is more useful to think in terms of themes that pervade many activities, such as low cost, a particular notion of customer service, or a particular conception of the value delivered. These themes are embodied in nests of tightly linked activities.

FIT AND SUSTAINABILITY

Strategic fit among many activities is fundamental not only to competitive advantage but also to the sustainability of that advantage. It is harder for a rival to match an array of interlocked activities than it is merely to imitate a particular sales-force approach, match a process technology, or replicate a set of product features. Positions built on systems of activities are far more sustainable than those built on individual activities. (See "Alternative Views of Strategy.")

Consider this simple exercise. The probability that competitors can match any activity is often less than one. The probabilities then quickly compound to make matching the entire system highly unlikely (.9 × .9 = .81; .9 × .9 × .9 × .9 = .66, and so on). Existing companies that try to reposition or straddle will be forced to reconfigure many activities. And even new entrants, though they do not confront the trade-offs facing established rivals, still face formidable barriers to imitation.

The more a company's positioning rests on activity systems with second- and third-order fit, the more sustainable its advantage will be. Such systems, by their very nature, are usually difficult to untangle from outside the company and therefore hard to imitate. And even if rivals can identify the relevant interconnections, they will have difficulty replicating them. Achieving fit is difficult because it requires the integration of decisions and actions across many independent subunits.

A competitor seeking to match an activity system gains little by imitating only some activities and not matching the whole. Performance does not improve; it can decline. Recall Continental Lite's disastrous attempt to imitate Southwest.

Finally, fit among a company's activities creates pressures and incentives to improve operational effectiveness, which makes imitation even harder. Fit means that poor performance in one activity will degrade the performance in others, so that weaknesses are exposed and more prone to get attention. Conversely, improvements in one activity will pay dividends in others. Companies with strong fit among their activities are rarely inviting targets. Their superiority in strategy and in execution only compounds their advantages and raises the hurdle for imitators.

Alternative Views of Strategy

The Implicit Strategy Model of the Past Decade

- One ideal competitive position in the industry
- Benchmarking of all activities and achieving best practice

- Aggressive outsourcing and partnering to gain efficiencies
- Advantages rest on a few key success factors, critical resources, core competencies
- Flexibility and rapid responses to all competitive and market changes

Sustainable Competitive Advantage
- Unique competitive position for the company
- Activities tailored to strategy
- Clear trade-offs and choices vis-à-vis competitors
- Competitive advantage arises from fit across activities
- Sustainability comes from the activity system, not the parts
- Operational effectiveness a given

When activities complement one another, rivals will get little benefit from imitation unless they successfully match the whole system. Such situations tend to promote winner-take-all competition. The company that builds the best activity system—Toys "R" Us, for instance—wins, while rivals with similar strategies—Child World and Lionel Leisure—fall behind. Thus finding a new strategic position is often preferable to being the second or third imitator of an occupied position.

The most viable positions are those whose activity systems are incompatible because of trade-offs. Strategic positioning sets the trade-off rules that define how individual activities will be configured and integrated. Seeing strategy in terms of activity systems only makes it clearer why organizational structure, systems, and processes need to be strategy-specific. Tailoring organization to strategy, in turn, makes complementarities more achievable and contributes to sustainability.

One implication is that strategic positions should have a horizon of a decade or more, not of a single planning cycle. Continuity fosters improvements in individual activities and the fit across activities, allowing an organization to build unique capabilities and skills tailored to its strategy. Continuity also reinforces a company's identity.

Conversely, frequent shifts in positioning are costly. Not only must a company reconfigure individual activities, but it must also realign entire systems. Some activities may never catch up to the vacillating strategy. The inevitable result of frequent shifts in strategy, or of failure to choose a distinct position in the first place, is "me-too" or hedged activity configurations, inconsistencies across functions, and organizational dissonance.

What is strategy? We can now complete the answer to this question. Strategy is creating fit among a company's activities. The success of a strategy depends on doing many things well—not just a few—and integrating among them. If there is no fit among activities, there is no distinctive strategy and little sustainability. Management reverts to the simpler task of overseeing independent functions, and operational effectiveness determines an organization's relative performance.

Rediscovering Strategy

THE FAILURE TO CHOOSE

Why do so many companies fail to have a strategy? Why do managers avoid making strategic choices? Or, having made them in the past, why do managers so often let strategies decay and blur? (See "Reconnecting with Strategy.")

Reconnecting with Strategy

Most companies owe their initial success to a unique strategic position involving clear trade-offs. Activities once were aligned with that position. The passage of time and the pressures of growth, however, led to compromises that were, at first, almost imperceptible. Through a succession of incremental changes that each seemed sensible at the time, many established companies have compromised their way to homogeneity with their rivals.

The issue here is not with the companies whose historical position is no longer viable; their challenge is to start over, just as a new entrant would. At issue is a far more common phenomenon: the established company achieving mediocre returns and lacking a clear strategy. Through incremental additions of product varieties, incremental efforts to serve new customer groups, and emulation of rivals' activities, the existing company loses its clear competitive position. Typically, the company has matched many of its competitors' offerings and practices and attempts to sell to most customer groups.

A number of approaches can help a company reconnect with strategy. The first is a careful look at what it already does. Within most well-established companies is a core of uniqueness. It is identified by answering questions such as the following:

- Which of our product or service varieties are the most distinctive?
- Which of our product or service varieties are the most profitable?
- Which of our customers are the most satisfied?
- Which customers, channels, or purchase occasions are the most profitable?
- Which of the activities in our value chain are the most different and effective?

Around this core of uniqueness are encrustations added incrementally over time. Like barnacles, they must be removed to reveal the underlying strategic positioning. A small percentage of varieties or customers may well account for most of a company's sales and especially its profits. The challenge, then, is to refocus on the unique core and realign the company's activities with it. Customers and product varieties at the periphery can be sold or allowed through inattention or price increases to fade away.

A company's history can also be instructive. What was the vision of the founder? What were the products and customers that made the company? Looking backward, one can reexamine the original strategy to see if it is still valid. Can the historical positioning be implemented in a modern way, one consistent with today's technologies and practices? This sort of thinking may lead to a commitment to renew the strategy and may challenge the organization to recover its distinctiveness. Such a challenge can be galvanizing and can instill the confidence to make the needed trade-offs.

Commonly, the threats to strategy are seen to emanate from outside a company because of changes in technology or the behavior of competitors. Although external changes can be the problem, the greater threat to strategy often comes from within. A sound strategy is undermined by a misguided view of competition, by organizational failures, and, especially, by the desire to grow.

Managers have become confused about the necessity of making choices. When many companies operate far from the productivity frontier, trade-offs appear unnecessary. It can seem that a well-run company should be able to beat its ineffective rivals on all dimensions simultaneously. Taught by popular management thinkers that they do not have to make trade-offs, managers have acquired a macho sense that to do so is a sign of weakness.

Unnerved by forecasts of hypercompetition, managers increase its likelihood by imitating everything about their competitors. Exhorted to think in terms of revolution, managers chase every new technology for its own sake.

The pursuit of operational effectiveness is seductive because it is concrete and actionable. Over the past decade, managers have been under increasing pressure to deliver tangible, measurable performance improvements. Programs in operational effectiveness produce reassuring progress, although superior profitability may remain elusive. Business publications and consultants flood the market with information about what other companies are doing, reinforcing the best-practice mentality. Caught up in the race for operational effectiveness, many managers simply do not understand the need to have a strategy.

Companies avoid or blur strategic choices for other reasons as well. Conventional wisdom within an industry is often strong, homogenizing competition. Some managers mistake "customer focus" to mean they must serve all customer needs or respond to every request from distribution channels. Others cite the desire to preserve flexibility.

Organizational realities also work against strategy. Trade-offs are frightening, and making no choice is sometimes preferred to risking blame for a bad choice. Companies imitate one another in a type of herd behavior, each assuming rivals know something they do not. Newly empowered employees, who are urged to seek every possible source of improvement, often lack a vision of the whole and the perspective to recognize trade-offs. The failure to choose sometimes comes down to the reluctance to disappoint valued managers or employees.

THE GROWTH TRAP

Among all other influences, the desire to grow has perhaps the most perverse effect on strategy. Trade-offs and limits appear to constrain growth. Serving one group of customers and excluding others, for instance, places a real or imagined limit on revenue growth. Broadly targeted strategies emphasizing low price result in lost sales with customers sensitive to features or service. Differentiators lose sales to price-sensitive customers.

Managers are constantly tempted to take incremental steps that surpass those limits but blur a company's strategic position. Eventually, pressures to grow or apparent saturation of the target market lead managers to broaden the position by extending product lines, adding new features, imitating competitors' popular services, matching processes, and even making acquisitions. For years, Maytag Corporation's success was based on its focus on reliable, durable washers and dryers, later extended to include dishwashers. However, conventional wisdom emerging within the industry supported the notion of selling a full line of products. Concerned with slow industry growth and competition from broad-line appliance makers, Maytag was pressured by dealers and encouraged by customers to extend its line. Maytag expanded into refrigerators and cooking products under the Maytag brand and acquired other brands—Jenn-Air, Hardwick Stove, Hoover, Admiral, and Magic Chef—with disparate positions. Maytag grew substantially from $684 million in 1985 to a peak of $3.4 billion in 1994, but return on sales declined from 8% to 12% in the 1970s and 1980s to an average of less than 1% between 1989 and 1995. Cost cutting will improve this performance, but laundry and dishwasher products still anchor Maytag's profitability.

Neutrogena may have fallen into the same trap. In the early 1990s, its U.S. distribution broadened to include mass merchandisers such as Wal-Mart Stores. Under the Neutrogena name, the company expanded into a wide variety of products—eye-makeup remover and shampoo, for example—in which it was not unique and which diluted its image, and it began turning to price promotions.

Compromises and inconsistencies in the pursuit of growth will erode the competitive advantage a company had with its original varieties or target customers. Attempts to compete in several ways at once create confusion and undermine organizational motivation and focus. Profits fall, but more revenue is seen as the answer. Managers are unable to make choices, so the company embarks on a new round of broadening and compromises. Often, rivals continue to match each other until desperation breaks the cycle, resulting in a merger or downsizing to the original positioning.

PROFITABLE GROWTH

Many companies, after a decade of restructuring and cost-cutting, are turning their attention to growth. Too often, efforts to grow blur uniqueness, create compromises, reduce fit, and ultimately undermine competitive advantage. In fact, the growth imperative is hazardous to strategy.

What approaches to growth preserve and reinforce strategy? Broadly, the prescription is to concentrate on deepening a strategic position rather than broadening and compromising it. One approach is to look for extensions of the strategy that leverage the existing activity system by offering features or services that rivals would find impossible or costly to match on a stand-alone basis. In other words, managers can ask themselves which activities, features, or forms of competition are feasible or less costly to them because of complementary activities that their company performs.

Deepening a position involves making the company's activities more distinctive, strengthening fit, and communicating the strategy better to those customers who should value it. But many companies succumb to the temptation to chase "easy" growth by adding hot features, products, or services without screening them or adapting them to their strategy. Or they target new customers or markets in which the company has little special to offer. A company can often grow faster—and far more profitably—by better penetrating needs and varieties where it is distinctive than by slugging it out in potentially higher growth arenas in which the company lacks uniqueness. Carmike, now the largest theater chain in the United States, owes its rapid growth to its disciplined concentration on small markets. The company quickly sells any big-city theaters that come to it as part of an acquisition.

Globalization often allows growth that is consistent with strategy, opening up larger markets for a focused strategy. Unlike broadening domestically, expanding globally is likely to leverage and reinforce a company's unique position and identity.

Companies seeking growth through broadening within their industry can best contain the risks to strategy by creating stand-alone units, each with its own brand name and tailored activities. Maytag has clearly struggled with this issue. On the one hand, it has organized its premium and value brands into separate units with different strategic positions. On the other, it has created an umbrella appliance company for all its brands to gain critical mass. With shared design, manufacturing, distribution, and customer service, it will be hard to avoid homogenization. If a given business unit attempts to compete with different positions for different products or customers, avoiding compromise is nearly impossible.

THE ROLE OF LEADERSHIP

The challenge of developing or reestablishing a clear strategy is often primarily an organizational one and depends on leadership. With so many forces at work against making choices and trade-offs in organizations, a clear intellectual framework to guide strategy is a necessary counterweight. Moreover, strong leaders willing to make choices are essential.

In many companies, leadership has degenerated into orchestrating operational improvements and making deals. But the leader's role is broader and far more important. General management is more than the stewardship of individual functions. Its core is strategy: defining and communicating the company's unique position, making trade-offs, and forging fit among activities. The leader must provide the discipline to decide which industry changes and customer needs the company will respond to, while avoiding organizational distractions and maintaining the company's distinctiveness. Managers at lower levels lack the perspective and the confidence to maintain a strategy. There will be constant pressures to compromise, relax trade-offs, and emulate rivals. One of the leader's jobs is to teach others in the organization about strategy—and to say no.

Strategy renders choices about what not to do as important as choices about what to do. Indeed, setting limits is another function of leadership. Deciding which target group of customers, varieties, and needs the company should serve is fundamental to developing a strategy. But so is deciding not to serve other customers or needs and not to offer certain features or services. Thus strategy requires constant discipline and clear communication. Indeed, one of the most important functions of an explicit, communicated strategy is to guide employees in making choices that arise because of trade-offs in their individual activities and in day-to-day decisions.

Improving operational effectiveness is a necessary part of management, but it is *not* strategy. In confusing the two, managers have unintentionally backed into a way of thinking about competition that is driving many industries toward competitive convergence, which is in no one's best interest and is not inevitable.

Managers must clearly distinguish operational effectiveness from strategy. Both are essential, but the two agendas are different.

The operational agenda involves continual improvement everywhere there are no trade-offs. Failure to do this creates vulnerability even for companies with a good strategy. The operational agenda is the proper place for constant change, flexibility, and relentless efforts to achieve best practice. In contrast, the strategic agenda is the right place for defining a unique position, making clear trade-offs, and tightening fit. It involves the continual search for ways to reinforce and extend the company's position. The strategic agenda demands discipline and continuity; its enemies are distraction and compromise.

Strategic continuity does not imply a static view of competition. A company must continually improve its operational effectiveness and actively try to shift the productivity frontier; at the same time, there needs to be ongoing effort to extend its uniqueness while strengthening the fit among its activities. Strategic continuity, in fact, should make an organization's continual improvement more effective.

A company may have to change its strategy if there are major structural changes in its industry. In fact, new strategic positions often arise because of industry changes, and new entrants unencumbered by history often can exploit them more easily. However, a company's choice of a new position must be driven by the ability to find new trade-offs and leverage a new system of complementary activities into a sustainable advantage. (See "Emerging Industries and Technologies.")

Emerging Industries and Technologies

Developing a strategy in a newly emerging industry or in a business undergoing revolutionary technological changes is a daunting proposition. In such cases, managers face a high level of uncertainty about the needs of customers, the products and services that will prove to be the most desired, and the best configuration of activities and technologies to deliver them. Because of all this uncertainty, imitation and hedging are rampant: unable to risk being wrong or left behind, companies match all features, offer all new services, and explore all technologies.

During such periods in an industry's development, its basic productivity frontier is being established or reestablished. Explosive growth can make such times profitable for many companies, but profits will be temporary because imitation and strategic convergence will ultimately destroy industry profitability. The companies that are enduringly successful will be those that begin as early as possible to define and embody in their activities a unique competitive position. A period of imitation may be inevitable in emerging industries, but that period reflects the level of uncertainty rather than a desired state of affairs.

In high-tech industries, this imitation phase often continues much longer than it should. Enraptured by technological change itself, companies pack more features—most of which are never used—into their products while slashing prices across the board. Rarely are trade-offs even considered.

The drive for growth to satisfy market pressures leads companies into every product area. Although a few companies with fundamental advantages prosper, the majority are doomed to a rat race no one can win.

Ironically, the popular business press, focused on hot, emerging industries, is prone to presenting these special cases as proof that we have entered a new era of competition in which none of the old rules are valid. In fact, the opposite is true.

Notes

1. I first described the concept of activities and its use in understanding competitive advantage in *Competitive Advantage* (New York: The Free Press, 1985). The ideas in this article build on and extend that thinking.

2. Paul Milgrom and John Roberts have begun to explore the economics of systems of complementary functions, activities, and functions. Their focus is on the emergence of "modern manufacturing" as a new set of complementary activities, on the tendency of companies to react to external changes with coherent bundles of internal responses, and on the need for central coordination—a strategy—to align functional managers. In the latter case, they model what has long been a bedrock principle of strategy. See Paul Milgrom and John Roberts, "The Economics of Modern Manufacturing: Technology, Strategy, and Organization," *American Economic Review* 80 (1990): 511–528; Paul Milgrom, Yingyi Qian, and John Roberts, "Complementarities, Momentum, and Evolution of Modern Manufacturing," *American Economic Review* 81 (1991) 84–88; and Paul Milgrom and John Roberts, "Complementarities and Fit: Strategy, Structure, and Organizational Changes in Manufacturing," *Journal of Accounting and Economics,* vol. 19 (March–May 1995): 179–208.

3. Material on retail strategies is drawn in part from Jan Rivkin, "The Rise of Retail Category Killers," unpublished working paper, January 1995. Nicolaj Siggelkow prepared the case study on The Gap.

2
Changing the Role of Top Management: Beyond Strategy to Purpose

Christopher A. Bartlett and Sumantra Ghoshal

Structure follows strategy. And systems support structure. Few aphorisms have penetrated Western business thinking as deeply as these two. Not only do they influence the architecture of today's largest corporations but they also define the role that top corporate managers play.

Yet these aphorisms and the management doctrine to which they have given rise are no longer adequate. The job they prescribe for senior management is no longer the job that needs to be done. Senior managers of today's large enterprises must move beyond strategy, structure, and systems to a framework built on purpose, process, and people.

The concepts that still define most senior managements' understanding of their roles have their roots in the 1920s, when Alfred Sloan at General Motors and a few of his contemporaries were engineering a new strategy: diversification. Those pioneers discovered that diversification benefited from a divisional structure and that tightly designed planning and control systems in turn supported that structure. From then on, the strategy-structure-systems link has been an article of faith reflected in the design of MBA programs, reinforced in consultants' reports, and confirmed in the actions and mind-sets of practicing managers worldwide. Top-level managers view themselves as the designers of the strategy, the architects of the structure, and the managers of the systems that direct and drive their companies.

For decades, this philosophy served companies well. It supported successive waves of growth as companies integrated horizontally in the 1950s, diversified in the 1960s, and expanded into global markets in the 1970s and early 1980s. But over the last decade, technological, competitive, and market changes have eroded its effectiveness. The problems of companies as diverse as GM and IBM in the United States, Philips and Daimler-Benz in Europe, and Matsushita and Hitachi in Japan can be traced, at least in part, to top management's cleaving to this philosophy too tightly and for too long.

The great power—and fatal flaw—of the strategy-structure-systems framework lay in its objective: to create a management system that could minimize the idiosyncrasies of human behavior. Indeed, the doctrine held that if the three elements were properly designed and effectively implemented, large, complex organizations could be run with people as replaceable parts. Over time, as corporate size and diversity expanded, strategies, structures, and reporting and planning systems became more and more complex. Employees' daily activities became increasingly fragmented and systematized.

In the benevolent, high-growth environment that followed World War II, strategy, structure, and systems offered much-needed discipline, focus, and control. Today's economic environment is different. Overcapacity and intense competition are the norm in most global businesses. The lines separating businesses have blurred as technologies and markets converge, creating new growth opportunities where traditional businesses intersect. And, most notably, the scarcest corporate resources are less often the financial funds that top management controls than the knowledge and expertise of the people on the front lines.

Analysts have many prescriptions for these challenges, and executives have rushed to adopt them: from focusing on strategic intent to inverting the organizational pyramid; from corporate reengineering to employee empowerment. Yet after five years of research in which we studied 20 large, vigorous European, U.S., and Japanese companies, we believe that these prescriptions address the artifacts of the problems and not their causes. They focus on partial, operational solutions. What managers need, however, is a fundamental change in doctrine.

Consider some examples. Over 30% of 3M's sales come from products introduced in the last five years. How has 3M managed to retain its innovative capability and entrepreneurial spirit despite its $14 billion bulk? What enabled ABB to transform two also-ran companies into the leaders in the global power-equipment industry while world markets were in recession? How has Canon managed to grow and renew itself, expanding from cameras to calculators to copiers to computers? And what has kept other large, complex companies like AT&T, Royal Dutch/Shell, Intel, Andersen Consulting, Kao, and Corning from succumbing to the so-called inevitable decline of large corporations?

Although the strategies, structures, and systems of these companies have little in common, their leaders share a surprisingly consistent philosophy. First, they place less emphasis on following a clear strategic plan than on building a rich, engaging corporate purpose. Next, they focus less on formal structural design and more on effective management processes. Finally, they are less concerned with controlling employees' behavior than with developing their capabilities and broadening their perspectives. In sum, they have moved beyond the old doctrine of strategy, structure, and systems to a softer, more organic model built on the development of purpose, process, and people. In this article, we examine the first element of the changing role of top management: shaping organizational purpose.

Such a transformation can start only with top management. Before senior managers can realign behavior and beliefs throughout the corporation, they need to change their own priorities and ways of thinking.

From Setting Strategy to Defining Purpose

Formulating strategy has long been the domain of top management. From Alfred Sloan to Lee Iacocca, the powerful, even heroic image of the CEO as omniscient strategist is ingrained in business history and folklore.

When companies were smaller and less diversified, setting business strategy was a straightforward task. As companies grew larger and more complex, however, senior executives needed elaborate systems and specialized staff to ensure that headquarters could review, influence, and approve the strategic plans of specific business units. Over time, the workings of increasingly formalized planning processes eclipsed the utility of the plans they produced: sterile generalities to which frontline managers felt little affinity or commitment.

Ironically, disaffection only increased as senior managers ceded responsibility for unit-level strategy to the divisional managers and shifted their own attention to crafting an overall corporate framework and logic. That shift led senior managers to explore the elusive concept of business synergies, to work on balancing cross-funded strategic portfolios, and, in recent years, to articulate notions of broad strategic vision or highly focused strategic intent. Meanwhile, the people actually running business units grew increasingly confused about their roles. The elaborate contortions required to fit their strategies into the corporate rationale frustrated them. Classification of their complex businesses into simplistic, portfolio-funding roles demotivated them. And strategic visions that seemed vague or definitions of strategic intent that were overly constraining made them cynical. All in all, top management's efforts to provide strategic leadership often had the opposite effect.

The problem is not the CEO but rather the assumption that the CEO *should* be the corporation's chief strategist, assuming full control of setting the company's objectives and determining its priorities. In an environment where the fast-changing knowledge and expertise required to make such decisions are usually found on the front lines, this assumption is untenable. Strategic information cannot be relayed to the top without becoming diluted, distorted, and delayed.

CEO Andy Grove, for example, acknowledges that for a long time neither he nor other top Intel executives were willing or able to see how the competitive environment had undermined the company's strategy of being a major player in both memory chips and microprocessors. Yet for two full years before top management woke up to this reality, various project leaders, marketing managers, and plant supervisors were busy refocusing Intel's strategy by shifting resources from memories to microprocessors. Management, Grove confessed, might have been "fooled by our strategic rhetoric, but those on the front lines could see that we had to retreat from memory chips. . . . People formulate strategy with their fingertips. Our most significant strategic decision was made not in response to some clear-sighted corporate vision but by the marketing and investment decisions of frontline managers who really knew what was going on."

Yet at the very time that top-level managers are acknowledging their own limits, many are also learning that the people who can "formulate strategy with their fingertips" are deeply disaffected. Neither the valueless quantitative terms of most planning and control processes nor the mechanical formulas of leveraged incentive systems nurture employees' commitment or motivation. In fact, even this fragile relationship is eroding as successive waves of restructuring, delayering, and retrenching weaken any reserve of corporate loyalty.

In most corporations today, people no longer know—or even care—

what or *why* their companies are. In such an environment, leaders have an urgent role to play. Obviously, they must retain control over the processes that frame the company's strategic priorities. But strategies can engender strong, enduring emotional attachments only when they are embedded in a broader organizational purpose.

This means creating an organization with which members can identify, in which they share a sense of pride, and to which they are willing to commit. In short, senior managers must convert the contractual employees of an economic entity into committed members of a purposeful organization.

Embedding Corporate Ambition

Traditionally, top-level managers have tried to engage employees intellectually through the persuasive logic of strategic analyses. But clinically framed and contractually based relationships do not inspire the extraordinary effort and sustained commitment required to deliver consistently superior performance. For that, companies need employees who care, who have a strong emotional link with the organization.

Prescriptions for forging such links surface regularly. One that is currently fashionable calls for building a Zen-like focus on strategic intent to challenge and eventually overcome less focused rivals. To create an obsession with winning, top management identifies a specific stretch target (typically defined in competitive terms) and drives the organization toward that goal through a series of operating challenges.

The flip side of this technique, however, is strategic myopia and inflexibility, because a laserlike focus risks constraining rather than liberating the organization. Consider Komatsu. During the mid- to late 1980s, Komatsu was widely cited as an example of the power of strategic intent. But even as management students in the West were admiring the company's obsession with beating the market leader, Caterpillar, Komatsu's leadership had decided that "Maru-C" (surround Caterpillar) had led to stagnation and stereotyped thinking. Over the last four years, President Tetsuya Katada has reoriented Komatsu toward a corporate agenda reflected in a new slogan, "Growth, Global, Groupwide," or the "Three Gs" for short. He describes it as "a much more abstract challenge than one focused on catching and beating Caterpillar, but it will stimulate people to think and discuss creatively what Komatsu can be." (See "From Strategic Intent to Corporate Purpose: The Remaking of Komatsu.")

From Strategic Intent to Corporate Purpose: The Remaking of Komatsu

When he succeeded his father as Komatsu's president in 1964, Ryoichi Kawai articulated an objective that the company would pursue for more than 20 years. Komatsu's strategic intent, Kawai announced, was to "catch up with and surpass Caterpillar."

The management approach Kawai adopted to pursue this goal became a well-studied and widely emulated model in the West. Each year, Kawai would define a clear and specific operating priority—for example, improving quality, reducing costs, or expanding exports—that used Caterpillar's performance as a standard and cited Caterpillar itself as the competitive target. Then each year's priority would be translated into detailed action plans through PDCA (plan, do, check, act), Komatsu's tightly controlled management system.

Kawai's strategy worked well, and by 1982, when he was choosing his successor, Komatsu had grown from a tiny local competitor with poor product quality to Cat's most serious global challenger in the construction equipment market. But the market was about to change. By 1989, when Tetsuya Katada became the third president to follow Kawai, worldwide demand for construction equipment was down, competition was up, and Komatsu's profits were in steady decline.

As Katada saw the situation, Komatsu's management had become so obsessed with catching Caterpillar that it had stopped thinking about strategic choices. For instance, its product development efforts were biased toward Cat's high-end bulldozers rather than toward smaller, lower-priced products like hydraulic excavators, for which market demand was growing. Katada worried that Komatsu's top management had stopped questioning the business the company was in. Further, he was concerned that the inflexible, top-down style that had become embedded at Komatsu had crushed "the spirit of enterprise" among middle and frontline managers.

Managers, Katada decided, "can no longer operate within the confines of a defined objective. They need to go out and see the needs and opportunities and operate in a creative and innovative way, always encouraging initiative from below." In other words, he told the company, "I want everyone to stop concentrating simply on catching up with Caterpillar."

At meetings and discussions, Katada challenged managers at several levels to find ways for the company to double its sales by the mid-1990s. What emerged from these and subsequent discussions was a new definition of the company. Rather than thinking of Komatsu as a construction equipment company trying to catch Cat, management began to describe it as a "total technology enterprise" with an opportunity to leverage its existing resources and expertise in electronics, robotics, and plastics.

Under a new banner of "Growth, Global, Groupwide" (the Three Gs), Katada encouraged management at all levels to find new growth opportunities through expanding geographically and leveraging competences. He appointed a Committee for the 1990s to determine how Komatsu could enrich its corporate philosophy, broaden its social contributions, and revitalize its human resources. His objective was to create an organization that could attract and stimulate the best people. "Compared with our old objective," Katado acknowledged, "the Three Gs slogan may seem abstract, but it was this abstract nature that stimulated people to ask what they could do and respond creatively."

More than a strategy, Komatsu now had a corporate purpose, to which its managers could commit and in which they had a voice. In the first three years after Katada articulated the Three Gs, Komatsu's sales, which had been declining since 1982, perked up. That surge was driven almost entirely by a 40% growth in Komatsu's nonconstruction equipment business.

Obviously, strategic visions can be so broad that they convey little meaning or guidance to people deep in the organization. Andy Grove is characteristically blunt in labeling most strategic vision statements "pap." Yet some of the elements of both strategic intent and strategic vision are evident in the efforts that Grove and other top-level managers are making to shed their uncomfortable and increasingly inappropriate role as strategic gurus. Their objective is neither to impose a tight strategic agenda on their line managers nor to inspire them toward some ineffable goal. Rather, they are working to embed a clearly articulated, well-defined ambition in the thinking of every individual while giving each person the freedom to interpret the company's broad objectives creatively.

Three characteristics distinguish this approach from previous practices. The executives we observed articulated the corporate ambition in terms designed to capture employees' attention and interest rather than in terms related to strategic or financial goals. They engaged the organization in developing, refining, and renewing the ambition. And they ensured that it was translated into measurable activities to provide a benchmark for achievement and a sense of momentum.

Capture Employees' Attention and Interest. Defining a company's objectives so that they have personal meaning for employees is hard. Most such statements are too vague to be useful to line managers, and often they are too out of touch with reality even to be credible. At AT&T, Bob Allen found himself atop a company that had to change from thinking and acting like a regulated utility and do so amidst industry turbulence. The formal planning process defined the key strategic task as loading more traffic onto the existing telecommunications network and developing products to meet the needs of an emerging infocom business. But Allen decided not to talk about AT&T's objectives in such rational and analytic terms. Nor did he choose a competitively focused strategic intent—countering Northern Telecom's invasion of AT&T's home market, for example—or a broad vision of futuristic information highways and virtual worlds. Instead, Allen chose very human terms, stating that the company was "dedicated to becoming the world's best at bringing people together—giving them easy access to each other and to the information and services they want and need—anytime, anywhere."

This simple statement captured AT&T's objective of providing network linkages as well as the attendant access to information and services—but in simple, personal language that anyone could understand. Equally important, employees could relate to and take pride in such a mission.

Other companies achieved a similar impact by focusing on the development of core capabilities. At Corning, for example, CEO Jamie Houghton challenged his organization to overlay its exceptional technological capability with a commitment to quality that would make the company truly world-class. To an organization that was feeling demotivated and even defeated, this commitment to quality provided a focus for rebuilding organizational pride and self-confidence while simultaneously boosting a crucial strategic competence.

Get the Organization Involved. A statement of corporate ambition is only a touchstone for the larger process of gaining organizational commitment. The statement must be broad enough to invite— and indeed require—the organization's involvement in interpreting, refining, and making it operational. In practice, this means tapping into the reservoir of knowledge and expertise that is widely distributed throughout the company. As Andy Grove observed about Intel's shift out of the memory business and the importance of inviting organizational discussion and debate, "The more successful we are as a microprocessor company, the more difficult it will be to become something else. . . . We need to soften the strategic focus at the top so we can generate new possibilities from within the organization."

For many top-level managers, softening the strategic focus isn't easy. They worry that the organization will interpret such an approach as strategic fuzziness, or worse, indecision. But these concerns evaporate when senior managers realize that they are not abandoning their responsibility for the strategic direction but rather improving the quality of its formulation and the odds of its implementation.

At AT&T, for example, Bob Allen challenged his entire organization to interpret and operationalize the deliberately broad "anytime, anywhere" statement. He also created a Strategy Forum and invited the company's 60 most senior managers to participate in two- or three-day meetings held five times a year. There they discussed and refined AT&T's overall objectives and direction.

Create Momentum. Top management's third challenge is to build and sustain commitment to the objectives the organization has helped to develop. Everyone needs to believe that the articulated ambition is legitimate and viable; that it is more than public relations rhetoric or motivational hype. By making tangible commitments to the defined objectives, senior managers substantiate such belief. They also provide people deep in the organization with the motivation that comes from making perceptible progress.

Jamie Houghton demonstrated the seriousness of his belief in Corning's quality crusade by appointing one of the company's most capable and respected senior managers to head the effort. Furthermore, despite a severe financial crunch, Houghton allocated $5 million to create a new Quality Institute to lead the massive program of education and organizational development. He also committed to boost training to 5% of every employee's total working hours. Corning's quality program quickly achieved Houghton's aim. As one executive committee member said, "It did a lot more than just improve quality. It put self-respect and confidence back in our people."

Bob Allen also backed his statement of corporate ambition with tangible commitments. The Strategy Forum's discussions led to the conclusion that "bringing people together anytime, anywhere" would require major investments in several complementary information technologies likely to become vital in the new communications highways. The resulting decisions to acquire NCR for $7.5 billion and McCaw Cellular for $12.6 billion were strong evidence of the vision's organizational legitimacy and a powerful mental jump-start to a belief in its viability.

Instilling Organizational Values

There are few more powerful or public signals of what a company stands for than the ways it defines and measures performance. Most companies focus almost entirely on financial results: the strategic objective to become number one or number two in the industry justifies the pressure to meet the budgeted 15% increase in sales. That goal in turn is crucial for the company to achieve its overall aim of a 20% return on net assets by mid-decade.

If managers' interest in such quantitative objectives flags or signs of organizational exhaustion appear, top management often responds by presenting the objectives in a more compelling way—linked to a highly leveraged incentive program, for example, or motivated by a crisis—real or manufactured.

But often, corporate leaders simply continue to explain and justify the objectives in greater detail in the hope that acceptance will follow understanding. GE's Jack Welch hoped that a more detailed explanation of his demanding profit objectives would build commitment to them, but it didn't help. In 1988, Welch made a highly polished presentation to top-level managers in which he depicted the company as a "growth engine" powered by a balanced capability to generate and apply funds. His charisma notwithstanding, Welch failed to generate the interest, excitement, and commitment he had hoped for. Instead, his dramatic but stark imagery increased some line managers' frustration with and alienation from a company that was already driving them hard. The presentation confirmed their feeling that they were little more than cogs in a perpetual-motion money machine.

Although achieving acceptable financial objectives is clearly important for a company's survival, a target ROI will rarely galvanize an organization into action. If people are to put out the extraordinary effort required to realize company targets, they must be able to identify with them. As one disaffected manager said, "It's fine to emphasiz what we must shoot for, but we also need to know what we stand for."

Identifying, communicating, and shaping organizational values is more difficult than articulating a strategic vision because it relies less on analysis and logic and more on emotion and intuition. Moreover, although every well-established company operates on a set of beliefs and philosophies, they usually remain implicit. Some companies even repress them so as not to distract employees from the business agenda or offend people who have other views. Financial objectives are popular performance measures in part because they are "safe"; people won't dispute them.

Companies that assert more boldly what they stand for typically attract and retain employees who identify with their values and become more deeply committed to the organization that embodies them. "In the end," observes Goran Lindahl, ABB's group executive vice president responsible for the company's power transmission and distribution business, "managers are loyal not to a particular boss or even to a company but to a set of values they believe in and find satisfying."

Nowhere is this powerful alignment between company and employee beliefs more evident than in The Body Shop, the U.K.-based beauty products retailer. Founder Anita Roddick has articulated a strong, clear business philosophy, which she acknowledges is "quirky." Nonetheless, the values she has created have attracted a group of employees (and a following of customers) who identify with the organization's commitment to environmental causes and with its belief that companies can be agents of social change. As Roddick describes her approach, "Most businesses focus all the time on profits, profits, profits. I think that is deeply boring. I want to create an electricity and passion that bonds people to the company. Especially with young people, you have to find ways to grab their imagination. You want them to feel they are doing something important. I'd never get that kind of motivation if we were just selling shampoo and body lotion."

Social altruism isn't the only way to give employees a strong emotional link to their companies. Ask the managers at Lincoln Electric how their little company has outlasted giants like Westinghouse and Airco to dominate the fiercely competitive welding equipment and supplies businesses. Lincoln Electric managers attribute most of the company's success to a philosophy that has allowed them to develop the industry's most productive workforce. Founded on a strong belief in the power of unfettered capitalism, the company is driven by a highly leveraged incentive program that retains many of the characteristics of a nineteenth-century piecework system. The program has survived because the company attracts employees who identify strongly with Lincoln's unshakable belief in individual accountability and the power of pure meritocracy.

For companies that have been less clear and consistent about what they stand for, the challenge is difficult but still achievable. Drawing again on the experiences in our study, we discerned three lessons for top management. First, build the new philosophy around the company's existing value and belief system. Second, maintain a high level of personal involvement in this activity over many years. And third, translate broad philosophical objectives into visible and measurable goals.

Build on Core Values. Today it is a truism that a company's culture—the values it embodies—influences the decisions and choices of its managers. As a result, some CEOs are using the same didactic methods to change their companies' values that they once reserved for driving down profit objectives. Moreover, they try to impose these new value sets almost as often as they used to revise budget targets. The result is an organizational cynicism that brushes off any new initiative as the "culture of the month."

New values cannot be instilled through a crash program, nor should existing belief systems be chucked or subverted without careful consideration of the effect on the relationship between the organization and its members. In fact, the goal for most companies should be to build on the strengths and modify the limitations of the existing set of values, not to make radical changes in values. And where value confrontation is essential, it requires careful attention, not a broadside attack.

Consider Corning. When Jamie Houghton assumed its leadership in 1983, Corning was experiencing difficult times. A major restructuring had reduced its worldwide payroll from 45,000 to 30,000. Its core businesses, mostly in mature segments, were under attack by foreign competition. To make matters worse, global recession seemed to guarantee that Corning's long-term decline in financial performance would continue. Within the company, a sense of drift and a lack of confidence were eroding the family-like atmosphere that had long bonded employees to Corning.

Houghton knew he had to eliminate the paternalism that had sustained a country-club culture at Corning for years. But he also understood that much in the company's existing but largely implicit value system—respect for the individual and a commitment to integrity, for example—were important and worthwhile. He wanted to highlight those values and sharpen their focus.

Houghton also wanted to add other values that he believed would be important to Corning's future self-identity. So he began to talk about the importance of corporate leadership and performance accountability, not only because they were crucial in the emerging competitive environment but also because they reflected the belief system of a new generation of Corning employees whom he wanted to attract. Gradually, Houghton overlaid these new values on the old.

Sow the Message. Planting new values takes more than inspiring speeches. At best, the speeches can only confirm the message sent by senior executives' daily actions. Management is the message; speeches only call attention to it.

Houghton set himself the task of visiting ten different corporate facilities each quarter to "talk, listen, and feel the atmosphere." During these visits, he reiterated Corning's new values and told stories that reflected their impact. This was no mere jawboning, however. Houghton translated abstract statements into action to make them real and relevant to all members of the organization. For example, to signal that he was serious about performance accountability, he terminated any budget presentation that did not meet corporate targets. Furthermore, he incorporated broad idealistic values into action programs—for example, one to break the company's glass ceiling for women, minorities, and non-U.S. nationals. Finally, he made sure that the company's business strategies were consistent with its core values. He divested or spun off businesses that did not match the company's professed identity as a market and technology leader.

Measure Progress. Despite their best efforts, many companies find that strategic and operating imperatives block or erode the values they strive to build. The reason is that such goals and objectives are inevitably quantified, whereas value statements usually offer neither clearly defined goals nor satisfactory methods for gauging their accomplishment. Unavoidably, the hard drives out the soft, and commitment to the desired values dissipates.

Like many companies, Corning had long allowed financial targets to dominate its objectives and thus had calibrated its performance in terms of growth, profitability, and ROI. Houghton realized that Corning needed an equally compelling way of tracking progress toward attaining its new culture.

In describing what he wanted Corning to become, Houghton repeatedly used the words "a world-class company." To ensure that this was not just empty rhetoric, he established a corporate objective: by the mid-1990s, Corning would be broadly and publicly recognized as among the world's most respected companies—by, for instance, its inclusion in the annual *Fortune* CEO poll of "America's most admired corporations." This standard included outstanding financial results but also encompassed superior performance on dimensions such as quality, innovation, and corporate responsibility. Equally important, employees could identify with the standard and take pride in achieving it.

Giving Meaning to Employees' Work

In the end, every individual extracts the most basic sense of purpose from the personal fulfillment he or she derives from being part of an organization. Creating that sense of fulfillment is the third challenge senior managers face as they strive to develop an energizing corporate purpose. Institutions like churches, communities, even families, which once provided individuals with identity, affiliation, meaning, and support, are eroding. The workplace is becoming a primary means for personal fulfillment. Managers need to recognize and respond to the reality that their employees don't just want to work for a company; they want to belong to an organization. More than just providing work, companies can help give meaning to people's lives.

To realize the value of a committed employee, an organization must bring its big ideas and bold initiatives down to a personal level. Senior managers must establish and maintain a link between the company and each of its employees. This is not to say that North American companies must shift from their characteristic impersonal contracts to the Japanese model of lifetime employment. But a link does imply a mutual commitment, in which the employer treats the employee not as a cost to be controlled but as an asset to be developed. Employees for their part commit not only their time but also their emotional energy to making their company as effective and competitive as they can. In short, the objective is to change the relationship from one in which employees feel they work for a company to one in which they recognize they belong to an organization. It is the difference between hiring out as a mercenary and becoming a Marine.

In the companies we studied that were best at achieving this new kind of relationship, top-level managers focused on three activities. They recognized employees' contributions and treated them like valuable assets. They committed to maximizing opportunities for personal growth and development. And they ensured that everyone not only understood how his or her role fit into the company's overall organizational purpose but also how he or she might contribute personally to achieving it.

Recognize Individual Accomplishments. As companies grow larger and more complex, employees can come to feel more like cogs in a machine than members of a team. To retain some sense of humanity, companies may publish in-house newsletters, sponsor social functions, or implement a casual dress code. But the impact of such exercises is seldom significant or enduring. Indeed, their very existence emphasizes the awkwardness and impersonality of organizations that can respond to human needs only in mechanistic ways.

Further, while most senior managers understand the need to recognize and celebrate the major contributions of star performers, few realize the importance of acknowledging the ongoing efforts of those who sustain the organization. IKEA, the world's largest home furnishings manufacturer and retailer, is an exception. Even after the company had grown to almost 50,000 employees in 20 countries, founder Ingvar Kamprad still tried to visit each of the chain's 75 outlets and meet every employee. He would often invite a store's employees to stay after closing for dinner at the in-house restaurant. It was a ritual that frontline associates would go to the buffet first, then managers, and last Kamprad. He would circulate and offer praise, encouragement, and advice to the people who worked for him.

Personal recognition must reflect genuine respect. People on the front lines are quick to recognize empty public relations gestures or attempts at manipulation. Andy Grove built an enormous reservoir of credibility and goodwill when he took extraordinary measures to retain employees during the memory-products bloodbaths of the mid-1980s. Grove tried to retain as many of the people as possible who had built this business for Intel, recognizing them as genuine company assets. To avoid layoffs, he first chose to sell a 20% interest in Intel to IBM in order to finance the company through its crisis. Next, he implemented the "125% solution" by asking employees to work ten hours more a week without compensation. Then he followed the "90% solution," a 10% across-the-board pay cut to minimize separations. Only after that did Grove resort to layoffs in the face of a $200 million loss.

Through actions such as these, born of genuine respect and concern for individual employees, senior managers develop the basis for mutual commitment. They can then build on this foundation by demonstrating equal concern for the growth and development of all the organization's members.

Commit to Developing Employees. As companies have delayered, restructured, and downsized, employees who were already feeling distanced and detached have become more disillusioned and even cynical. Too often, layoffs have been the aftermath of grand corporate visions that promised personal opportunities. Companies tout the "partnerships" they have with their organization's members, then shower them with pink slips. It's not surprising that employees are unlikely to commit to new goals or values until they're convinced that the future holds new opportunities for *them*.

Top-level managers must take a broader view of employee training and development and make a much stronger commitment to it than they traditionally have. Instead of simply training employees for job skills, companies must develop their capacity for personal growth. In her colorful way, Anita Roddick explained The Body Shop's decision to establish an education center offering not only courses on company products, skin care, and customer service but also sessions on topics like sociology, AIDS, aging, and urban survival. "You can train dogs," says Roddick. "We wanted to *educate* our people and help them realize their full potential."

Poul Andreassen, CEO of Danish-based ISS, believes that one reason his commercial cleaning business has grown into a $2 billion enterprise employing 114,000 people in 16 countries is his respect for workers, which he backs by investing in their development. Despite a strong philosophy of decentralization—headquarters has only 50 people—ISS still manages training centrally. Andreassen believes that training is key to transforming workers into professionals. Beyond teaching his employees basic job skills, he uses training as "a demonstration of caring" that motivates, bonds, and gives people confidence. For cleaning-team supervisors, for example, a five-stage training program covers basic skills and broader topics such as financial knowledge, interpersonal skills, problem solving, and customer relations. These people, once regarded as little more than work-gang bosses, have grown to be effective team builders and new-business generators. ISS's labor turnover is 40% below the industry average, and its cleaning crews have become an important source of innovative practices and entrepreneurial ideas for the company.

Andersen Consulting views the development of its people as a goal in itself and makes no proprietary claims to the skills and knowledge it develops. Its recruiting brochure promises that "after training with us, you could work for anyone anywhere—or you could work for yourself." The result is an exceptionally well-trained and extremely loyal group of associates.

Foster Individual Initiative. In a few companies, individual effort and personal contribution still constitute the bedrock of organizational process. 3M is one. Since the 1920s, when the company's fortunes were turned around by the development of waterproof sandpaper and adhesive tape, 3M management has valued the enormous potential of the entrepreneurs in its midst. Management developed a culture that recognizes individual initiative as the source of the company's growth, and it confirmed and institutionalized that strongly held belief through its policies and procedures. For example, the "15% rule" allows employees to spend up to 15% of their time on bootleg projects that they believe have potential for the company. As bootlegged innovations developed into major businesses, company folklore became filled with stories of entrepreneurial heroes whose impact was direct and tangible. Through the stories and its organizational infrastructure, 3M keeps alive the highly motivating belief that individual effort is important and has real impact on the company's performance.

Likewise at Kao, the Tokyo-based branded packaged-goods company, CEO Yoshio Maruta has developed an organizational culture and management philosophy that rejects authoritarianism and fosters individual initiative in a variety of ways. First, the company shares information openly; everyone can know what anyone can know and can use the information to do his or her job more effectively. Further, Kao's internal environment encourages cooperation, and the twin tasks of teaching and learning are ingrained as a major responsibility of every employee. Finally, the decision-making process is open and transparent—literally, in open-space areas—so that those with relevant knowledge and expertise are embraced by the process, not locked out of it. By translating his philosophy into norms and practices, Maruta built an organizational environment in which employees right down to the front line know that they are connected with and are contributing to overall corporate goals.

From Economic Entity to Social Institution

A fundamental philosophical difference separates senior executives who see themselves as designers of corporate strategy from those who define their task more broadly as shaping institutional purpose. Strategy makers view the companies they head as profit-maximizing entities with a narrowly defined role in a large and complex social environment. In their view, companies are simply agents of economic exchange in a broader marketplace. They are dependents of their shareholders, customers, employees, and larger communities, and the purpose of strategy is to manage these often conflicting dependencies for the maximum benefit of the company they serve.

This minimalist, passive, and self-serving definition grossly understates reality. Corporations are one of the most, if not the most, important institutions of modern society. A company today is more than just a business. As important repositories of resources and knowledge, companies shoulder a huge responsibility for generating wealth by continuously improving their productivity and competitiveness. Furthermore, their responsibility for defining, creating, and distributing value makes corporations one of society's principal agents of social change. At the micro level, companies are important forums for social interaction and personal fulfillment.

Purpose is the embodiment of an organization's recognition that its relationships with its diverse stakeholders are interdependent. In short, purpose is the statement of a company's moral response to its broadly defined responsibilities, not an amoral plan for exploiting commercial opportunity.

The three aspects of top management's task in building a sense of purpose are mutually interdependent and collectively reinforcing. If corporate ambition begins to focus on the company's narrow self-interest, it eventually loses the excitement, support, and commitment that emerge when objectives are linked to broader human aspirations. When organizational values become merely self-serving, companies quickly lose the sense of identification and pride that makes them attractive not only to employees but also to customers and others. And when management's respect for and attention to its employees' ideas and inputs is diluted, motivation and commitment fade.

Purpose—not strategy—is the reason an organization exists. Its definition and articulation must be top management's first responsibility.

3
Building Your Company's Vision

James C. Collins and Jerry I. Porras

We shall not cease from exploration
And the end of all our exploring
Will be to arrive where we started
And know the place for the first time.

—T.S. ELIOT, FOUR QUARTETS

Companies that enjoy enduring success have core values and a core purpose that remain fixed while their business strategies and practices endlessly adapt to a changing world. The dynamic of preserving the core while stimulating progress is the reason that companies such as Hewlett-Packard, 3M, Johnson & Johnson, Procter & Gamble, Merck, Sony, Motorola, and Nordstrom became elite institutions able to renew themselves and achieve superior long-term performance. Hewlett-Packard employees have long known that radical change in operating practices, cultural norms, and business strategies does not mean losing the spirit of the HP Way—the company's core principles. Johnson & Johnson continually questions its structure and revamps its processes while preserving the ideals embodied in its credo. In 1996, 3M sold off several of its large mature businesses—a dramatic move that surprised the business press—to refocus on its enduring core purpose of solving unsolved problems innovatively. We studied companies such as these in our research for *Built to Last: Successful Habits of Visionary Companies* and found that they have outperformed the general stock market by a factor of 12 since 1925.

Truly great companies understand the difference between what

Exhibit 3-1　Articulating a Vision

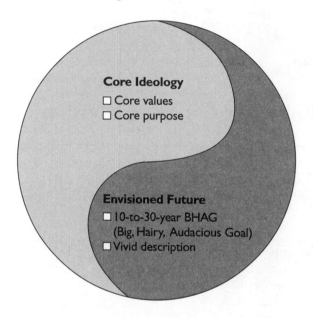

Core Ideology
☐ Core values
☐ Core purpose

Envisioned Future
☐ 10-to-30-year BHAG
　(Big, Hairy, Audacious Goal)
☐ Vivid description

should never change and what should be open for change, between what is genuinely sacred and what is not. This rare ability to manage continuity and change—requiring a consciously practiced discipline—is closely linked to the ability to develop a vision. Vision provides guidance about what core to preserve and what future to stimulate progress toward. But *vision* has become one of the most overused and least understood words in the language, conjuring up different images for different people: of deeply held values, outstanding achievement, societal bonds, exhilarating goals, motivating forces, or raisons d'être. We recommend a conceptual framework to define vision, add clarity and rigor to the vague and fuzzy concepts swirling around that trendy term, and give practical guidance for articulating a coherent vision within an organization. It is a prescriptive framework rooted in six years of research and refined and tested by our ongoing work with executives from a great variety of organizations around the world.

A well-conceived vision consists of two major components: *core ideology* and *envisioned future*. (See Exhibit 3-1.) Core ideology, the yin in our scheme, defines what we stand for and why we exist. Yin is unchanging and complements yang, the envisioned future. The envisioned future is what we aspire to become, to achieve, to create—something that will require significant change and progress to attain.

Core Ideology

Core ideology defines the enduring character of an organization—a consistent identity that transcends product or market life cycles, technological breakthroughs, management fads, and individual leaders. In fact, the most lasting and significant contribution of those who build visionary companies is the core ideology. As Bill Hewlett said about his longtime friend and business partner David Packard upon Packard's death not long ago, "As far as the company is concerned, the greatest thing he left behind him was a code of ethics known as the HP Way." HP's core ideology, which has guided the company since its inception more than 50 years ago, includes a deep respect for the individual, a dedication to affordable quality and reliability, a commitment to community responsibility (Packard himself bequeathed his $4.3 billion of Hewlett-Packard stock to a charitable foundation), and a view that the company exists to make technical contributions for the advancement and welfare of humanity. Company builders such as David Packard, Masaru Ibuka of Sony, George Merck of Merck, William McKnight of 3M, and Paul Galvin of Motorola understood that it is more important to know who you are than where you are going, for where you are going will change as the world around you changes. Leaders die, products become obsolete, markets change, new technologies emerge, and management fads come and go, but core ideology in a great company endures as a source of guidance and inspiration.

Core ideology provides the glue that holds an organization together as it grows, decentralizes, diversifies, expands globally, and develops workplace diversity. Think of it as analogous to the principles of Judaism that held the Jewish people together for centuries without a homeland, even as they spread throughout the Diaspora. Or think of the truths held to be self-evident in the Declaration of Independence, or the enduring ideals and principles of the scientific community that bond scientists from every nationality together in the common purpose of advancing human knowledge. Any effective vision must embody the core ideology of the organization, which in turn consists of two distinct parts: core values, a system of guiding principles and tenets; and core purpose, the organization's most fundamental reason for existence.

Core Values. Core values are the essential and enduring tenets of an organization. A small set of timeless guiding principles, core values require no external justification; they have *intrinsic* value and importance to those inside the organization. The Walt Disney Company's core values of imagination and wholesomeness stem not from market requirements but from the founder's inner belief that imagination and wholesomeness should be nurtured for their own sake. William Procter and James Gamble didn't instill in P&G's culture a focus on product excellence merely as a strategy for success but as an almost religious tenet. And that value has been passed down for more than 15 decades by P&G people. Service to the customer—even to the point of subservience—is a way of life at Nordstrom that traces its roots back to 1901, eight decades before customer service programs became stylish. For Bill Hewlett and David Packard, respect for the individual was first and foremost a deep personal value; they didn't get it from a book or hear it from a management guru. And Ralph S. Larsen, CEO of Johnson & Johnson, puts it this way: "The core values embodied in our credo might be a competitive advantage, but that is not *why* we have them. We have them because they define for us what we stand for, and we would hold them even if they became a competitive *dis*advantage in certain situations."

The point is that a great company decides for itself what values it holds to be core, largely independent of the current environment, competitive requirements, or management fads. Clearly, then, there is no universally right set of core values. A company need not have as its core value customer service (Sony doesn't) or respect for the individual (Disney doesn't) or quality (Wal-Mart Stores doesn't) or market focus (HP doesn't) or teamwork (Nordstrom doesn't). A company might have operating practices and business strategies around those qualities without having them at the essence of its being. Furthermore, great companies need not have likable or humanistic core values, although many do. The key is not *what* core values an organization has but that it has core values at all.

Companies tend to have only a few core values, usually between three and five. In fact, we found that none of the visionary companies we studied in our book had more than five: most had only three or four. (See "Core Values Are a Company's Essential Tenets.") And, indeed, we should expect that. Only a few values can be truly *core*—that is, so fundamental and deeply held that they will change seldom, if ever.

Core Values Are a Company's Essential Tenets

Merck

- Corporate social responsibility
- Unequivocal excellence in all aspects of the company
- Science-based innovation
- Honesty and integrity
- Profit, but profit from work that benefits humanity

Nordstrom

- Service to the customer above all else
- Hard work and individual productivity
- Never being satisfied
- Excellence in reputation; being part of something special

Philip Morris

- The right to freedom of choice
- Winning—beating others in a good fight
- Encouraging individual initiative
- Opportunity based on merit; no one is entitled to anything
- Hard work and continuous self-improvement

Sony

- Elevation of the Japanese culture and national status
- Being a pioneer—not following others; doing the impossible
- Encouraging individual ability and creativity

Walt Disney

- No cynicism
- Nurturing and promulgation of "wholesome American values"

- Creativity, dreams, and imagination
- Fanatical attention to consistency and detail
- Preservation and control of the Disney magic

To identify the core values of your own organization, push with relentless honesty to define what values are truly central. If you articulate more than five or six, chances are that you are confusing core values (which do not change) with operating practices, business strategies, or cultural norms (which should be open to change). Remember, the values must stand the test of time. After you've drafted a preliminary list of the core values, ask about each one, If the circumstances changed and *penalized* us for holding this core value, would we still keep it? If you can't honestly answer yes, then the value is not core and should be dropped from consideration.

A high-technology company wondered whether it should put quality on its list of core values. The CEO asked, "Suppose in ten years quality doesn't make a hoot of difference in our markets. Suppose the only thing that matters is sheer speed and horsepower but not quality. Would we still want to put quality on our list of core values?" The members of the management team looked around at one another and finally said no. Quality stayed in the *strategy* of the company, and quality-improvement programs remained in place as a mechanism for stimulating progress; but quality did not make the list of core values.

The same group of executives then wrestled with leading-edge innovation as a core value. The CEO asked, "Would we keep innovation on the list as a core value, no matter how the world around us changed?" This time, the management team gave a resounding yes. The managers' outlook might be summarized as, "We always want to do leading-edge innovation. That's who we are. It's really important to us and always will be. No matter what. And if our current markets don't value it, we will find markets that do." Leading-edge innovation went on the list and will stay there. A company should not change its core values in response to market changes; rather, it should change markets, if necessary, to remain true to its core values.

Who should be involved in articulating the core values varies with the size, age, and geographic dispersion of the company, but in many situations we have recommended what we call a *Mars Group*. It works like this: Imagine that you've been asked to re-create the very best attributes of your organization on another planet but you have seats on the rocket ship for only five to seven people. Whom should you send? Most likely, you'll choose the people who have a gut-level understanding of your core values, the highest level of credibility with their peers, and the highest levels of competence. We'll often ask people brought together to work on core values to nominate a Mars Group of five to seven individuals (not necessarily all from the assembled group). Invariably, they end up selecting highly credible representatives who do a super job of articulating the core values precisely because they are exemplars of those values—a representative slice of the company's genetic code.

Even global organizations composed of people from widely diverse cultures can identify a set of shared core values. The secret is to work from the individual to the organization. People involved in articulating the core values need to answer several questions: What core values do you personally bring to your work? (These should be so fundamental that you would hold them regardless of whether or not they were rewarded.) What would you tell your children are the core values that you hold at work and that you hope *they* will hold when they become working adults? If you awoke tomorrow morning with enough money to retire for the rest of your life, would you continue to live those core values? Can you envision them being as valid for you 100 years from now as they are today? Would you want to hold those core values, even if at some point one or more of them became a competitive disadvantage? If you were to start a new organization tomorrow in a different line of work, what core values would you build into the new organization regardless of its industry? The last three questions are particularly important because they make the crucial distinction between enduring core values that should not change and practices and strategies that should be changing all the time.

Core Purpose. Core purpose, the second part of core ideology, is the organization's reason for being. An effective purpose reflects people's idealistic motivations for doing the company's work. It doesn't just describe the organization's output or target customers; it captures the soul of the organization. (See "Core Purpose Is a Company's Reason for Being.") Purpose, as illustrated by a speech David Packard gave to HP employees in 1960, gets at the deeper reasons for an organization's existence beyond just making money. Packard said,

> I want to discuss why a company exists in the first place. In other words, why are we here? I think many people assume, wrongly, that a company exists simply to make money. While this is an important result of a company's existence, we have to go deeper and find the real reasons for our being. As we investigate this, we

inevitably come to the conclusion that a group of people get together and exist as an institution that we call a company so they are able to accomplish something collectively that they could not accomplish separately—they make a contribution to society, a phrase which sounds trite but is fundamental. . . . You can look around [in the general business world and] see people who are interested in money and nothing else, but the underlying drives come largely from a desire to do something else: to make a product, to give a service—generally to do something which is of value.[1]

Purpose (which should last at least 100 years) should not be confused with specific goals or business strategies (which should change many times in 100 years). Whereas you might achieve a goal or complete a strategy, you cannot fulfill a purpose; it is like a guiding star on the horizon—forever pursued but never reached. Yet although purpose itself does not change, it does inspire change. The very fact that purpose can never be fully realized means that an organization can never stop stimulating change and progress.

Core Purpose Is a Company's Reason for Being

3M: To solve unsolved problems innovatively

Cargill: To improve the standard of living around the world

Fannie Mae: To strengthen the social fabric by continually democratizing home ownership

Hewlett-Packard: To make technical contributions for the advancement and welfare of humanity

Lost Arrow Corporation: To be a role model and a tool for social change

Pacific Theatres: To provide a place for people to flourish and to enhance the community

Mary Kay Cosmetics: To give unlimited opportunity to women

McKinsey & Company: To help leading corporations and governments be more successful

Merck: To preserve and improve human life.

Nike: To experience the emotion of competition, winning, and crushing competitors

Sony: To experience the joy of advancing and applying technology for the benefit of the public

Telecare Corporation: To help people with mental impairments realize their full potential

Wal-Mart: To give ordinary folk the chance to buy the same things as rich people

Walt Disney: To make people happy

In identifying purpose, some companies make the mistake of simply describing their current product lines or customer segments. We do not consider the following statement to reflect an effective purpose: "We exist to fulfill our government charter and participate in the secondary mortgage market by packaging mortgages into investment securities." The statement is merely descriptive. A far more effective statement of purpose would be that expressed by the executives of the Federal National Mortgage Association, Fannie Mae: "To strengthen the social fabric by continually democratizing home ownership." The secondary mortgage market as we know it might not even exist in 100 years, but strengthening the social fabric by continually democratizing home ownership can be an enduring purpose, no matter how much the world changes. Guided and inspired by this purpose, Fannie Mae launched in the early 1990s a series of bold initiatives, including a program to develop new systems for reducing mortgage underwriting costs by 40% in five years; programs to eliminate discrimination in the lending process (backed by $5 billion in underwriting experiments); and an audacious goal to provide, by the year 2000, $1 trillion targeted at 10 million families that had traditionally been shut out of home ownership—minorities, immigrants, and low-income groups.

Similarly, 3M defines its purpose not in terms of adhesives and abrasives but as the perpetual quest to solve unsolved problems innovatively—a purpose that is always leading 3M into new fields. McKinsey & Company's purpose is not to do management consulting but to help corporations and governments be more successful: in 100 years, it might involve methods other than consulting. Hewlett-Packard doesn't exist to make electronic test and measurement equipment but to make technical contributions that improve people's lives—a purpose that has led the company far afield from its origins in electronic instruments. Imagine if Walt Disney had conceived of his company's purpose as to make cartoons, rather than to make people happy; we probably wouldn't have Mickey Mouse, Disneyland, EPCOT Center, or the Anaheim Mighty Ducks Hockey Team.

One powerful method for getting at purpose is the *five whys*. Start with the descriptive statement We make X products or We deliver X services, and then ask, Why is that important? five times. After a few whys, you'll find that you're getting down to the fundamental purpose of the organization.

We used this method to deepen and enrich a discussion about purpose when we worked with a certain market-research company. The executive team first met for several hours and generated the following statement of purpose for their organization: To provide the best market-research data available. We then asked the following question: Why is it important to provide the best market-research data available? After some discussion, the executives answered in a way that reflected a deeper sense of their organization's purpose: To provide the best market-research data available so that our customers will understand their markets better than they could otherwise. A further discussion let team members realize that their sense of self-worth came not just from helping customers understand their markets better but also from making a *contribution* to their customers' success. This introspection eventually led the company to identify its purpose as: To contribute to our customers' success by helping them understand their markets. With this purpose in mind, the company now frames its product decisions not with the question Will it sell? but with the question Will it make a contribution to our customers' success?

The five whys can help companies in any industry frame their work in a more meaningful way. An asphalt and gravel company might begin by saying, We make gravel and asphalt products. After a few whys, it could conclude that making asphalt and gravel is important because the quality of the infrastructure plays a vital role in people's safety and experience; because driving on a pitted road is annoying and dangerous; because 747s cannot land safely on runways built with poor workmanship or inferior concrete; because buildings with substandard materials weaken with time and crumble in earthquakes. From such introspection may emerge this purpose: To make people's lives better by improving the quality of man-made structures. With a sense of purpose very much along those lines, Granite Rock Company of Watsonville, California, won the Malcolm Baldrige National Quality Award—not an easy feat for a small rock quarry and asphalt company. And Granite Rock has gone on to be one of the most progressive and exciting companies we've encountered in *any* industry.

Notice that none of the core purposes fall into the category "maximize shareholder wealth." A primary role of core purpose is to guide and inspire. Maximizing shareholder wealth does not inspire people at all levels of an organization, and it provides precious little guidance.

Maximizing shareholder wealth is the standard off-the-shelf purpose for those organizations that have not yet identified their true core purpose. It is a substitute—and a weak one at that.

When people in great organizations talk about their achievements, they say very little about earnings per share. Motorola people talk about impressive quality improvements and the effect of the products they create on the world. Hewlett-Packard people talk about their technical contributions to the marketplace. Nordstrom people talk about heroic customer service and remarkable individual performance by star salespeople. When a Boeing engineer talks about launching an exciting and revolutionary new aircraft, she does not say, "I put my heart and soul into this project because it would add 37 cents to our earnings per share."

One way to get at the purpose that lies beyond merely maximizing shareholder wealth is to play the "Random Corporate Serial Killer" game. It works like this: Suppose you could sell the company to someone who would pay a price that everyone inside and outside the company agrees is more than fair (even with a very generous set of assumptions about the expected future cash flows of the company). Suppose further that this buyer would guarantee stable employment for all employees at the same pay scale after the purchase but with no guarantee that those jobs would be in the same industry. Finally, suppose the buyer plans to kill the company after the purchase—its products or services would be discontinued, its operations would be shut down, its brand names would be shelved forever, and so on. The company would utterly and completely cease to exist. Would you accept the offer? Why or why not? What would be lost if the company ceased to exist? Why is it important that the company continue to exist? We've found this exercise to be very powerful for helping hard-nosed, financially focused executives reflect on their organization's deeper reasons for being.

Another approach is to ask each member of the Mars Group, How could we frame the purpose of this organization so that if you woke up tomorrow morning with enough money in the bank to retire, you would nevertheless keep working here? What deeper sense of purpose would motivate you to continue to dedicate your precious creative energies to this company's efforts?

As they move into the twenty-first century, companies will need to draw on the full creative energy and talent of their people. But why should people give full measure? As Peter Drucker has pointed out, the best and most dedicated people are ultimately volunteers, for they have the opportunity to do something else with their lives. Confronted with an increasingly mobile society, cynicism about corporate life, and an expanding entrepreneurial segment of the economy, companies more than ever need to have a clear understanding of their purpose in order to make work meaningful and thereby attract, motivate, and retain outstanding people.

Discovering Core Ideology

You do not create or set core ideology. You *discover* core ideology. You do not deduce it by looking at the external environment. You understand it by looking inside. Ideology has to be authentic. You cannot fake it. Discovering core ideology is not an intellectual exercise. Do not ask, What core values should we hold? Ask instead, What core values do we truly and passionately hold? You should not confuse values that you think the organization ought to have—but does not—with authentic core values. To do so would create cynicism throughout the organization. ("Who're they trying to kid? We all know that isn't a core value around here!") Aspirations are more appropriate as part of your envisioned future or as part of your strategy, not as part of the core ideology. However, authentic core values that have weakened over time can be considered a legitimate part of the core ideology—as long as you acknowledge to the organization that you must work hard to revive them.

Also be clear that the role of core ideology is to guide and inspire, not to differentiate. Two companies can have the same core values or purpose. Many companies could have the purpose to make technical contributions, but few live it as passionately as Hewlett-Packard. Many companies could have the purpose to preserve and improve human life, but few hold it as deeply as Merck. Many companies could have the core value of heroic customer service, but few create as intense a culture around that value as Nordstrom. Many companies could have the core value of innovation, but few create the powerful alignment mechanisms that stimulate the innovation we see at 3M. The authenticity, the discipline, and the consistency with which the ideology is lived—not the content of the ideology—differentiate visionary companies from the rest of the pack.

Core ideology needs to be meaningful and inspirational only to people inside the organization; it need not be exciting to outsiders. Why not? Because it is the people inside the organization who need to commit to the organizational ideology over the long term. Core ideology can also play a role in determining who *is* inside and who is not. A clear and well-articulated ideology attracts to the company people whose personal values are compatible with the company's core values; conversely, it repels those whose personal values are incompatible. You cannot impose new core values or purpose on people. Nor are core values and purpose things people can buy into. Executives often ask, How do we get people to share our core ideology? You don't. You can't. Instead, find people who are predisposed to share your core values and purpose; attract and retain those people; and let those who do not share your core values go elsewhere. Indeed, the very process of articulating core ideology may cause some people to leave when they realize that they are not personally compatible with the organization's core. Welcome that outcome. It is certainly desirable to retain within the core ideology a diversity of people and viewpoints. People who share the same core values and purpose do not necessarily all think or look the same.

Don't confuse core ideology itself with core ideology statements. A company can have a very strong core ideology without a formal statement. For example, Nike has not (to our knowledge) formally articulated a statement of its core purpose. Yet, according to our observations, Nike has a powerful core purpose that permeates the entire organization: to experience the emotion of competition, winning, and crushing competitors. Nike has a campus that seems more like a shrine to the competitive spirit than a corporate office complex. Giant photos of Nike heroes cover the walls, bronze plaques of Nike athletes hang along the Nike Walk of Fame, statues of Nike athletes stand alongside the running track that rings the campus, and buildings honor champions such as Olympic marathoner Joan Benoit, basketball superstar Michael Jordan, and tennis pro John McEnroe. Nike people who do not feel stimulated by the competitive spirit and the urge to be ferocious simply do not last long in the culture. Even the company's name reflects a sense of competition: Nike is the Greek goddess of victory. Thus, although Nike has not formally articulated its purpose, it clearly has a strong one.

Identifying core values and purpose is therefore not an exercise in wordsmithery. Indeed, an organization will generate a variety of statements over time to describe the core ideology. In Hewlett-Packard's archives, we found more than half a dozen distinct versions of the HP Way, drafted by David Packard between 1956 and 1972. All versions stated the same principles, but the words used varied depending on the era and the circumstances. Similarly, Sony's core ideology has been stated many different ways over the company's history. At its founding, Masaru Ibuka described two key elements of Sony's ideology: "We shall welcome technical difficulties and focus on highly sophisticated technical products that have great usefulness for society regardless of the quantity involved; we shall place our main emphasis on ability, performance, and personal character so that each individual can show the best in ability and skill."[2] Four decades later, this same concept appeared in a statement of core ideology called Sony Pioneer Spirit: "Sony is a pioneer and never intends to follow others. Through progress, Sony wants to serve the whole world. It shall be always a seeker of the unknown. . . . Sony has a principle of respecting and encouraging one's ability . . . and always tries to bring out the best in a person. This is the vital force of Sony."[3] Same core values, different words.

You should therefore focus on getting the content right—on capturing the essence of the core values and purpose. The point is not to create a perfect statement but to gain a deep understanding of your organization's core values and purpose, which can then be expressed in a multitude of ways. In fact, we often suggest that once the core has been identified, managers should generate their own statements of the core values and purpose to share with their groups.

Finally, don't confuse core ideology with the concept of core competence. Core competence is a strategic concept that defines your organization's capabilities—what you are particularly good at—whereas core ideology captures what you stand for and why you exist. Core competencies should be well aligned with a company's core ideology and are often rooted in it; but they are not the same thing. For example, Sony has a core competence of miniaturization—a strength that can be strategically applied to a wide array of products and markets. But it does not have a core *ideology* of miniaturization. Sony might not even have miniaturization as part of its strategy in 100 years, but to remain a great company, it will still have the same core values described in the Sony Pioneer Spirit and the same fundamental reason for being—namely, to advance technology for the benefit of the general public. In a visionary company like Sony, core competencies change over the decades, whereas core ideology does not.

Once you are clear about the core ideology, you should feel free to change absolutely *anything* that is not part of it. From then on, whenever someone says something should not change because "it's part of our culture" or "we've always done it that way" or any such excuse, mention this simple rule: If it's not core, it's up for change. The strong version of the rule is, *If it's not core, change it!* Articulating core ideology is just a starting point, however. You also must determine what type of progress you want to stimulate.

Envisioned Future

The second primary component of the vision framework is *envisioned future*. It consists of two parts: a 10-to-30-year audacious goal plus vivid descriptions of what it will be like to achieve the goal. We recognize that the phrase *envisioned future* is somewhat paradoxical. On the one hand, it conveys concreteness—something visible, vivid, and real. On the other hand, it involves a time yet unrealized—with its dreams, hopes, and aspirations.

Vision-level BHAG. We found in our research that visionary companies often use bold missions—or what we prefer to call *BHAGs* (pronounced BEE-hags and shorthand for Big, Hairy, Audacious Goals)—as a powerful way to stimulate progress. All companies have goals. But there is a difference between merely having a goal and becoming committed to a huge, daunting challenge—such as climbing Mount Everest. A true BHAG is clear and compelling, serves as a unifying focal point of effort, and acts as a catalyst for team spirit. It has a clear finish line, so the organization can know when it has achieved the goal; people like to shoot for finish lines. A BHAG engages people—it reaches out and grabs them. It is tangible, energizing, highly focused. People get it right away; it takes little or no explanation. For example, NASA's 1960s moon mission didn't need a committee of wordsmiths to spend endless hours turning the goal into a verbose, impossible-to-remember mission statement. The goal itself was so easy to grasp—so compelling in its own right—that it could be said 100 different ways yet be easily understood by everyone. Most corporate statements we've seen do little to spur forward movement because they do not contain the powerful mechanism of a BHAG.

Although organizations may have many BHAGs at different levels operating at the same time, vision requires a special type of BHAG—a vision-level BHAG that applies to the entire organization and requires 10 to 30 years of effort to complete. Setting the BHAG that far into the future requires thinking beyond the current capabilities of the organization and the current environment. Indeed, inventing such a goal forces an executive team to be visionary, rather than just strategic or tactical. A BHAG should not be a sure bet—it will have perhaps only a 50% to 70% probability of success—but the organization must believe that it can reach the goal anyway. A BHAG should require extraordinary effort and perhaps a little luck. We have helped companies create a vision-level BHAG by advising them to think in terms of four broad categories: target BHAGs, common-enemy BHAGs, role-model BHAGs, and internal-transformation BHAGs. (See "Big, Hairy, Audacious Goals Aid Long-Term Vision.")

Vivid Description. In addition to vision-level BHAGs, an envisioned future needs what we call *vivid description*—that is, a vibrant, engaging, and specific description of what it will be like to achieve the BHAG. Think of it as translating the vision from words into pictures, of creating an image that people can carry around in their heads. It is a question of painting a picture with your words. Picture painting is essential for making the 10-to-30-year BHAG tangible in people's minds.

Big, Hairy, Audacious Goals Aid Long-Term Vision

Target BHAGs can be quantitative or qualitative

- Become a $125 billion company by the year 2000 (Wal-Mart, 1990)
- Democratize the automobile (Ford Motor Company, early 1900s)
- Become the company most known for changing the worldwide poor-quality image of Japanese products (Sony, early 1950s)
- Become the most powerful, the most serviceable, the most far-reaching world financial institution that has ever been (City Bank, predecessor to Citicorp, 1915)
- Become the dominant player in commercial aircraft and bring the world into the jet age (Boeing, 1950)

Common-enemy BHAGs involve David-versus-Goliath thinking

- Knock off RJR as the number one tobacco company in the world (Philip Morris, 1950s)
- Crush Adidas (Nike, 1960s)
- *Yamaha wo tsubusu!* We will destroy Yamaha! (Honda, 1970s)

Role-model BHAGs suit up-and-coming organizations

- Become the Nike of the cycling industry (Giro Sport Design, 1986)
- Become as respected in 20 years as Hewlett-Packard is today (Watkins-Johnson, 1996)
- Become the Harvard of the West (Stanford University, 1940s)

Internal-transformation BHAGs suit large, established organizations

- Become number one or number two in every market we serve and revolutionize this company to have the strengths of a big company combined with the leanness and agility of a small company (General Electric Company, 1980s)

- Transform this company from a defense contractor into the best diversified high-technology company in the world (Rockwell, 1995)

- Transform this division from a poorly respected internal products supplier to one of the most respected, exciting, and sought-after divisions in the company (Components Support Division of a computer products company, 1989)

For example, Henry Ford brought to life the goal of democratizing the automobile with this vivid description: "I will build a motor car for the great multitude. . . . It will be so low in price that no man making a good salary will be unable to own one and enjoy with his family the blessing of hours of pleasure in God's great open spaces. . . . When I'm through, everybody will be able to afford one, and everyone will have one. The horse will have disappeared from our highways, the automobile will be taken for granted . . . [and we will] give a large number of men employment at good wages."

The components-support division of a computer-products company had a general manager who was able to describe vividly the goal of becoming one of the most sought-after divisions in the company: "We will be respected and admired by our peers. . . . Our solutions will be actively sought by the end-product divisions, who will achieve significant product `hits' in the marketplace largely because of our technical contribution. . . . We will have pride in ourselves. . . . The best up-and-coming people in the company will seek to work in our division. . . . People will give unsolicited feedback that they love what they are doing. . . . [Our own] people will walk on the balls of their feet. . . . [They] will willingly work hard because they want to. . . . Both employees and customers will feel that our division has contributed to their life in a positive way."

In the 1930s, Merck had the BHAG to transform itself from a chemical manufacturer into one of the preeminent drug-making companies in the world, with a research capability to rival any major university. In describing this envisioned future, George Merck said at the opening of Merck's research facility in 1933, "We believe that research work carried on with patience and persistence will bring to industry and commerce new life; and we have faith that in this new laboratory, with the tools we have supplied, science will be advanced, knowledge increased, and human life win ever a greater freedom from suffering and disease. . . . We pledge our every aid that this enterprise shall merit the faith we have in it. Let your light so shine—that those who seek the Truth, that those who toil that this world may be a better place to live in, that those who hold aloft that torch of science and knowledge through these social and economic dark ages, shall take new courage and feel their hands supported."

Passion, emotion, and conviction are essential parts of the vivid description. Some managers are uncomfortable expressing emotion about their dreams, but that's what motivates others. Churchill understood that when he described the BHAG facing Great Britain in 1940. He did not just say, "Beat Hitler." He said, "Hitler knows he will have to break us on this island or lose the war. If we can stand up to him, all Europe may be free, and the life of the world may move forward into broad, sunlit uplands. But if we fail, the whole world, including the United States, including all we have known and cared for, will sink into the abyss of a new Dark Age, made more sinister and perhaps more protracted by the lights of perverted science. Let us therefore brace ourselves to our duties and so bear ourselves that if the British Empire and its Commonwealth last for a thousand years, men will still say, `This was their finest hour.'"

A Few Key Points. Don't confuse core ideology and envisioned future. In particular, don't confuse core purpose and BHAGs. Managers often exchange one for the other, mixing the two together or failing to articulate both as distinct items. Core purpose—not some specific goal—is the reason why the organization exists. A BHAG is a clearly articulated goal. Core purpose can never be completed, whereas the BHAG is reachable in 10 to 30 years. Think of the core purpose as the star on the horizon to be chased forever; the BHAG is the mountain to be climbed. Once you have reached its summit, you move on to other mountains.

Identifying core ideology is a discovery process, but setting the envisioned future is a creative process. We find that executives often have a great deal of difficulty coming up with an exciting BHAG. They want to analyze their way into the future. We have found, therefore, that some executives make more progress by starting first with the vivid description and backing from there into the BHAG. This approach involves starting with questions such as, We're sitting here in 20 years; what would we love to see? What should this company look like?

What should it feel like to employees? What should it have achieved? If someone writes an article for a major business magazine about this company in 20 years, what will it say? One biotechnology company we worked with had trouble envisioning its future. Said one member of the executive team, "Every time we come up with something for the entire company, it is just too generic to be exciting—something banal like `advance biotechnology worldwide.'" Asked to paint a picture of the company in 20 years, the executives mentioned such things as "on the cover of *Business Week* as a model success story . . . the *Fortune* most admired top-ten list . . . the best science and business graduates want to work here . . . people on airplanes rave about one of our products to seatmates . . . 20 consecutive years of profitable growth . . . an entrepreneurial culture that has spawned half a dozen new divisions from within . . . management gurus use us as an example of excellent management and progressive thinking," and so on. From this, they were able to set the goal of becoming as well respected as Merck or as Johnson & Johnson in biotechnology.

It makes no sense to analyze whether an envisioned future is the right one. With a creation—and the task is creation of a future, not prediction—there can be no right answer. Did Beethoven create the right Ninth Symphony? Did Shakespeare create the right *Hamlet?* We can't answer these questions; they're nonsense. The envisioned future involves such essential questions as Does it get our juices flowing? Do we find it stimulating? Does it spur forward momentum? Does it get people going? The envisioned future should be so exciting in its own right that it would continue to keep the organization motivated even if the leaders who set the goal disappeared. City Bank, the predecessor of Citicorp, had the BHAG "to become the most powerful, the most serviceable, the most far-reaching world financial institution that has ever been"—a goal that generated excitement through multiple generations until it was achieved. Similarly, the NASA moon mission continued to galvanize people even though President John F. Kennedy (the leader associated with setting the goal) died years before its completion.

To create an effective envisioned future requires a certain level of unreasonable confidence and commitment. Keep in mind that a BHAG is not just a goal; it is a Big, Hairy, Audacious Goal. It's not reasonable for a small regional bank to set the goal of becoming "the most powerful, the most serviceable, the most far-reaching world financial institution that has ever been," as City Bank did in 1915. It's not a tepid claim that "we will democratize the automobile," as Henry Ford said. It was almost laughable for Philip Morris—as the sixth-place player with 9% market share in the 1950s—to take on the goal of defeating Goliath RJ Reynolds Tobacco Company and becoming number one. It was hardly modest for Sony, as a small, cash-strapped venture, to proclaim the goal of changing the poor-quality image of Japanese products around the world. (See "Putting It All Together: Sony in the 1950s.") Of course, it's not only the audacity of the goal but also the level of commitment to the goal that counts. Boeing didn't just envision a future dominated by its commercial jets; it bet the company on the 707 and, later, on the 747. Nike's people didn't just talk about the idea of crushing Adidas; they went on a crusade to fulfill the dream. Indeed, the envisioned future should produce a bit of the "gulp factor": when it dawns on people what it will take to achieve the goal, there should be an almost audible gulp.

Putting It All Together: Sony in the 1950s

Core Ideology

Core Values

- Elevation of the Japanese culture and national status
- Being a pioneer—not following others; doing the impossible
- Encouraging individual ability and creativity

Purpose

To experience the sheer joy of innovation and the application of technology for the benefit and pleasure of the general public

Envisioned Future

BHAG

Become the company most known for changing the worldwide poor-quality image of Japanese products

Vivid Description

We will create products that become pervasive around the world. . . . We will be the first Japanese company to go into the U.S. market and distribute directly. . . . We will succeed with innovations that U.S. companies have failed at—such as the transistor radio. . . . Fifty years from now, our brand name will be as well known as any in the world . . . and will signify innovation and quality that rival the most innovative companies anywhere. . . . "Made in Japan" will mean something fine, not something shoddy.

But what about failure to realize the envisioned future? In our research, we found that the visionary companies displayed a remarkable ability to achieve even their most audacious goals. Ford did democratize the automobile; Citicorp did become the most far-reaching bank in the world; Philip Morris did rise from sixth to first and beat RJ Reynolds worldwide; Boeing did become the dominant commercial aircraft company; and it looks like Wal-Mart will achieve its $125 billion goal, even without Sam Walton. In contrast, the comparison companies in our research frequently did not achieve their BHAGs, if they set them at all. The difference does not lie in setting easier goals: the visionary companies tended to have even more audacious ambitions. The difference does not lie in charismatic, visionary leadership: the visionary companies often achieved their BHAGs without such larger-than-life leaders at the helm. Nor does the difference lie in better strategy: the visionary companies often realized their goals more by an organic process of "let's try a lot of stuff and keep what works" than by well-laid strategic plans. Rather, their success lies in building the strength of their organization as their primary way of creating the future.

Why did Merck become the preeminent drugmaker in the world? Because Merck's architects built the best pharmaceutical research and development organization in the world. Why did Boeing become the dominant commercial aircraft company in the world? Because of its superb engineering and marketing organization, which had the ability to make projects like the 747 a reality. When asked to name the most important decisions that have contributed to the growth and success of Hewlett-Packard, David Packard answered entirely in terms of decisions to build the strength of the organization and its people.

Finally, in thinking about the envisioned future, beware of the We've Arrived Syndrome—a complacent lethargy that arises once an organization has achieved one BHAG and fails to replace it with another. NASA suffered from that syndrome after the successful moon landings. After you've landed on the moon, what do you do for an encore? Ford suffered from the syndrome when, after it succeeded in democratizing the automobile, it failed to set a new goal of equal significance and gave General Motors the opportunity to jump ahead in the 1930s. Apple Computer suffered from the syndrome after achieving the goal of creating a computer that nontechies could use. Start-up companies frequently suffer from the We've Arrived Syndrome after going public or after reaching a stage in which survival no longer seems in question. An envisioned future helps an organization only as long as it hasn't yet been achieved. In our work with companies, we frequently hear executives say, "It's just not as exciting around here as it used to be; we seem to have lost our momentum." Usually, that kind of remark signals that the organization has climbed one mountain and not yet picked a new one to climb.

Many executives thrash about with mission statements and vision statements. Unfortunately, most of those statements turn out to be a muddled stew of values, goals, purposes, philosophies, beliefs, aspirations, norms, strategies, practices, and descriptions. They are usually a boring, confusing, structurally unsound stream of words that evoke the response "True, but who cares?" Even more problematic, seldom do these statements have a direct link to the fundamental dynamic of visionary companies: preserve the core and stimulate progress. That dynamic, not vision or mission statements, is the primary engine of enduring companies. Vision simply provides the context for bringing this dynamic to life. Building a visionary company requires 1% vision and 99% alignment. When you have superb alignment, a visitor could drop in from outer space and infer your vision from the operations and activities of the company without ever reading it on paper or meeting a single senior executive.

Creating alignment may be your most important work. But the first step will always be to recast your vision or mission into an effective context for building a visionary company. If you do it right, you shouldn't have to do it again for at least a decade.

Notes

1. David Packard, speech given to Hewlett-Packard's training group on March 8, 1960; courtesy of Hewlett-Packard Archives.
2. See Nick Lyons, *The Sony Vision* (New York: Crown Publishers, 1976). We also used a translation by our Japanese student Tsuneto Ikeda.
3. Akio Morita, *Made in Japan* (New York: E.P. Dutton, 1986), p. 147.

PART

III

Making Change Happen:
Become a Change Agent

1
Changing the Way We Change

**Richard Tanner Pascale, Mark Millemann, and
Linda Gioja**

More and more companies are trying to make a fundamental
change in the way they operate. For years, they've struggled with
growing competition by introducing improvements (or at least improvement programs) into every function and process. But the competitive pressures keep on getting worse, the pace of change keeps ac-
celerating, and companies keep pouring executive energy into the
search for ever higher levels of quality, service, and overall business
agility. The treadmill moves faster, companies work harder, results improve slowly or not at all.

The problem is not the programs, some of which have worked won-
ders. The problem is that the whole burden of change typically rests
on so few people. In other words, the number of people *at every level*
who make committed, imaginative contributions to organizational
success is simply too small. More employees need to take a greater interest and a more active role in the business. More of them need to
care deeply about success. Companies achieve real agility only when
every function, office, strategy, goal, and process—when every person—is able and eager to rise to every challenge. This type and degree
of fundamental change, commonly called *revitalization* or *transformation,* is what more and more companies seek but all too rarely achieve.

Surveys confirm that executives have begun to give revitalization a
high priority. With a few notable exceptions, however, most of their
efforts to achieve it have met with frustration—partly because large
organizations have such a remarkable capacity to resist change of *all*

This article is based on research and consulting work carried out jointly with CSC Index.

kinds, and partly because the kind of change being sought is so much more radical and uncomfortable than anything required by a shift in strategy or process or corporate structure. For that matter, corporate revitalization often includes shifts in strategy or process or structure, but revitalization means a good deal more—it means a permanent rekindling of individual creativity and responsibility, a lasting transformation of the company's internal and external relationships, an honest-to-God change in human behavior on the job. Revitalization is not incremental change. Its realizable goal is a discontinuous shift in organizational capability—a resocialization so thorough that employees feel they are working for a different company, a leap in a company's ability to meet or exceed industry benchmarks, a jump in bottom-line results.

This kind of sustained organizational renewal would not be easy even if companies had a reliable road map to make the journey a reasonable bet. As it is, most of what's been written about transformational change is either too conceptual and therefore too impractical, too inspirational and therefore too vague, or too company specific and therefore too hard to apply to one's own situation. We have been inept at transforming troubled organizations—or even at maintaining the vitality of healthy ones—because we have never before identified the factors that produce sustainable revitalization.

In essence, there are three concrete interventions that will restore companies to vital agility and then keep them in good health: *incorporating employees* fully into the process of dealing with business challenges, *leading from a different place* so as to sharpen and maintain employee involvement and constructive stress, and *instilling mental disciplines* that will make people behave differently and then help them sustain their new behavior into the future. Done properly, these three interventions will create a landmark shift in an organization's operating state or culture by significantly altering the way people experience their own *power* and *identity* and the way they deal with *conflict* and *learning.*

We discovered these sources of revitalization by tracking the change efforts, in good times and bad, of three of the world's largest organizations: Sears, Roebuck & Company, Royal Dutch Shell, and the United States Army. Sears (with $36 billion in revenues and 310,000 employees), Shell (with $100 billion in revenues and 110,000 employees), and the U.S. Army (with a $62 billion operating budget, 750,000 civilian and active-duty employees, and another 550,000 in the Army Reserve) share traits of size, geographical dispersion, and managerial complexity. They also share the distinction of having beaten the odds. All three have survived for 100 years or more and have retained their essential identity—they have been neither swallowed up by others nor disaggregated into fragments.

The events that triggered transformation efforts at Sears, Shell, and the army were quite different. In all three organizations, however, the 800-pound gorilla that impaired performance and stifled change was culture. The trouble is, there are as many different definitions of *culture* as there are articles on change management, and none of them give us much help in telling us how, or even what, to fix. Nevertheless, in our study of what might loosely be called *culture* at Sears, Shell, and the army, we found four distinct indicators that are highly predictive of performance in both good times and bad. These four indicators can serve managers in much the same way that vital signs serve physicians in appraising the health of the human body.

This analogy of vital signs is important. The reason so many early forms of healing failed was that practitioners were treating only the most obvious symptoms of some larger malfunctioning system they knew little or nothing about. Gradually, however, medical science identified these invisible systems, figured out how they worked, studied their interdependencies, and learned to pay close attention to key indicators of a patient's physical well-being. Today physicians begin an examination by checking these vital signs—pulse, blood pressure, pulmonary function, reflexes—to form a general but still fairly accurate impression of how each complex subsystem and the organism as a whole are faring.

Organizations have similar systems and symptomatologies. Their vital signs reveal a great deal about their overall health and adaptability, and about the strength and vigor of their functional systems. The four vital signs we identified at Sears, Shell, and the army give us a working definition of culture and tell us most of what we need to know about the operating state of any company:

Power. Do employees believe they can affect organizational performance? Do they believe they have the power to make things happen?

Identity. Do individuals identify rather narrowly with their professions, working teams, or functional units, or do they identify with the organization as a whole?

Conflict. How do members of the organization handle conflict? Do they smooth problems over, or do they confront and resolve them?

Learning. How does the organization learn? How does it deal with new ideas?

Organizational Drift

As a result of age, size, or competitive intensity, most organizations exhibit a deterioration in vital signs that is inconsistent with—in fact, often destructive to—their ambitions and purposes.

The members of start-up organizations have a sense of individual and collective power; they feel they can make a big difference in the pursuit of the goals they all share. Employees identify with the enterprise as a whole; alignment and informal teamwork are commonplace. When conflicts occur, people handle them directly and almost never allow them to interfere with getting things done. The whole organization is open to learning; trial and error are the norm.

As organizations grow older and larger, however, the vigor of these four vital signs deteriorates. Instead of power, people often develop a sense of resignation in response to seemingly insurmountable obstacles or to lack of support from their superiors in the daily hassle of getting things done. As organizations become more complicated and demanding, people strive to carve out private patches of turf where they can exercise responsibility, protect themselves, and keep the world at bay. When it comes to their identity, therefore, employees lose their sense of teamwork and alignment with the entire enterprise and begin to seek the safety of their particular profession, union, function, team, or location. People in mature organizations tend to avoid conflict for fear of blame or of having someone take their disagreement personally. Alternatively, they may take part in a succession of routine collisions that lead to stalemate rather than resolution. As for learning, larger and older organizations tend to be less receptive to new ideas than their younger counterparts. In place of inquiry and experimentation, ideas get studied to death in hopes of ferreting out every possible weakness before making a commitment. The precondition for action is certain knowledge.

The Sears story is a useful illustration of a company culture's natural drift away from good health. It also illustrates one CEO's well-orchestrated but ultimately ineffective efforts to reverse the drift and another CEO's remarkable success at breathing new life into the enterprise.

Ed Brennan's 12-year tenure at Sears's helm cannot be faulted for a lack of intelligence, energy, or good intentions. He put the Sears Tower up for sale, slimmed down headquarters, and moved the central organization to an open campus in Chicago's suburbs. He called for an end to Sears's tradition of insisting that customers use only Sears credit cards. He launched Brand Central, which offered for the first time such non-Sears appliances as GE, Maytag, and Panasonic. He diversified into financial services through the acquisition of Dean Witter (for $607 million) and Coldwell Banker (for $202 million), and he invested $1 billion to launch the Discover Card. (When he spun off these assets in 1993, Sears's market capitalization had risen to $36 billion from $8 billion when he took the job, and the cumulative profit from financial services had accounted for approximately two-thirds of Sears's consolidated earnings for the preceding five years.) Brennan also did his best to rebuild Sears as a retail store. He reduced employment by 48,000 jobs, simplified logistics, moved into women's apparel, took steps to streamline the buying organization, and piloted new formats such as stand-alone automotive outlets, as well as home-furnishing and home-improvement stores. But it was Brennan's successor, Arthur Martinez, who became famous for revitalizing the retail side of Sears.

Where Brennan fell down—in contrast to Martinez—was in failing to grapple with the Sears culture; that is, Brennan failed to address the deterioration of the company's vital signs. Unlike Martinez, he never quite came to terms with the insight that culture was as strategic as his product and market initiatives were, and that fixing the vital signs would go a long way toward fixing the company.

When Martinez took over in 1992, few employees had any sense of power; most felt nothing but resignation. As one regional manager put it, "It was a company of `salute and obey.' Directives came from above, and we did our best to follow them. There was no maneuvering room to make sensible market decisions. As bad press began in the 1970s, there was widespread depression and an unwillingness to admit at cocktail parties that we worked at Sears. It all seemed so big and complex and out of control. We felt defeated and powerless."

In terms of identity, Sears had drifted a long way from the vibrancy that prevailed from its founding in 1880 through 1956, when General Robert Wood retired as its fourth CEO. For much of that period, the central buying staff and equally strong territory managers kept each other honest through a system of checks and balances. Beginning in the mid-1950s, however, a succession of caretaker CEOs allowed this precise tension between the field and the home office to degenerate into an empty ritual. Territory managers ran their stores like baronies and stonewalled strategic direction from above. This tilt toward regional fragmentation and a more local identity unquestionably contributed to Sears's inability to respond early to the threats posed by

Wal-Mart and Toys "R" Us. "Too small to worry about" or "Not a problem in my region" were the typical reactions.

Brennan tried to correct the excesses of decentralization but pushed the pendulum too far back in the opposite direction. He eliminated the position of territory manager along with most other echelons in the regional hierarchy. Once-powerful store managers were relegated to "keeping the lights on and the doors open," as one store manager put it. "As a result, our knowledge at the fingertips was lost. Executive management ushered in an era of drive-by merchandising. Experts from headquarters would visit a store three times a month and would believe they understood your local market better than you did."

Under enormous pressure to meet their performance targets and threatened by further layoffs, store management teams hunkered down and concentrated on their own turf. As a consequence, the stores became a merchandising hodgepodge, and poor service and frequent out-of-stock conditions alienated customers. Many of Brennan's efforts to achieve sweeping change snagged in the concertina wire of the stores' defensive perimeters. Brennan was trying to build a companywide identity by edict. Predictably, the center did not hold, and the effort failed. In the fallout, identity fragmented more than ever as people everywhere in the company looked out for themselves.

The third of Sears's vital signs to show serious deterioration was its capacity for constructive conflict. The company's initial operating model was built on a vibrant tension between home and regional offices. This struggle between policy from headquarters and inventive execution at the stores was mediated by a succession of four very strong and accessible CEOs whose careers spanned the first 76 years of Sears's history. These men were not threatened by conflict; they encouraged and harnessed it. But by the time Ed Brennan succeeded to the chairmanship, the former mix of initiatives and controls had long since given way to compliance and acquiescence. Pushing back or resisting directives meant "not being a team player."

As for learning, Sears had drifted to the most extreme condition of denial and complacency. Negative reports by business analysts beginning in 1974 were interpreted at Sears as bad journalism and unfair treatment. In 1990, when Sears was accused of widespread dishonesty in its automotive repairs (a sting operation by the State of California Consumer Affairs Department found fraud in 85% of its visits to Sears Auto Centers, and 44 states subsequently filed suit), Brennan's first line of defense was to deny all allegations and to stonewall. An even more troubling example: Sears began including Wal-Mart among its competitor benchmarks only in 1992, by which time Wal-Mart was 60% larger than Sears. Sears's strongly inbred culture was deeply implicated in this capacity for denial. Throughout Brennan's tenure, only one of 100 top executives had a non-Sears career background. "Sears is different" or "We tried that once and it didn't work" were frequent responses to new ideas.

Incorporating Employees

Sears, Shell, and the U.S. Army are currently engaged in efforts to revitalize their organizations. All three are doing their best to transform the way their people experience power, identity, conflict, and learning. All three, in one fashion or another, are using the same three interventions to achieve this improvement in their vital signs.

The first intervention is to incorporate employees into the activity of the organization. This is not the same as communicating or motivating or rolling out plans hatched at the top. It is resocialization. It means engaging employees as meaningful contributors (not just doers) in the principal challenges facing the enterprise. It means seeing employees as volunteers who decide each day whether or not to contribute the extra ounce of discretionary energy that will differentiate the enterprise from its rivals. Although incorporation shares DNA with such familiar ideas as consensus management, employee involvement, and self-managed teams, it is something more. Its distinct properties include the use of concrete, pressing business problems to generate a sense of urgency; the cascading involvement of every employee beginning at the very top of the enterprise and continuing down through the ranks; and the generation of initiatives conceived and staffed by employees across hierarchy and function.

We can see one leader's efforts to reverse drift through incorporation in the turnaround of Shell Malaysia. Its British chairman, Chris Knight, had the benefit of three career rotations in Malaysia prior to his appointment as chairman. When he arrived in 1992, he saw that the organization was in trouble. The company was overstaffed; traditional revenues from oil and gas were in decline; service standards with wholesale customers were in disarray; and the once-dormant government-owned oil company, Petronas, had become an aggressive competitor in the vehicle-fuel market.

Knight wanted to build a much more agile and less costly enterprise, but he had watched several predecessors try and fail to alter Shell

Malaysia's vital signs. Most employees felt that as the largest private oil company in the country, Shell should try not to make waves. This ultraconservative philosophy led employees to avoid any deviation from usual practice and stifled in the cradle any impulse to use their power of initiative. Within a cocoon of comfortable oligopoly, their identity was located in small, defensible silos. Refining quarreled with transport, and everyone fought the crazy ideas that came from marketing and sales, but all these conflicts were distinctly muted. Malaysian employees are from cultures sensitive to saving face and therefore tend to approach impasses by highly circuitous routes. "Smooth and avoid" was the norm. Finally, there was little learning. Knight observed a frustrating lack of concern, even of curiosity, when competitor Caltex gobbled up 10% of domestic market share.

For more than a year, Knight tried to achieve authentic alignment among his eight-person executive team. Somehow, the goal always eluded his grasp. In exasperation, he scheduled an incorporation event in Kuching, Borneo, and asked all 260 of Shell's senior and midlevel managers to attend.

The leader of a middle-management strategic-initiative team kicked off the two-and-a-half-day meeting with a brief presentation of two key proposals aimed at repositioning Shell and regaining competitive advantage. The first proposal envisioned a daring partnership with Shell's biggest competitor, Petronas, in order to engage in joint procurement, thus lowering costs for both companies and putting their competitors at a disadvantage. The second proposal was to streamline and improve Shell's ragged relationships with its 3,000 franchised service stations by creating a single point of contact in a customer service center.

Assembled in small groups, the managers were then asked to identify the soft spots in these strategic proposals. When the entire assembly reconvened, some groups suggested improvements from the floor, but on balance there was general agreement with the proposals. The next step was an organizational audit. Each of several large teams of participants took one facet of the company—strategy, structure, systems—and described how it affected current performance and the impact it might have on the two proposals. When these analyses were shared in plenary session, it was evident to most people that Shell's operating practices would seriously compromise the new initiatives. Over the course of the meeting, many of Knight's management cadre became aware of the emerging competitive pressures affecting the company and were mobilized to take part in developing a response.

Such mobilization is the aim of any well-designed incorporation process.

Just below the surface of this off-site meeting, another development was taking place. As lower-level managers gained firsthand knowledge of business priorities and saw where the chairman wished to take the company, the vast majority of them bought into the plan, which left obstructionist senior managers isolated and exposed. One senior British expatriate, recognizing that his hand had been called, chose the final ten minutes of the meeting to air his differences with the chairman publicly. Knight dismissed him 48 hours later—a firing heard round the world of Shell, where this sort of thing was never done.

But the firing raises an obvious question: How does dismissal for disagreement fit together with the notion of encouraging constructive conflict? Knight's position was that he fired the man not for disagreeing but for never disagreeing in the previous 13 months of high-level discussions or at any time during the meeting except in the concluding minutes. Moreover, most Shell employees—at least those in Malaysia—accepted this explanation. Rather than create a fear of openness, the termination of an executive widely seen as an opponent of change was regarded as a defining moment in the progress of the broader involvement and deeper commitment that is incorporation.

Incorporation doesn't begin and end with one off-site meeting, however uplifting it might be. Knight's next move was to sponsor one-day events called *valentines,* a name and concept that he borrowed from Ford. In these exercises, gatherings of 100 salaried and hourly employees split into smaller groups of peers from each of the major functional units within the downstream organization—refining, logistics, engineering, customer service, accounting, and so forth. At issue was the new concept proposed in the second strategic initiative outlined in Kuching—the customer service center. Knight's goal was, first, to give customers a single point of contact with Shell through a toll-free number and, second, to empower the customer service center to break logjams and satisfy customer needs. The second of these twin objectives was the wolf in sheep's clothing. It is easy enough to recruit an around-the-clock staff of operators to cover a toll-free number. It is quite another matter to shift organizational power so radically that customer-service-center representatives will be able to break deadlocks and redeploy resources. This is the stuff over which organizational blood is spilled—and a challenge that did not play into the historical strengths of Shell's downstream functions.

The valentines exercise is a vehicle for conflict resolution. Each functional team is required to write a succinct description of its grievances with any of the other teams in the room, pinpointing what it does to inhibit productivity and what is likely to get in the way of a successful customer-service center. When each group has received, say, half a dozen of these valentines, its members are given time to sift and discuss them, and then to select two issues they think particularly important to resolve. The group then gets two hours to come up with, first, a detailed plan for corrective action that it can implement within 60 days; second, the name of a member of its own team who will be accountable for delivering the action; and third, the name of a so-called committed partner from the team that sent the valentine who will share responsibility for making the new solution work.

Back in plenary session, each person assigned an action stands and explains the grievance and the proposed solution, and names the team's nominee for committed partner—often the individual seen as most likely to sabotage the proposal and therefore the person most essential to its success. The committed partner then stands, and a fascinating negotiation unfolds. Tension mounts, and the room falls silent. With coaching from the facilitator, the two principals air conflicts and express their deep-seated distrust of each other's motives. A robust solution is the usual result.

Making good use of these and other techniques, Shell Malaysia reversed its ten-year drift. It fostered a new level of individual power, a new sense of identity with the enterprise as a whole, a new kind of open and productive conflict, and a new appetite for learning that persists to this day.

Leading from a Different Place

An organization coming unfrozen under an overload of experimentation and new ideas is a terrifying thing for traditional leaders. Matters seem out of control, which to a degree they are. But as leaders weather this storm, they begin to undergo a shift in mind-set. From thinking, "I've got to stay in control" or "This is too fast," they develop an ability to operate outside their comfort zone and accept ambiguity and adversity as a part of the design. The second of the three interventions—a new approach to leadership—requires them to establish focus and urgency, maintain healthy levels of stress, and not feel compelled to come to the rescue with a lot of answers. They learn to stay the course until guerrilla leaders at lower levels come forward with initiatives that address the company's shortcomings.[1]

Arthur Martinez did precisely all these things at Sears. And from the very beginning, he did one important thing that Brennan had not done: he began telling the truth. For seven successive years, retail executives at Sears had lied to themselves. They set annual goals and came back at year's end below plan. The targets were set lower each time around, but they were never low enough. Market surveys showed Sears perilously close to breaking its last remaining links with its retail customers. It was the Sears credit card, delivering 70% of the profits, that was carrying the retail group. All of this was painful to face. Martinez held up the mirror.

To generate a sense of urgency, Martinez set difficult goals. Within two years, Sears would quadruple its margins to achieve industry parity, reverse its loss of market share, and improve customer satisfaction by 15%. Then came the hard part. Like Sears under Brennan, most organizations are submerged in their numbing but familiar lethargy, their somnambulant operating state. It's like being stirred from your dreams by a strange noise in the night: in the fog of semiconsciousness, one part of you struggles to focus on whether it's an intruder or the cat; but another part resists the possibility of bad news and struggles to go back to sleep. Similarly, people in organizations resist undertakings that would pull them from their familiar world. When a leader raises an issue and generates urgency around it, the guaranteed first line of defense is for the organization to turn back to the leader for an answer. "We need a plan . . . more direction . . . more resources" are the words to this predictable refrain. Many leaders take the bait. Martinez did not. He refused to give his team of top-level managers the answers, and the authenticity of his refusal was powerful. He didn't *have* the answers. No one did. Sears's management had to create the answers on the basis of what Martinez did provide— which was truth, urgency, and enough productive stress to alter thinking and behavior.

Leading from a different place always requires resocialization of the kind Martinez achieved at Sears. Nowhere is the transformational power of resocialization more evident than at three highly unusual U.S. Army training centers—at Fort Irwin, California; Fort Polk, Louisiana; and Hoenfelds, Germany. In fact, the training is sufficiently remarkable to have been studied by the chief education officers at Shell, Sears, Motorola, and GE, and by senior delegations from every country in Western Europe, Russia, and most nations of Asia, Latin America, and the Middle East. Perfected over the past 15 years, the training is widely recognized to have almost single-handedly transformed the army, the largest employer in the United States.

Over a grueling two-week period, an entire organizational unit of 3,000 to 4,000 people goes head-to-head with a competitor of like size in a simulation so realistic that no participant comes away unscathed. The exercise often alters forever the way executives—in this case, army officers—lead. Critical to its impact is a cadre of 600 instructors, one assigned to every person with leadership or supervisory responsibilities. These *observer/controllers,* as they are called, shadow their counterparts through day after 18-hour day of intense activity. They provide personal coaching and facilitate a nonhierarchical team debriefing called an After Action Review (AAR), in which participants struggle to understand what went wrong and how to correct their shortcomings. These AARs are in fact the focal point of an organizational exercise that can range across 650,000 acres (at Fort Irwin in the Mojave Desert) and cost $1 million a day.

For many, the juxtaposition of *U.S. Army* with words like *revitalization, experimentation,* and *nonhierarchical* amounts to a contradiction in terms. But that view is out of date. According to General Gordon R. Sullivan, the army's recently retired chief of staff, "The paradox of war in the Information Age is one of managing massive amounts of information and resisting the temptation to overcontrol it. The competitive advantage is nullified when you try to run decisions up and down the chain of command. All platoons and tank crews have real-time information on what is going on around them, the location of the enemy, and the nature and targeting of the enemy's weapons system. Once the commander's intent is understood, decisions must be devolved to the lowest possible level to allow these frontline soldiers to exploit the opportunities that develop."

A number of factors have contributed to the army's extraordinary, sustained transformation, including higher-quality soldiers, one outcome of a volunteer army. But inside and outside observers agree that the National Training Command (NTC) has been the crucible in which it has all come together. Since the NTC was established, the army's more than half a million men and women in uniform have rotated through its programs several times—most upper-, mid-, and lower-level officers and NCOs, five times. As one officer put it, "The NTC experience leaves no room for debate. Day after day, you are confronted with the hard evidence of discrepancies between intentions and faulty execution, between what you wanted the enemy to do and what he actually did."

Leading from a different place requires great resolve both to stay the course and to resist the temptation to provide the answer. The solutions, and the commitment to deliver on them, must come from the ranks. Leaders must maintain the pressure until followers see that *they* are going to have to make things happen, until guerrilla leaders step forward and begin to engage in leaderlike acts. Not everyone is a guerrilla leader, but sustained stress will eventually produce enough such leaders to begin shifting the tide of vital signs.

Leading from a different place also entails a transformation in the operating state of leaders themselves. They become a microcosm of the shift in vital signs that they want to see in their organizations. From resigning themselves to the limits of their power to make things happen (and to the implausibility of expecting middle managers to help), they move toward the possibility of genuinely distributed intelligence; from taking on an identity as the person in charge, they become clearinghouses for the different ways an enrolled organization handles its responsibilities; from avoiding straight talk, they develop an ability to handle and even encourage constructive conflict; from assuming that they must provide a detailed road map for the journey, they begin to accept learning as a form of inquiry in action. Leaders must place themselves squarely in the zone of discomfort and learn to tolerate ambiguity. We are all much more likely to act our way into a new way of thinking than to think our way into a new way of acting, and that is the essence of leading from a different place.

Instilling Mental Disciplines

We know that when incorporation slackens or vanishes—as it did at Sears for a long time before Martinez or in the army before and during Vietnam—stagnation and entropy are almost invariably the results. We have seen at Sears, Shell, and the U.S. Army that incorporation combined with a different type of leadership was able to reverse an organization's drift and restore its cultural vitality. But if an organization is to change the way its people think and act and interact, and if this resocialization is not to evaporate the moment financial results improve and people start to believe the worst is over, then people must internalize a set of principles or disciplines that shape their reactions and govern their behavior. Disciplines of this kind might also be called enduring social patterns, but they are a good deal more than unconscious habits. Habits are automatic and therefore mindless. Disciplines are mindful. We can see these disciplines at work in the After Action Review, which constitutes the heart of the NTC experience.

Each afternoon, the commander of the brigade undergoing training receives an assignment, such as "penetrate enemy defenses" or "defend your sector against a superior force." Inside crowded command tents, 30 to 40 staff officers and senior fighting-unit commanders study the situation and endeavor to hammer out a winning strategy. Later that afternoon, this strategy begins to filter out to 3,000 soldiers dispersed across many square miles of rugged terrain. Tank crews and platoons are briefed, minefields laid, artillery and helicopters coordinated, reconnaissance initiated. Commencing at midnight, both friendly and enemy probes get under way.

By dawn, the day's battle is in full swing. The "enemy" (the 11th Armored Cavalry Regiment) is permanently stationed at Fort Irwin. It knows the terrain, behaves unpredictably, and almost always devastates the unit in training. And all the action is recorded. Perched on mountaintops, powerful video cameras zoom in on the hot spots. An elaborate laser-based technology precisely tracks when and where each weapon is fired, electronically disabling any fighting unit that is hit. Audiotapes record communication and confusion over the voice network. By 11 A.M., the outcome has been decided, and within 90 minutes, the observer/controllers have pulled each combat team together near terrain that has been pivotal in its piece of the battle.

Let us take a closer look at an AAR in progress.[2] A company team of two platoons with two tanks, four armored personnel carriers, and an HMMV (the modern version of a jeep) have pulled into a tight circle under the shade of a desert outcropping. The crews lean back against tank treads, a flip chart slung over the HMMV antenna. The fighting is in its fifth day. Exhaustion is evident. The observer/controller has created a sand table on the ground, a miniature of the terrain in which this unit was annihilated in the day's battle. He asks a gunnery sergeant to come forward, position the company's armor on the sand table, and explain the unit's mission.

Sergeant: Our overall mission was to destroy the enemy at objective K-2.

Observer/controller: Why was this important? What was your tank's particular role in all this?

Sergeant: I'm not sure.

Observer/controller: Can anyone help?

A trickle of comments gradually builds into a flood of discussion. It begins to appear that only the lieutenant in charge understood the mission. There had been no coordination of individual tanks and vehicles, and none had been given a particular sector in which to concentrate its fire. No one had understood that the unit's main task was to drive the enemy column away from a weak point in the defenses and into a zone where it would be within range of friendly tanks and artillery.

Key lessons for the next day are recorded on the flip chart. The soldiers all come away with a picture of what they were involved in but could not see. Each soldier has contributed to a composite grasp of the engagement, supplemented by video clips and hard data from the observer/controller. Day after day, particular themes are reinforced: all members of the unit must understand the big picture; they all need to *think;* they must always put themselves in the shoes of an uncooperative enemy; they must prepare to the point that surprise will no longer surprise them; they must set aside hierarchy, exercise self-criticism, work as a team.

"The After Action Review has democratized the army," says Brigadier General William S. Wallace, current commander of the NTC. "It has instilled a discipline of relentlessly questioning everything we do. Above all, it has resocialized three generations of officers to move away from a command-and-control style of leadership to one that takes advantage of distributed intelligence. It has taught us never to become too wedded to our script for combat and to remain versatile enough to exploit the broken plays that inevitably develop in the confusion of battle."

The success of the NTC experience and the After Action Review is the result of carefully designed imperatives that can be applied in any organization or corporation. First, take a team of people who must work together across functions and hierarchies and immerse it in a prolonged, intense learning experience. Have the team take on a very tough project or a very tough competitor. Under the right conditions, stress and exhaustion will unfreeze old patterns of behavior and create an opening for new understanding and behavior to take root. Second, in order to eliminate subjectivity and debate, collect hard data on what has transpired. Let the data, not the trainers, point the finger. Third, utilize highly skilled facilitators who have a deep knowledge of what they are observing. Never criticize. Use Socratic questioning to evoke self-discovery. Fourth, do not evaluate performance. The experience is not about success or failure. It is about how much each individual can learn. Make it safe to learn.

There are seven disciplines embedded in the After Action Review, and all seven are as relevant in business as they are in combat.

1. Build an intricate understanding of the business. An organization's members do best when line-of-sight understanding bridges the gap between overall strategy and individual performance. This is harder than it looks. On the one hand, troops need to understand the principal aims of each engagement ("move to establish contact but don't precipitate an all-out fight" or "block the enemy at this line but don't commit to a counterattack") and how it fits into the larger strategic context. On the other hand, soldiers need solid individual skills. Both requirements are essential. The idea is to prevent soldiers from behaving like automatons. They are not there simply to obey orders but to apply their skills and intelligence to a larger goal.

The first requirement—conveying the big picture to the small unit—is easy to overlook in the heat of preparing for battle. In the AAR close-up above, we saw how the lieutenant commanding the armored unit had neglected to communicate the big picture and how his men then failed to achieve a goal of which they were unaware. To carry out the second requirement, developing individual areas of expertise, the army has borrowed a concept from the total quality movement and has distilled all the facets of a military action down to three: the key *tasks* involved, the *conditions* under which each task may need to be performed, and the acceptable *standards* for success. (For example, at a range of 2,000 yards, hit an enemy tank moving at 20 miles per hour over uneven terrain at night with an 80% success rate.)

Sears has shown an exemplary grasp of this discipline. To convey the larger strategic picture to every employee, the company uses learning maps—large murals with elaborate legends on the borders—to communicate essential business conditions to small groups of employees working with a facilitator. One map takes people through the shifts in the competitive environment from 1950 to 1990. Another map, laid out like a game, asks employees to place bets on the sources and uses of funds as they flow from customers' wallets to the bottom line. Sears then asks its employees to use what they've absorbed from the learning maps to come up with a list of three or four highly practical actions that can be taken immediately at the store level to correct deficiencies and improve customer service.

Sears anchors the proficiency side of this discipline with training to improve its interface with customers, then adds performance measures that focus attention on individual and team performance with respect to customer satisfaction. Together, these initiatives enable employees to perform to high standards and to understand how they each contribute to Sears's success.

2. Encourage uncompromising straight talk. The AAR is predicated on a frank exchange among soldiers as they sort through the confusion of battle and figure out where things went wrong. Such an exchange will not occur if people are showing deference to their superiors or holding back for fear of hurting someone's feelings. As we noted earlier, observer/controllers are skilled at using objective data to point the finger—fostering healthy give-and-take and creating a safe environment for candor.

Sears practiced this discipline from the top down (Martinez helped his top-level managers confront the truth about Sears's past performance) and from the bottom up (town hall meetings cultivated a new and much more straightforward style of communication). We also saw Shell Malaysia emphasize this discipline with its valentines exercise.

3. Manage from the future. Hardship for its own sake is clearly not the army's intention, but attaining excellence can be painful. Be All That You Can Be is more than the army's recruiting slogan. It challenges every element of the institution—from the private soldier to the logistics command—to stretch itself. Being all you can be is not a destination to be reached but a mind-set to manage from.

Organizations often "use up" their future, and that is precisely what happened to the U.S. Army after the high-water mark of World War II, to Sears after General Wood's retirement, and to Shell in the 1980s. Once the members of an organization believe they have reached the future, they begin to codify their past successes. Drift and loss of vitality follow "winning formulas" of this kind just as surely as night follows day.

The most essential aspect of managing from the future is to alter the institution's point of view. We all tend to look toward the future as a distant goal. By contrast, this discipline means internalizing some future goal so the institution can plant its feet in that future and manage the present from there. At Shell Malaysia, Knight inherited a company that had used up its future, a company content to keep a low profile as it tried to avoid further market-share losses to Caltex, Mobil, and Petronas. Knight shifted this mind-set entirely, asserting that the future of the industry was regional, not national. He insisted that Shell and Petronas needed to join forces and make Malaysia the dominant low-cost player in Southeast Asia. Once this perspective was accepted as a valid view of the future, a stream of beneficial results flowed from it for both companies.

4. Harness setbacks. NTC participants know from the outset that they are fighting an enemy far tougher than any they are likely to meet in the field. Observer/controllers remind them daily that their maneuvers are not about winning but about learning. Harnessing setbacks is a matter of recontextualizing failure, treating breakdowns as breakthroughs, seeing defeat as opportunity. But this requires considerably more self-discipline than most managers realize. Human beings are hardwired to react adversely to mistakes by blaming themselves (guilt or shame), others (finger-pointing), or bad luck (resignation and fatalism). Day after day, observer/controllers hammer on the benefits of controlled failure until every soldier learns to embrace setbacks as windows to learning.

This discipline has been directly applied at Sears, where Gus Pagonis (one in a long line of increasingly sought-after U.S. Army generals who have landed top corporate posts) heads Sears's far-flung logistics empire. Pagonis has brought the entire AAR process directly to Sears. Daily sessions of 10 to 12 employees representing every level from warehouse to headquarters scrutinize 24-hour updates on late or wrong shipments and chip away at corrective action.

5. Promote inventive accountability. The tasks, conditions, and standards in the first discipline create the benchmarks of acceptable performance, and soldiers are trained to meet or exceed these benchmarks so that their units can count on them in combat. But there is more to it than that. Close battles are won by exploiting the enemy's broken plays. Mastery of a combat assignment requires not just replicable skills but also the capacity to improvise. Observer/controllers single out and reward creative acts of initiative that are built on a solid platform of proficiency.

The new emphasis on "the softer side of Sears" has brought the company into competition with Nordstrom, which, according to Martinez, sets the world standard in striking the proper tension between improvisation and accountability. Nordstrom encourages inventiveness with the motto Respond to Unreasonable Customer Requests (for example, delivering an over-the-phone purchase to a frantic customer at the airport who is about to catch a plane). Salespeople keep scrapbooks of their heroics in providing exceptional service, and these heroics figure into promotions and storewide recognition. On the accountability side, each department tracks the sales per hour of each salesperson and posts the information publicly every two weeks—from the top of the list (worst) to the bottom (best). A sales associate unable to meet a threshold level of sales on a three-month rolling average is dismissed—an infrequent occurrence, since topping the list several times in a row leads most poor performers to move on of their own free will.

6. Understand the quid pro quo. Organizational agility and the disciplines that sustain it make enormous demands on people. Organizations must make sure that their members receive commensurate returns. Once upon a time, corporations were like ocean liners. Anyone fortunate enough to secure a berth cruised right through to disembarkation at retirement. In return for loyalty, sacrifice, and the occasional aggravating boss, employees at Sears, Shell, and the army, among others, enjoyed implicit or explicit job security.

We have now witnessed a decade of continuous job attrition in which companies have downsized, delayered, reengineered, and outsourced. From 1980 to 1996, Sears has laid off more than 100,000 employees. The U.S. Army has reduced its ranks by 300,000 soldiers from a high of 1.2 million during the Gulf War. Worldwide, Shell has cut 150,000 jobs since 1980.

Understanding the quid pro quo is a demanding discipline. A genuinely transformational employment contract has four levels—three more than the reward-and-recognition that was once considered adequate. The second level is employability—the training and skills that enhance people's marketability. Valuable as this element of the contract may be over the long run, it is nevertheless overrated as an incentive. Enhanced employability will inspire no one to offer the kind of deep, creative commitment and enthusiasm that companies struggling for revitalization so badly need. Employee involvement at that level cannot be bought or enticed, and it is not likely to emerge naturally from the individualistic, transactional employment contracts that are typical for many kinds of credentialed experts and specialists.

It takes more than compensation and employability to produce transformational participation. It also takes a sense of meaning in the work strong enough to generate intrinsic satisfaction. And finally, employees must understand where the enterprise is going and have some say in shaping its destiny. Shell, Sears, and the army are all wrestling with these four components of the quid pro quo. In the army, the AAR is the engine of a powerful learning and resocialization experience, driven in part by people's clear perception that defending their country is important work. Senior officers take part in more dramatic changes of perception than their juniors; but even the lowest-ranking soldier has a hand, day after day, in altering the army's culture and, ultimately, its destiny.

7. Create relentless discomfort with the status quo. The After Action Review is based on the notion that individuals can improve—in most cases, improve dramatically—on everything they do. Observer/controllers continually reinforce the notion that AAR disciplines can be applied elsewhere to other activities, and a protocol like the AAR does tend to get under a person's skin. Soldiers carry the ideas back to their home bases. Once internalized, the discipline of relentless discomfort begins to reveal itself in repeated, gnawing questions: How can we do this still better (faster, cheaper)? Is there a radical new approach that we haven't thought of yet? Day in and day out, throughout the army, the AAR format and disciplines are employed to critique performance and to make improvements as soldiers and employees at every level begin to see acceptable performance levels as insufficient for sustained vitality.

Sears and Shell struggle to turn episodic attention to improvement into a vigorous daily discipline. Among their benchmarks is USAA, long a top performer in the insurance industry. USAA has adopted a practice it calls "painting the bridge"—a reference to the fact that the task is never complete. (As soon as painters on the Golden Gate or any other large bridge finish the job, it's time to go back and start over.) In brief, an independent team of 14 organizational experts starts at one end of USAA and works its way to the other, one unit at a time. Its mission is to work with departmental teams and question everything they do. Is the role teams perform necessary? Can it be streamlined or improved? Can the team be merged with another unit? Can it be eliminated? Not surprisingly, people in the company have ambivalent feelings about this once-every-two-year regimen. But it reliably delivers improvements and, equally important, reinforces USAA's unending effort to become a better company.

Researchers at the Harvard Business School recently tracked the impact of change efforts among the *Fortune* 100. Virtually all these companies implemented at least one change program between 1980 and 1995, but only 30% of those initiatives produced an improvement in bottom-line results that exceeded the company's cost of capital, and only 50% led to an improvement in market share price. This discouraging result was not for lack of trying. On average, each of the companies invested $1 billion in change programs over the 15-year period.[3]

Frustration with such results is naturally widespread because the effort and the outcome are so hugely disproportionate. Or to be more precise, the effort of some people in a company is so much greater than the outcome for all. The solution is to focus on the *all*, to shift the attention from incremental change to the tools that can transform the attitudes and behavior of every last employee.

Notes

1. See Ronald A. Heifetz and Donald L. Laurie, "The Work of Leadership," *Harvard Business Review* 75, no. 1 (1997): 124–134.

2. The following description is taken from a video presentation of an After Action Review at Fort Irwin, titled *Mojavia: In Pursuit of Agility* (New York: Marc Gerstein Associates, 1997).

3. Nitin Nohria, "From the M-form to the N-form: Taking Stock of Changes in the Large Industrial Corporation," working paper 96-054, Harvard Business School, Boston, Mass.

2
Breaking the Functional Mind-Set in Process Organizations

Ann Majchrzak and Qianwei Wang

Thousands of businesses have reengineered work in order to focus employees on processes that clearly provide value to customers. They have done away with their functional silos and created new organizational structures—process-complete departments—each able to perform all the cross-functional steps or tasks required to meet customers' needs. Although many of these efforts have paid off in the form of lower costs, shorter cycle times, and greater customer satisfaction, many others have resulted in disappointment: companies have endured the trauma of reengineering only to discover that their performance is no better—and in some cases actually worse—than before.

What caused things to go wrong? There certainly are a variety of possibilities, among them a failure to focus on parts of the business that were significant to customers and a failure to integrate autonomous, functionally focused information systems into a shared, process-focused database and network. But something else that is often overlooked is the tendency of managers and reengineering teams to underestimate the actions required to transform the way employees behave and work with one another. They assume that simply changing their organizational structures from functional units into process-complete departments will cause people to shed their func-

A grant from the National Center for Manufacturing Sciences helped support the research for this article. The authors would like to thank the members of the ACTION project team for their willingness to share their experiences and ideas, and for guiding the research on which the article was based.

tional mind-sets and will forge them instantly into a team intent on achieving common goals.

Over the last three years, we conducted a study of U.S. electronics manufacturers that proved that this assumption is wrong. At each of the companies, which ranged in size from small concerns to such corporate giants as Texas Instruments, Hewlett-Packard, and Unisys, we examined a department whose responsibilities included manufacturing—or, to be more specific, assembling a printed circuit board, inserting the board into an electronic commercial product, or both. Each manufacturing department had been identified by management as the one with the best practices in the company. Each had fewer than 300 workers. We chose these departments because they were sufficiently homogeneous—in terms of their production processes, their national cultural influences, and the market conditions they faced—to permit a comparison of their performances.

Of the 86 departments, 31 could be classified as process complete because they were responsible for most manufacturing steps, support tasks, and interfaces with customers. Those responsibilities included creating the schedule; acquiring the orders and the needed parts and people; training workers; moving parts; setting up, maintaining, and repairing equipment; transforming the parts into a final product; inspecting and reworking the product; delivering the finished product to customers; obtaining feedback from customers and making modifications in the product to meet their needs; and evaluating and improving the process. Reengineering experts such as Michael Hammer and James Champy would call this set of jobs the order-fulfillment process. We classified the remaining 55 departments as functional because they did not have responsibility for most of those activities.

We obtained data on cycle times, conducted detailed work-flow analyses, identified who was responsible for each step in the process, documented the organizational structure, observed how the department coordinated work, and interviewed managers and workers. We interviewed more than 1,500 people. To compare performances, we focused mainly on cycle times, for three reasons. First, cycle times are a major competitive factor in the electronics industry, and many companies in our sample embraced process-centered structures specifically to shorten their cycle times. Second, it was possible to compare cycle times in a uniform fashion. Finally, cycle times included time spent reworking parts and therefore could serve as a process-quality metric, too.[1]

To our surprise, we found that process-complete departments did *not* necessarily have faster cycle times than functional departments. In fact, the only ones that did were those whose managers had taken steps to cultivate a collective sense of responsibility among workers that went beyond merely changing the organization's structure. We found that such collective responsibility could be fostered in a variety of ways: by structuring jobs with overlapping responsibilities, basing rewards on group performance, laying out the work area so that people can see one another's work, and designing procedures so that employees with different jobs are better able to collaborate.

Interestingly, the particular method or number of methods employed did not seem to matter. Process-complete departments that had adopted all four methods did not have significantly faster cycle times than those that had adopted only one or two. What did matter was whether a company had embraced *any* of the methods—whether the company recognized that it needed to do more than merely restructure the organization to foster a collaborative culture.

And it mattered considerably. (See Exhibit 2-1.) Process-complete departments that had acted on the insight had cycle times as much as 7.4 times faster than those that hadn't. Even more startling, the latter departments had much longer cycle times—as much as 3.5 times longer—than the functional departments. The process-complete departments with longer cycle times had one or several of the following critical deficiencies: jobs with narrow responsibilities, employees with many different titles, rewards based solely on individual performance, physical layouts that discouraged people from seeing one another's work, and no explicit procedures for knitting employees together. In other words, those departments maintained functional distinctions and a narrow focus on specific tasks, thereby negating the potential benefits of a process-focused structure.

Changing the Culture

In the course of conducting this study and other research, we have asked many managers who are reengineering their businesses to explain why they are moving toward process-complete departments. They always answer that such a change will reduce the time and effort required to integrate and monitor the work of autonomous units, thereby reducing cycle times and instilling in workers a common understanding of what they have to do to satisfy customers. But when we ask managers to describe the changes that must take place for their

Exhibit 2-1 **How Ways of Promoting Collaboration Improve Cycle Times**

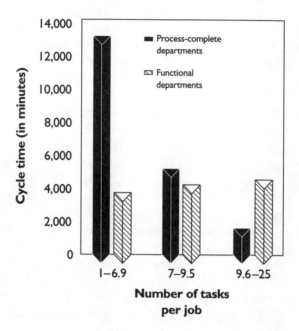

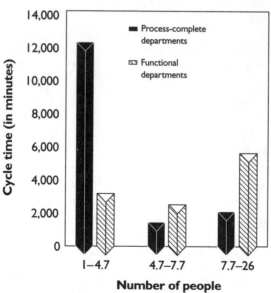

Exhibit 2-1 (continued)

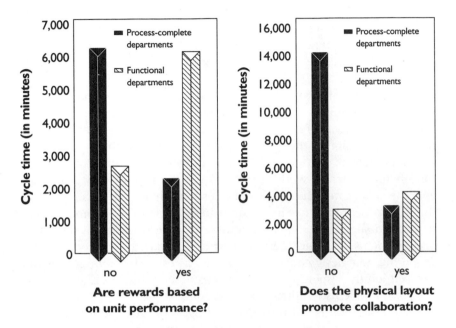

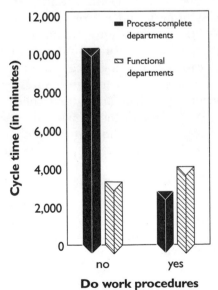

organizations to achieve those objectives, they speak mainly of melding multiple functions into customer-focused teams responsible for an entire process. Most of the managers assume that this structural change will naturally create a common understanding of, and a collective sense of responsibility for, customers' needs. Surprisingly few can define the type of collaboration they want employees to achieve, let alone the means they might employ to encourage such collaboration.

For example, one organization had restructured procurement and manufacturing engineering by melding the two functions into customer-focused teams responsible for the entire process—from the initial price quotation to the customer to the delivery of the product. The individual jobs of the manufacturing engineers and the procurement officers on the teams were broadened but did not overlap. Although every team was now supposed to be responsible for customer satisfaction, the procurement officers continued to spend their time buying parts from suppliers, and the manufacturing engineers continued to occupy themselves with designing and manufacturing products and proposing new designs to customers. As a result, the two groups did not feel jointly responsible for total customer satisfaction and retention, and problems fell through the cracks.

Such a situation is not unusual. Managers often underestimate the difficulty of breaking the functional mind-set. During the re-engineering process, they spend enormous amounts of money defining which tasks the process-centered units should perform and which people should be assigned to those units, but they give relatively little thought to restructuring incentive systems, reconfiguring the work space, or designing jobs and procedures within the process-based units to encourage collaboration and collective responsibility. They also give little thought to their own jobs. Many managers do away with functions but fail to change their own positions. They continue to act like functional chiefs even though the functions no longer formally exist.

Such managers overlook the importance of changing their organization's culture. They fail to see that collective responsibility is an attitude, a value, a concern. It means taking an interest in one's colleagues and in improving the outcome of mutual (as opposed to individual) efforts. People who feel collectively responsible are willing to work especially hard to avoid letting the team down. They will take the initiative in offering a colleague a helping hand with a work problem even though doing so might make it more difficult for them to meet their own deadlines. Changing the organizational structure alone will not instill such values or behavior.

Our research indicates that if companies are not ready to take the steps required to change their culture, they may be better off leaving their functional departments intact. After all, coordination among functions can be greatly improved without reorganizing around complete processes.

The high-performing functional departments we studied showed, for example, that members of a function can be encouraged to help outsiders if they are given cross-functional responsibilities. Information networks can be installed to distribute information more widely, more quickly, and in a more useful form. The links among functions can be strengthened by having fewer sign-offs for unusual requests, by introducing specific and clearly stated outcome-based performance criteria, and by inviting individuals from other functions to frequent milestone-review meetings.

Reengineering experts suggest that such changes will not go far enough to make employees feel collectively responsible for producing the outcomes required to satisfy customers. Our research, however, indicates that companies may reap greater benefits by strengthening the ties among their functions than by creating process-complete departments that lack a collaborative culture.

Cultivating Collective Responsibility

In our study, we focused on the impact of the four critical means of building a collaborative culture. Of the 31 process-complete departments, none had adopted all four methods. The best performers had employed an average of 3, while the worst had employed an average of 2.7—a difference that is not statistically significant. Let's examine each method in more detail.

MAKE RESPONSIBILITIES OVERLAP

In our sample, process-complete departments made responsibilities overlap by designing jobs with a relatively broad range of duties, by having a relatively small number of job titles, or both. The cycle times of the 20 departments with broadened jobs (jobs with responsibility for about 10 to 25 different activities in the process) were, on average,

7.4 times faster than the cycle times of departments that did not have broad jobs (jobs with responsibility for fewer than 7 activities). Similarly, the cycle times of the 10 departments with few job titles (departments in which about eight or more people had the same title) were, on average, 5.8 times faster than the cycle times of departments with many titles (those in which fewer than five people had the same title).[2]

One department in our sample that had made responsibilities overlap by designing broad jobs and using few titles was a 61-person unit that assembled printed circuit boards. The department, part of a 1,600-person facility owned by one of North America's largest computer-hardware manufacturers, was responsible for all the steps involved in fulfilling customers' orders. Whereas many similarly sized departments in our sample had as many as 13 titles, this department had only 4: operators, process operators/inspectors (higher-skilled operators), maintenance technicians (for complex repairs), and quality-control people (for suggesting improvements to the process). The 29 operators and 25 operators/inspectors performed most of the department's tasks, and the two technicians and four quality-control people served as expert consultants. All 60 employees reported to a single supervisor.

The department also tried to break down the boundaries between positions by assigning people to multiple teams, by rotating assignments within teams weekly, and by holding unitwide meetings twice a month to discuss improvements to the process. As a result, every employee could perform most of the department's functions.

Designing jobs so that employees can at least partially perform most of the functions assigned to a department helps create a shared sense of responsibility because people understand one another's work and thus share a common language and similar constraints and objectives. More important, if a process-complete department does not make responsibilities overlap, it will end up with a set of specialized jobs by default and may inadvertently re-create the same coordination problems and high overhead that bedevil organizations with functional departments.

BASE REWARDS ON UNIT PERFORMANCE

Rewards may take the form of bonuses, raises, or nonfinancial recognition. In our sample, 12 of the process-complete departments rewarded their members for meeting or exceeding unitwide targets or standards. The cycle times of the 12 departments were, on average, 2.7 times faster than those of the departments that based rewards on individual performance alone.

Rewarding unit performance is important because it prevents employees from placing their individual or functional needs above customers' needs. For example, if employees are rewarded for reducing processing times at their individual workstations, they probably will not feel compelled to examine ways of reducing cycle times at the places between or outside their workstations (such as in inventory control, purchasing, or order preparation). In contrast, employees rewarded for achieving high levels of customer satisfaction or reductions in the department's total cycle time are more likely to be motivated to solve what they traditionally would consider other people's problems.

One high-performing department with unit-based rewards chose to tie a percentage of the monthly bonuses for all employees directly to customer satisfaction. It tied another percentage to the plant's performance, using such measures as revenue and profit. It based the remainder on group and individual performance in meeting product-quality standards. This complex reward system was possible because the department had accurate measures and tightly monitored processes. For example, quality levels for critical process equipment were monitored and reported automatically in real time. Management set upper and lower limits, which operators used to track their own performance; they could obtain information on daily, weekly, and monthly trends within seconds. Alarms sounded when the equipment began to go out of control. As a result, employees became aware of problems immediately and were motivated to work together to solve them.

CHANGE THE PHYSICAL LAYOUT

The layout of a work site can either inhibit or promote collective responsibility. In our study, process-complete departments with layouts that permitted people to see others' work had cycle times 4.4 times faster than those with layouts that didn't.

Layouts can encourage people to share information about one another's work and try out new ideas openly. One such layout organizes processing equipment in a circle or U-shaped cell with workers performing their tasks inside the cell. This kind of layout, used at several of the sites we studied, allows workers to share tasks easily, to observe when others are in trouble, and to offer assistance without letting their own performance deteriorate.

Another type of collaborative layout we observed was a special area for continuous improvement. A place for the work group to sit and discuss problems, such an area contains all the data relevant to the manufacturing floor (either in computers or on wall charts), as well as the tools for documenting, analyzing, designing, and building prototypes. This type of area makes it easier for people to analyze problems together, build prototypes, and discuss their individual and group-inspired ideas.

In contrast, certain layouts can prevent people from spontaneously sharing information, seeing how others do their work, and noticing opportunities for assisting others. Machine tools installed back-to-back with control panels facing outward are an example of this kind of layout: the operator of one machine tool cannot see the work of the operator of the other. Another example is a traditional long assembly line in which the assembler at the beginning of the line is unable to see what an assembler is doing farther down the line. When people cannot see others at work, misperceptions arise both about the nature of their jobs and about the pace, pressures, and commitment of those employees. The "I work harder than you do" mentality can easily develop.

REDESIGN WORK PROCEDURES

We asked employees to tell us to what extent their departments' formal and informal work procedures encouraged them to do the following three things: share ideas for improvement with people in other disciplines, involve everyone who would be affected by a decision in making that decision, and help others do their work even if it caused their own productivity to suffer. In 24 of the process-complete departments, employees reported that those three ways of relating to one another were integral to their work. By *integral*, they meant that such behavior was encouraged by management, was systematically monitored, and occurred frequently. The cycle times of the 24 departments were, on average, 3.3 times faster than those of the other 7 in our sample.

For example, in one 57-person department that assembled computers (part of a 2,700-person company), there were no teams or broad jobs. Although it was a supervisor-directed unit, not a self-managed one, and had narrowly defined jobs, workers reported that management strongly encouraged them to collaborate with coworkers and with support staff.

One way management encouraged collaboration in this department was by providing all workers with a computer terminal that connected them to an E-mail network and an electronic problem-reporting-and-tracking system. Managers actively used the E-mail network to keep workers informed of customer, cost, and market data. They also encouraged workers to use the reporting and tracking system to log problems and to comment on those that others encountered. The problems and comments were routed to the people assigned to provide the solutions. Because the problems, the responses, and the speed of the responses were tracked and measured, the engineers and other support people whose job it was to solve the problems were motivated to heed the workers.

The department's managers guaranteed that support staff would arrive on the scene within three to five minutes of receiving word of a line stoppage. (Workers knew whom to notify, and the department's E-mail and pager systems ensured that the messages got through. In addition, managers tracked response times.) This approach made the workers feel confident that the role of support staff really was to support them—to help them solve problems quickly.

Finally, the managers made themselves available for informal discussions in the cafeteria with anyone who wished to join them. Workers reported that they could discuss problems freely at these sessions. All in all, the message came through clearly that management considered collaboration extremely important.

Customizing the Design

There is no single cookie-cutter design for achieving a collective sense of responsibility—that is, no one approach is appropriate for all process-complete departments, even within the same organization. Neither does it seem to matter how many different methods are employed. What counts is how well any one method is implemented. The implication: When redesigning their organizations, managers should not be overly influenced by what other units in their companies or other "best practice" departments are doing. Instead, they should ask their own employees what they would need in order to work well together. In addition, managers should consider the constraints and possibilities provided by technology, the work process, the existing organizational culture, and the organization's strategic mission.

For example, changes in the physical layout are likely to facilitate a collective sense of responsibility only when face-to-face interaction is essential—such as when workers in different disciplines with different professional languages must examine a prototype together or listen to the odd noises emanating from a machine tool to reach a common understanding of a problem and come up with the best solution. In an organization where workers already share a common professional language and are not tied to their desks, changes in the physical layout may not be sufficiently compelling to create a collective sense of responsibility. Instead, such workers may benefit from team-based rewards or overlapping responsibilities.

Our study suggests that the success of business-process reengineering depends on how well managers create a collective sense of responsibility. Restructuring by process can lead to faster cycle times, greater customer satisfaction, and lower costs, but only if the organization has a collaborative culture. Combining the boxes on the organization chart alone will not create such a culture.

Notes

1. The cycle time of each department was the total throughput time for the three products that accounted for the highest percentage of the department's output during the most recent six-month period. Total throughput time was the time from order to delivery and included times for operation, setup, queuing, transportation between work sites, inspection, testing, and rework.

2. For each of the four methods of cultivating a collaborative culture, we determined through statistical analysis that it was highly likely (at a 95% level of confidence) that the particular method we were studying—and not one of the other three—was responsible for the difference in the cycle times of the departments that had employed that method and the departments that hadn't. This means that 95% of the time, departments that employ the particular method will have faster cycle times than departments that don't.

3
Fix the Process, Not the Problem

Harold Sirkin and George Stalk Jr.

In 1983, the CEO of a paper company faced a difficult decision. His board of directors had just met to consider alternatives to filing Chapter 11 for a subsidiary, a paper mill acquired two years earlier that was losing more than $1 million a month. The acquisition had been made to grow the company, but it now confronted management with the prospect of a major write-down. The price of the company's shares had already fallen 40%.

One year later, the mill was just about breaking even. Today it is very profitable. Earnings per share for the entire company tripled from 1983 to 1989, adjusted for stock splits, while price per share rose almost tenfold. Many of the mill managers can look forward to a comfortable retirement based on the value of their stake in the transformed company.

What happened? The short answer is that everyone at the paper mill became a problem solver. Together, managers and mill workers learned to take the initiative not just for identifying problems but also for developing better processes for fixing problems and improving products. Their approach did not depend on key senior executives taking charge and telling people what to do. Instead, the entire organization learned how to learn. The key to their success: a multi-year learning process in which employees developed four progressively more sophisticated problem-solving loops: fix-as-fail, prevention, finding root causes, and anticipation. (Exhibit 3-1 illustrates these four loops.)

Exhibit 3-1   How the Mill Solved Its Problems

The mill worked through the four loops, progressing from problem solving on a fix-as-fail basis to anticipating problems before they arose.

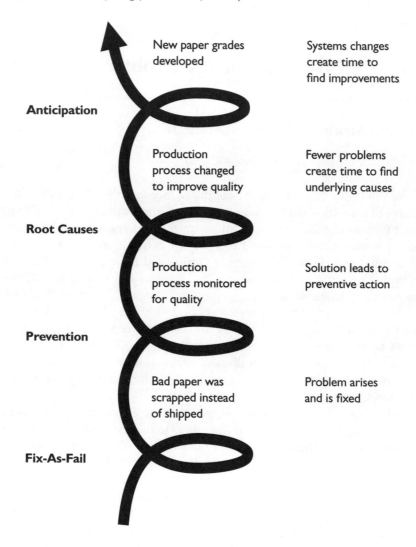

Anticipation

New paper grades
developed

Systems changes
create time to
find improvements

Production
process changed
to improve quality

Fewer problems
create time to find
underlying causes

Root Causes

Production
process monitored
for quality

Solution leads to
preventive action

Prevention

Bad paper was
scrapped instead
of shipped

Problem arises
and is fixed

Fix-As-Fail

Setting the Stage

For the company's CEO and his senior managers, starting the learning process was neither easy nor obvious. It was simply the only alternative that could give the mill a chance.

In the two months following the board meeting, the management team made several hard but necessary decisions. It shut down a small, inefficient, costly pulp mill and three paper-making machines. It laid off roughly 25% of the work force, delivering a serious blow to the small town in which the mill was the largest employer. It fired the mill's general manager. But these actions, management knew, could only slow the mill's losses. At best, it would buy one year's breathing time to turn the operation around. Success would depend on shifting the mix of products sold by the mill. And at first that seemed an insuperable problem.

Of the 13 product lines the mill produced, only 4 were profitable or had the potential to become profitable because of the mill's special manufacturing expertise and equipment. The rest of its products made little or no money and were nothing more than filler to keep the machinery operating. Shutting down three machines had eliminated some of these undesirable products, but those machines had accounted for only 20% of the mill's production capacity. That left significant volume with limited profitability, but it could not be eliminated immediately if the mill was to sustain even a scaled-back overhead level.

Clearly, the mill had to expand its volume in the four attractive product lines fast. Cutting prices to attract business was out because it would destroy any potential for profitability. That left improving quality and service—areas in which the mill's reputation was conspicuously poor. (The mill had always had problems with quality and meeting delivery dates. Adding to the difficulty was the fact that the mill had sustained a long, nasty strike that had ended only a few months earlier. During the strike, the CEO discovered on his way home one night that his brake lines had been slashed. Management's relations with the employees were adversarial at best.)

Management's first approach to the mill's problems was top-down. The senior managers met, analyzed the problems—as seen through their own eyes—and decided on ten key actions the mill would have to take to survive. Many of these actions required large amounts of capital and additional people, however—resources the company for the most part could not afford and that would not be available from the parent in the quantities needed. Moreover, the plans focused on solving specific problems, often in a slow and very costly way: for example, rebuilding two of the mill's paper-making machines to correct paper-thickness inconsistencies across the width and length of a sheet. The rebuilding would take two years and cost over $23 million; whether it would actually solve the problem was not clear.

The moment of truth came when the CEO's controller took the plans key managers had submitted and laid out the overall timetable for implementing them. The result startled the management team. Reaching break-even would take at least five years. With losses mounting daily, that was time the company did not have. Management had to find a way to improve results more quickly. After further discussion, the executives identified four approaches: add resources; fix fewer but higher leverage problems; fix problems faster; and learn from each experience to make subsequent efforts more effective. But the only way to make enough resources available was to enlist the entire organization's help to improve the mill's quality and service levels.

The idea of turning to your people and asking them to solve business problems sounds less bold and risky now than it did in 1983. But even so, knowing something has worked for others and moving onto unfamiliar ground yourself can be very different things. In this case, the CEO and the mill's new general manager began by taking their description of the mill's problems to lower and middle management. They discussed the mill's difficulties frankly and outlined what the product focus would have to be if the mill were to survive.

Making the stakes clear, the top managers pledged their commitment to the mill and made it tangible in important ways. They promised that the parent company would make capital investments when needed, despite the possibility of failure—a critical point, since the mill had not seen capital in many years. They promised to be available whenever called and passed out their home telephone numbers. They established a bonus plan for all the employees—from the mill manager to the janitors—that was pegged to improvements in individual product-line margins or volume but contingent on the mill's overall profitability. (For bonus purposes, the mill's financial performance would be assessed after six months and at six-month intervals thereafter.)

On the other hand, the downside was just as clear. Employees who weren't committed to saving the mill were invited to leave. (None did.) And the CEO left no question that the mill would be shut down if this effort did not succeed. Then, knowing that most of the employees trusted lower level management, he asked those managers to get the message to everyone at the mill and to solicit their help.

At the same time, in an effort to narrow the field of problems needing attention, the CEO implemented a new organization structure designed to make it easier for everyone to focus on problems that mattered to customers, instead of on individual functional goals. He created five product teams, one for each of the four attractive lines and one to manage the remaining products during the transition period. These teams were composed of seven middle managers, one from each of the key functional areas, and were headed up by the product-line salespeople (to reinforce focusing on customers). These managers were charged with enlisting the help of all the employees in their areas and urged to give everyone a chance to contribute.

To keep the teams from making the same mistake management had almost made—focusing on the immediately obvious problems and trying to solve them all at once—and to find further opportunities to narrow the list to problems with the greatest leverage, the CEO suggested that each product team take the next few weeks to talk with key customers to learn their needs and develop plans for responding. Beyond this, he let the team managers set their own agendas. He simply reminded them from time to time that they always had direct access to him and the general manager. And he reiterated his promise that resources would be found. To signal his commitment, he put the corporate jet at their disposal and used commercial flights for his own visits to other operations.

Learning to Learn

In the weeks that followed, each team expanded from its seven-manager core to draw in line operators, clerks, and other employees whose work related to its product line. To give the teams time to meet, the CEO created time—by authorizing everyone to ignore the crisis and stop fighting fires. Predictably, the first month was a disaster, with problems piling up and seemingly nothing to show in return. But before long, management's faith in the learning process began to pay off.

To illustrate what this process entailed, we will concentrate on the activities of one team, the food-service product team. For the turnaround to succeed, its products had to become the mill's largest line, doubling the existing volume. At the start, this looked like an impossible goal. Food-service product lines got more customer complaints than any other product, and they had gradually been losing market share.

Within ten days of its formation, the team had met with its three largest customers, all of whom rearranged their calendars to accommodate the team's schedule because they so badly wanted a reliable source of paper. These customers told the team in detail about the consequences of the mill's poor service and quality problems. Late deliveries could shut down their plants, so they compensated by holding large amounts of inventory and purchasing paper from other suppliers. Quality problems, such as holes in the paper, ruined their own end products, so they incurred additional costs inspecting incoming paper and also bought from the mill's competitors. These discussions highlighted how shipping poor paper cost the mill business. The team returned to the plant determined to solve these and other quality problems.

Team members had now seen and heard their customers' needs firsthand. They had talked with equipment operators, salespeople, and receiving employees as well as with the buyers. And they learned things they never had before—for example, the effect on a customer's operation of the mill's paper-winding procedures. Wound one way, the paper moved smoothly through the customer's equipment. Wound the other, nothing worked right. It was as easy for the mill operators to wind the paper one way as the other. But before, no one had ever known it made a difference.

Back at the mill, team members talked with everyone in their individual areas and reported what they had learned in the customers' plants. More importantly, they enlisted everyone's help in resolving the problems and brought along people from all levels, including machine operators and shipping clerks, on subsequent customer visits.

Loop One: Fix-As-Fail

Operators at the mill knew all about the line's quality problems. But poor quality paper had always been shipped to make tonnage goals set by the CEO and agreed to by the mill manager. The team decided on its own to do its best to stop shipping defective rolls, whatever the cost of rejecting paper. A team member checked every roll and, if there were problems, set it aside. To show customers that quality mattered, the team also asked the mill's general manager to be the final inspector and sign every roll. At first, half the rolls were rejected and later salvaged by removing the defective portions. This salvage process was costly and time consuming, but customers were not sent low-quality rolls. The team had developed its first important problem-solving loop.

Put simply, fix-as-fail means that when something goes wrong, the product or service is fixed before it is sent to the customer. It is the most basic kind of problem-solving loop, one that every company engages in to some degree or it could not remain in business. But many organizations get stuck in a fix-as-fail problem-solving mode, guaranteeing static performance and limited gains in productivity. The frequent need for last-minute fixes, the unpredictability with which problems crop up, the recurrence of the same old problems—all lead to stress, extra hours, and finger-pointing throughout the organization. Production processes come to seem uncontrollable. Operations often fall further and further behind with no apparent hope of catching up, since problems seem to accumulate faster than they can be solved. Improvement looks—and is—impossible because an ever-growing number of resources must be thrown into dealing with continual crises.

Loop Two: Prevention

To avoid or escape a fix-as-fail cycle, an organization must be able to engage in a second kind of problem-solving loop: developing processes to keep problems from occurring. For food-service product team members, this loop began when they looked at the buildup of scrap from rejected rolls and realized they had to find a way to stop solving quality problems through inspection. Realizing that they had to walk before they could run, they agreed as a first step to assign an inspector to watch as each roll was produced. When a defect appeared, the inspector would tell the machine operator, who could adjust the equipment immediately and prevent further problems. Adding the extra person was expensive, but productivity (as measured by good output per person) improved measurably. Scrap rates dropped dramatically, the quality of the product remained high, and the reject rate fell by some 75%.

As this example indicates, prevention does not depend on tracing problems to their root causes but on developing learning loops to feed information rapidly from the point where problems can be discovered to the people who can keep them from recurring. At one level, therefore, second-order learning is simply a matter of resource allocation. Investing one person in increasing the effectiveness of this problem-solving loop, as the paper company did, can free up 10 or 15 downstream people, who had been correcting problems on a fix-as-fail basis, and give them the time—and motivation—to embark on the third stage of learning, finding root causes.

At another level, however, second-order learning is also an organizational issue. Unless they are tackled head-on, old habits can enter in to keep people from moving beyond fix-as-fail problem solving. The corporate culture may block change. Employees may not have the tools to find and institute an effective problem-prevention process. Everyone may have accepted problems as a normal and inevitable part of doing business—especially if they are routinely rewarded for solving rather than forestalling them.

Loop Three: Find the Root Cause

Six months out, the team had the production process under control, and customers were beginning to notice a marked difference in quality. One of the mill's best customers called and said it would increase its orders if the quality level held. The team was pleased but not satisfied. Assigning someone to watch every roll was inefficient, and scrap rates remained much higher than desired. It was time to look for root causes, a process in which operators, not managers, would take the lead because they understood better than anyone how the machines worked.

Holes in the paper continued to be one of the team's biggest problems. By experimenting with the many variables that control paper quality, the operators and team members learned that they could produce paper with fewer holes if they changed the wire mesh in the paper-forming machine more frequently. They tested their finding, confirming that more frequent changes produced higher quality paper. Then they asked the mill manager if they could integrate this new procedure into the process permanently. He granted permission on the spot.

The operators also found that they could raise quality and lower the total cost per ton of good paper by using pulp furnish that was slightly more expensive. (Furnish is the mix of pulps that constitutes the raw material for a paper-making machine.) The team made this change too, without asking for approval from the mill manager until it could demonstrate the positive effect. Scrap rates fell further, and quality steadily improved. Before long, the team was able to do away with the in-process inspector because the machines were producing quality paper almost all of the time. The root causes of the quality problem had been found and eliminated.

By the end of the year, satisfied customers were giving the mill increasing shares of their business, the volume of the top four products had doubled, and profit margins had improved. The change in morale was equally dramatic. People knew they were winning the fight to save the mill. Friction between management and labor all but disappeared. Everyone knew more about the mill's operation and customers' needs. Customers who had previously been discouraged from visiting the mill were invited to tour the cleaner facility. The organization now felt strong enough to move from defense to offense.

Loop Four: Anticipation

One of the keys to the food-service product team's success was its new understanding of its customers' needs and how their businesses worked. Such understanding would have been unimaginable while the mill's people were spending most of their time fixing problems. Perhaps the most dramatic example of this understanding came when a machine operator's suggestion led to the discovery of an unsuspected competitive advantage.

As part of the team's effort to learn about one customer's business, the operator had gone to one of its plants and spent a long time watching the machines and talking with their line operators. He returned to the mill convinced that the customer could run slightly thinner paper just as efficiently as the paper it was then using, and he proposed that the mill offer it as an alternative. The team liked the idea, but the mill manager was not convinced, since paper is sold by the ton and thinner paper weighs less. Rather than reject the idea outright, however, the manager and the team reviewed the proposal with other teams, key functional managers, and key customers.

The breakthrough came when the mill manager realized that their key competitor did not have machines that could produce lower basis-weight paper. If the mill reduced its paper's weight, it could provide a low-cost alternative that competitors could not match. The mill could therefore raise its price per ton and make more money, while the customer's cost would go down since it would need less paper (by weight) to make its product. Everyone was ahead except the competitor.

After this, operators were invited to work with the team to develop new grades of paper. With experience, the team found new combinations of furnish and additives that let them make lower cost varieties that they had not been able to manufacture before. The operators were also able to alert the team to potential manufacturing problems before the new papers were put into production.

The food-service product team's volume did not just double, it quadrupled, while the number of employees stayed the same. The mill went from being the fifth of five suppliers to being the industry's number-one supplier for its products in two-and-one-half years. By 1986, the mill had to expand the capacity of its machines to meet demand. The organization had moved from being a mill that faced shutdown into the lead mill of the group.

Despite their success, mill employees are healthily dissatisfied. They want to know more about their company, their customers, their suppliers, and their competitors. Team members and operators have purchased samples of competitors' products to study and analyze. They have also asked for, and are receiving, training in management techniques as well as in new skills. Formally, the organization chart looks the same. But informally the organization has been revamped. Operators move from one machine to another as necessary or where there is a problem. People participate and make suggestions without worrying about layoffs. Bonuses (averaging 10% to 12% of compensation) have allayed workers' fears that management might get more than its fair share.

Patience Makes Progress

One mark of a world-class organization is that its managers seem to have easy jobs. Operations flow smoothly, and people put more time and energy into making improvements than reacting to problems. Such an organization will typically spend 80% of its time on root-cause and anticipatory problem-solving loops. In contrast, a lesser performer is likely to spend 90% of its effort in the fix-as-fail loop.

Executives from lesser performing companies often return from visits to superior operations charged up to achieve similar results. In their enthusiasm, however, many overlook the fact that the effectiveness they admire comes from steady progress through increasingly sophisticated problem-solving loops. And that progress, as we have seen through the paper mill's experience, takes time. Although the mill began to see the effects of its learning in three to six months (a typical time frame, in our experience, for the first signs of progress to become apparent), it took two years to reach the fourth loop. Depending on circumstances, a company may need as many as five years to work through the entire cycle.

Given this, it is easy to understand why many managers itch to short-circuit the process and jump to root-cause problem solving at once. But most companies that take this approach achieve unsatisfactory results, both because the organization does not truly understand its problems or the processes needed to resolve them and because it lacks the necessary resources. Instead of better performance, the net effect is overworked employees who neither solve problems well nor do a good job of maintaining the day-to-day business.

A better, more systematic approach to organizational problem solving should begin with a few simple questions:

- What are the critical problem-solving loops in our company? For a manufacturer, for example, these might include engineering change notices and warranty-claim resolution, while a service company might focus on satisfying nonroutine requests and its response to customer complaints.
- How well does our operation work from the customer's perspective? Do we respond to problems quickly and well or are we slow and unreliable?
- Do we learn from problems or are we continually fixing the same problems over and over again?
- Where do we spend most of our effort: on identifying and responding to specific problems or on resolving underlying causes and finding new ways to improve?

Progressing through this four-loop cycle is both a natural and an unnatural experience. Moving from fix-as-fail to prevention demands a great deal of effort, but there is little subtlety about what needs to be done. The problems that need attention are clearly identifiable. The demanding task is getting people to organize around them, if only because something else will always seem more important to one or more of the critical players. By the time the organization is ready to move from root cause to anticipation, however, this balance typically shifts. By then, problem-solving processes are familiar, so everyone is likely to be much more at ease. But the problem-solving loops that will yield meaningful improvements to the business (as the operator's suggestion did at the paper mill) are much more subtle and often depend on finding creative ways to expose employees at all levels to the right people in customers' organizations.

As an organization establishes more sophisticated problem-solving loops and begins to learn, its fundamental culture changes. But unless management supports this change by rewarding new performance metrics as well as those it has traditionally used, no one is likely to stay the course. At the paper mill, for example, the CEO took a number of unusual steps to let people know it was safe to expand beyond the old ways of working. He rewarded early change makers by recognizing their accomplishments publicly. He promoted people who were trying hard to manage the right processes and to make the right decisions, even if their efforts were not entirely successful. Perhaps most dramatic, though, was the way he handled the mill's first six-month bonus review. By the numbers, the mill just missed making its profit hurdle. Performance had pulled up a lot, but not quite enough to meet the plan. Nevertheless, the CEO decided (and the board agreed) to pay maximum bonuses anyway to support and reinforce what was happening. They knew that customers' perceptions change slowly and blamed the shortfall on history, not on the efforts under way.

In the pressure to get things done, many managers fear being patient. They focus on short-term fixes to existing problems rather than on instituting processes to solve and eventually prevent problems and to identify unsuspected opportunities. But as in the fable of the tortoise and the hare, the companies that seem to move most slowly and laboriously at the start often lead their industries by the end of the day.

4
Good Communication That Blocks Learning

Chris Argyris

Twenty-first-century corporations will find it hard to survive, let alone flourish, unless they get better work from their employees. This does not necessarily mean harder work or more work. What it does necessarily mean is employees who've learned to take active responsibility for their own behavior, develop and share first-rate information about their jobs, and make good use of genuine empowerment to shape lasting solutions to fundamental problems.

This is not news. Most executives understand that tougher competition will require more effective learning, broader empowerment, and greater commitment from everyone in the company. Moreover, they understand that the key to better performance is better communication. For 20 years or more, business leaders have used a score of communication tools—focus groups, organizational surveys, management-by-walking-around, and others—to convey and to gather the information needed to bring about change.

What *is* news is that these familiar techniques, used correctly, will actually inhibit the learning and communication that twenty-first-century corporations will require not just of managers but of every employee. For years, I have watched corporate leaders talking to subordinates at every level in order to find out what actually goes on in their companies and then help it go on more effectively. What I have observed is that the methods these executives use to tackle relatively simple problems actually prevent them from getting the kind of deep information, insightful behavior, and productive change they need to cope with the much more complex problem of organizational renewal.

Years ago, when corporations still wanted employees who did only what they were told, employee surveys and walk-around management were appropriate and effective tools. They can still produce useful information about routine issues like cafeteria service and parking privileges, and they can still generate valuable quantitative data in support of programs like total quality management. What they do *not* do is get people to reflect on their work and behavior. They do not encourage individual accountability. And they do not surface the kinds of deep and potentially threatening or embarrassing information that can motivate learning and produce real change.

Let me give an example of what I mean. Not long ago, I worked with a company conducting a TQM initiative. TQM has been highly successful at cutting unnecessary costs, so successful that many companies have raised it to the status of a management philosophy. In this particular case, a TQM consultant worked with top management to carry out a variety of surveys and group meetings to help 40 supervisors identify nine areas in which they could tighten procedures and reduce costs. The resulting initiative met its goals one month early and saved more money than management had anticipated. The CEO was so elated that he treated the entire team to a champagne dinner to celebrate what was clearly a victory for everyone involved.

I had regular conversations with the supervisors throughout the implementation, and I was struck by two often-repeated comments. First, the supervisors told me several times how easy it had been to identify the nine target areas since they knew in advance where the worst inefficiencies might be found. Second, they complained again and again that fixing the nine areas was long overdue, that it was high time management took action. As one supervisor put it, "Thank God for TQM!"

I asked several supervisors how long they had known about the nine problem areas, and their responses ranged from three to five years. I then asked them why, if they'd known about the problems, they'd never taken action themselves. "Why `Thank God for TQM'?" I said. "Why not `Thank God for the supervisors'?"

None of the supervisors hesitated to answer these questions. They cited the blindness and timidity of management. They blamed interdepartmental competitiveness verging on warfare. They said the culture of the company made it unacceptable to get others into trouble for the sake of correcting problems. In every explanation, the responsibility for fixing the nine problem areas belonged to someone else. The supervisors were loyal, honest managers. The blame lay elsewhere.

What was really going on in this company? To begin with, we can identify two different problems. Cost reduction is one. The other is a group of employees who stand passively by and watch inefficiencies develop and persevere. TQM produces the simple learning necessary to effect a solution to the first problem. But TQM will not prevent a recurrence of the second problem or cause the supervisors to wonder why they never acted. To understand why this is so, we need to know more about how learning takes place and about at least two mechanisms that keep it from taking place at all.

As I have emphasized in my previous articles on learning in the workplace, learning occurs in two forms: single-loop and double-loop. Single-loop learning asks a one-dimensional question to elicit a one-dimensional answer. My favorite example is a thermostat, which measures ambient temperature against a standard setting and turns the heat source on or off accordingly. The whole transaction is binary.

Double-loop learning takes an additional step or, more often than not, several additional steps. It turns the question back on the questioner. It asks what the media call follow-ups. In the case of the thermostat, for instance, double-loop learning would wonder whether the current setting was actually the most effective temperature at which to keep the room and, if so, whether the present heat source was the most effective means of achieving it. A double-loop process might also ask why the current setting was chosen in the first place. In other words, double-loop learning asks questions not only about objective facts but also about the reasons and motives behind those facts.

Here is a simple illustration of the difference between these two kinds of learning: A CEO who had begun to practice his own form of management-by-walking-around learned from his employees that the company inhibited innovation by subjecting every new idea to more than 275 separate checks and sign-offs. He promptly appointed a task force to look at this situation, and it eliminated 200 of the obstacles. The result was a higher innovation rate.

This may sound like a successful managerial intervention. The CEO discovers a counterproductive process and, with the cooperation of others, produces dramatic improvement. Yet I would call it a case of single-loop learning. It addresses a difficulty but ignores a more fundamental problem. A more complete diagnosis—that is to say, a double-loop approach to this situation—would require the CEO to ask the employees who told him about the sign-offs some tougher questions about company culture and their own behavior. For example, "How long have you known about the 275 required sign-offs?" Or "What goes on in this company that prevented you from questioning these practices and getting them corrected or eliminated?"

Why didn't the CEO ask these questions of the supervisor? And why didn't the 40 supervisors ask these questions of themselves? There are two closely related mechanisms at work here—one social, the other psychological.

The social reason that the CEO did not dig deeper is that doing so might have been seen as putting people on the spot. Unavoidably, digging deeper would have uncovered the employees' collusion with the inefficient process. Their motives were probably quite decent—they didn't want to open Pandora's box, didn't want to be negative. But their behavior—and the behavior of the CEO in ignoring this dimension of the problem—combined with everyone's failure to examine his or her individual behavior and blocked the kind of learning that is crucial to organizational effectiveness.

In the name of positive thinking, in other words, managers often censor what everyone needs to say and hear. For the sake of "morale" and "considerateness," they deprive employees and themselves of the opportunity to take responsibility for their own behavior by learning to understand it. Because double-loop learning depends on questioning one's own assumptions and behavior, this apparently benevolent strategy is actually *anti*learning. Admittedly, being considerate and positive can contribute to the solution of single-loop problems like cutting costs. But it will never help people figure out why they lived with problems for years on end, why they covered up those problems, why they covered up the cover-up, why they were so good at pointing to the responsibility of others and so slow to focus on their own. The 40 supervisors said it was high time that management took steps. None of them asked why they themselves had never even drawn management's attention to nine areas of waste and inefficiency.

What we see here is managers using socially "up-beat" behavior to inhibit learning. What we do not see, at least not readily, is why anyone should want to inhibit learning. The reason lies in a set of deeper and more complex psychological motives.

Consider again the story of the 40 supervisors. TQM's rigorous, linear reasoning solves a set of important, single-loop problems. But while we see some effective single-loop learning, no double-loop learning occurs at all. Instead, the moment the important problems involve potential threat or embarrassment, rigorous reasoning goes right out the window and *defensive reasoning* takes over. Note how the supervisors deftly sidestep all responsibility and defend themselves against the charge of inaction–or worse, collusion—by blaming others. In fact, what I call defensive reasoning serves no purpose except self-protection, though the people who use it rarely acknowledge that they are protecting themselves. It is the group, the department, the organization that they are protecting, in the name of being positive. They believe themselves to be using the kind of rigorous thinking employed in TQM, which identifies problems, gathers objective data, postulates causes, tests explanations, and derives corrective action, all along relatively scientific lines. But the supervisors' actual techniques—gathering data selectively, postulating only causes that do not threaten themselves, testing explanations in ways that are sloppy and self-serving—are a parody of scientific method. The supervisors are not protecting others; they are blaming them. They have learned this procedure carefully over time, supported at each step by defensive organizational rationalizations like "caring" and "thoughtfulness."

The reason the supervisors fail to question their own rather remarkable behavior—the reason they so instinctively and thoroughly avoid double-loop learning—is psychological. It has to do with the mental models that we all develop early in life for dealing with emotional or threatening issues.

In the process of growing up, all of us learn and warehouse master programs for dealing with difficult situations. These programs are sets of rules we use to design our own actions and interpret the actions of others. We retrieve them whenever we need to diagnose a problem or invent or size up a solution. Without them, we'd have to start from scratch each time we faced a challenge.

One of the puzzling things about these mental models is that when the issues we face are embarrassing or threatening, the master programs we actually use are rarely the ones we think we use. Each of us has what I call an *espoused theory of action* based on principles and precepts that fit our intellectual backgrounds and commitments. But most of us have quite a different *theory-in-use* to which we resort in moments of stress. And very few of us are aware of the contradiction between the two. In short, most of us are consistently inconsistent in the way we act.

Espoused theories differ widely, but most theories-in-use have the same set of four governing values. All of us design our behavior in order to remain in unilateral control, to maximize winning and minimize losing, to suppress negative feelings, and to be as rational as possible, by which we mean laying out clear-cut goals and then evaluating our own behavior on the basis of whether or not we've achieved them.

The purpose of this strategy is to avoid vulnerability, risk, embarrassment, and the appearance of incompetence. In other words, it is a deeply defensive strategy and a recipe for ineffective learning. We might even call it a recipe for antilearning, because it helps us avoid reflecting on the counterproductive consequences of our own behavior. Theories-in-use assume a world that prizes unilateral control and winning above all else, and in that world, we focus primarily on controlling others and on making sure that we are not ourselves controlled. If any reflection does occur, it is in the service of winning and controlling, not of opening ourselves to learning.

Defensive strategies discourage reflection in another way as well. Because we practice them most of our lives, we are all highly skilled at carrying them out. Skilled actions are second nature; we rarely reflect on what we take for granted.

In studies of more than 6,000 people, I have found this kind of defensive theory-in-use to be universal, with no measurable difference by country, age, sex, ethnic identity, education, wealth, power, or experience. All over the world, in every kind of business and organization, in every kind of crisis and dilemma, the principles of defensive reasoning encourage people to leave their own behavior unexamined and to avoid any objective test of their premises and conclusions.

As if this individual defensive reasoning were not enough of a problem, genuine learning in organizations is inhibited by a second universal phenomenon that I call *organizational defensive routines*. These consist of all the policies, practices, and actions that prevent human beings from having to experience embarrassment or threat and, at the same time, prevent them from examining the nature and causes of that embarrassment or threat.

Take face-saving. To work, it must be unacknowledged. If you tell your subordinate Fred that you are saving his face, you have defeated your own purpose. What you do tell Fred is a fiction about the success of his own decision and a lie about your reasons for rescinding it. What's more, if Fred correctly senses the mixed message, he will almost certainly say nothing.

The logic here, as in all organizational defensive routines, is unmistakable: send a mixed message ("Your decision was a good one, and I'm overruling it"); pretend it is not mixed ("You can be proud of your contribution"); make the mixed message and the pretense undiscussable ("I feel good about this outcome, and I'm sure you do too"); and, finally, make the undiscussability undiscussable ("Now that I've explained everything to your satisfaction, is there anything *else* you'd like to talk about?").

Defensive reasoning occurs when individuals make their premises and inferences tacit, then draw conclusions that cannot be tested except by the tenets of this tacit logic. Nothing could be more detrimental to organizational learning than this process of elevating individual defensive tactics to an organizational routine.

Yet whenever managers are trying to get at the truth about problems that are embarrassing or threatening, they are likely to stumble into the same set of predictable pitfalls. Asked to examine their own behavior or the behavior of subordinates, people in this situation are likely

- To reason defensively and to interact with others who are reasoning defensively;
- To get superficial, single-loop responses that lead to superficial, single-loop solutions;
- To reinforce the organizational defensive routines that inhibit access to valid information and genuine learning;
- To be unaware of their own defenses because these are so skilled and automatic; and
- To be unaware that they are producing any of these consequences, or, if they *are* aware of defensiveness, to see it only in others.

Given all these built-in barriers to self-understanding and self-examination under threatening conditions, it is a wonder that organizational learning takes place at all. It is an even greater wonder when we realize that many of the forms of communication that management works so hard to perfect actually reinforce those barriers. Yet this is exactly what they do.

We have seen a couple of examples of management's "benevolent" censorship of true but negative messages. In addition, we have looked at the psychological mechanisms that lead employees, supervisors, managers, and executives to engage in personal and collective defensive routines. The question we still have to answer is precisely how modern corporate communications succeed in actually contributing to this censorship and these defensive routines.

They do so in two explicit ways. First, they create a bias against personal learning and commitment in the way they parcel out roles and responsibilities in every survey, dialogue, and conversation. Second, they open a door to defensive reasoning—and close one on individual self-awareness—in the way they continuously emphasize extrinsic as opposed to intrinsic motivation.

First, consider the way roles and responsibilities are assigned in manager-employee (or leader-subordinate) conversations, interviews, and surveys. There seem to be two rules. Rule number one is that employees are to be truthful and forthcoming about the world they work in, about norms, procedures, and the strengths and weaknesses of their superiors. All other aspects of their role in the life of the organization—their goals, feelings, failings, and conflicted motives—are taken for granted and remain unexamined. Rule number two is that top-level managers, who play an intensely scrutinized role in the life of the company, are to assume virtually all responsibility for employee well-being and organizational success. Employees must tell the truth as they see it; leaders must modify their own and the company's behavior. In other words, employees educate, and managers act.

Take the case of Acme, a large, multinational energy company with 6,000 employees. Under increasing competitive pressure, the company was forced to downsize, and to no one's surprise, morale was failing fast. To learn as much as possible about its own shortcomings and how to correct them, Acme management designed and conducted an employee survey with the help of experts, and 95% of employees responded. Of those responding, 75% agreed on five positive points:

- They were proud to work for Acme.
- Their job satisfaction was very high.
- They found their immediate supervisors fair and technically competent.
- They believed management was concerned for their welfare.
- They felt competent to perform their own jobs. Some 65% of the respondents also indicated some concerns:
- They were skeptical about management's capacity to take initiative, communicate candidly, and act effectively.
- They described Acme's corporate culture as one of blame.
- They complained that managers, while espousing empowerment, were strongly attached to their own unilateral control.

The CEO read the first set of findings to mean that employees were basically satisfied and loyal. He saw the second set as a list of problems that he must make a serious effort to correct. And so the CEO replaced several top managers and arranged for the reeducation of the whole management team, including himself and his direct reports. He announced that Acme would no longer tolerate a culture of blame. He introduced training programs to make managers more forthright and better able to take initiative. And he promised to place greater emphasis on genuine empowerment.

The CEO's logic went like this: My employees will identify the problems. I'll fix them by creating a new vision, defining new practices and policies, and selecting a top management team genuinely committed to them. Change will inevitably follow.

I think most managers would call this a success story. If we dig deeper, however, we see a pattern I've observed hundreds of times. Underneath the CEO's aggressive action, important issues have been bypassed, and the bypass has been covered up.

When the CEO took his new team on a five-day retreat to develop the new strategy and plan its implementation, he invited me to come along. In the course of the workshop, I asked each participant to write a simple case in a format I have found to be a powerful tool in predicting how executives will deal with difficult issues during implementation. The method also reveals contradictions between what the executives say and what they do and highlights their awareness of these discrepancies.

I asked each member of the team to write one or two sentences describing one important barrier to the new strategy and another three or four sentences telling how they would overcome that barrier. Then I asked them to split the rest of the page in half. On one side, they were to write an actual or imagined dialogue with a subordinate about the issue in question. On the other side, they were to note any unsaid or unsayable thoughts or feelings they might have about this conversation. I asked them to continue this script for several pages. When they were finished, the group as a whole discussed each case at some length, and we recorded the discussions. The ability to replay key sections made it easier for the participants to score themselves on candor, forthrightness, and the extent to which their comments and behavior encouraged genuine employee commitment—the three values that the CEO had directed the executives to foster.

All of the executives chose genuinely important issues around resistance to change. But all of them dealt with the resistance they expected from subordinates by easing in, covering up, and avoiding candor and plain speaking. They did so in the name of minimizing subordinates' defensiveness and in hopes of getting them to buy into change. The implicit logic behind their scripts went something like this:

- Hide your fears about the other person's likely resistance to change. Cover this fear with persistent positiveness. Pretend the two of you agree, especially when you know you don't.
- Deal with resistant responses by stressing the problem rather than the resistance. Be positive. Keep this strategy a secret.
- If this approach doesn't work, make it clear that you won't take no for an answer. After all, you're the boss.

Imagine this kind of logic applied to sensitive issues in hundreds of conversations with employees. It's not hard to guess what the response will be, and it certainly isn't buy-in.

What happened to candor, forthrightness, and commitment building? All the executives failed to walk their talk, and all were unaware of their own inconsistency. When I pointed out the gap between action and intention, most saw it at once. Most were surprised that they hadn't seen it before. Most were quick to recognize inconsistency in others, but their lack of awareness with regard to their own inconsistency was systematic.

I know of only one way to get at these inconsistencies, and that is to focus on them. In the Acme case, the CEO managed to ignore the fact that the survey results didn't compute: on the one hand, employees said they were proud to work for the company and described management as caring; on the other, they doubted management's candor and competence. How could they hold both views? How could they be proud to work for a company whose managers were ineffective and inconsistent?

The CEO did not stop to explore any of these contradictions before embarking on corrective action. Had he done so, he might have discovered that the employees felt strong job satisfaction precisely *because* management never asked them to accept personal responsibility for Acme's poor competitive performance. Employees could safely focus their skepticism on top management because they had learned to depend on top management for their welfare. They claimed to value empowerment when in reality they valued dependence. They claimed commitment to the company when in reality they were committed only to the principle that management should make all the tough decisions, guarantee their employment, and pay them fairly. This logic made sense to employees, but it was *not* the kind of commitment that management had in mind.

None of these issues was ever discussed with employees, and none was raised in the leadership workshops. No effort was made to explore the concept of loyalty that permitted, indeed encouraged, managers to think one thing and say another. No attempt was made to help employees understand the role they played in the "culture of blame" that they'd named in the survey as one of their chief concerns. Above all, no one tried to untangle the defensive logic that contributed so mightily to these inconsistencies and that so badly needed critical examination. In fact, when I asked the management team why they had not discussed these questions, one person told me, "Frankly, until you started asking these questions, it just didn't occur to us. I see your point, but trying to talk to our people about this could be awfully messy. We're really trying to be *positive* here, and this would just stir things up."

The Acme story is a very common one: lots of energy is expended with little lasting progress. Employee surveys like the one Acme conducted—and like most other forms of leader-subordinate communication—have a fundamentally antimanagement bias whenever they deal with double-loop issues. They encourage employees *not* to reflect on their own behavior and attitudes. By assigning all the responsibility for fixing problems to management, they encourage managers *not* to relinquish the top-down, command-and-control mind-set that prevents empowerment.

The employees at Acme, like the 40 supervisors who were wined and dined for their TQM accomplishments, will continue to do what's asked of them as long as they feel adequately rewarded. They will follow the rules, but they will not take initiative, they will not take risks, and they are very unlikely to engage in double-loop learning. In short, they will not adopt the new behaviors and frames of reference so critical to keeping their companies competitive.

Over the last few years, I have come in contact with any number of companies struggling with this transition from command-and-control hierarchy to employee empowerment and organizational learning, and every one of them is its own worst enemy. Managers embrace the language of intrinsic motivation but fail to see how firmly mired in the old extrinsic world their communications actually are. This is the second explicit way in which corporate communications contribute to nonlearning.

Take the case of the 1,200-person operations division of what I'll call Europabank, where employee commitment to customer service was about to become a matter of survival. The bank's CEO had decided to spin off the division, and its future depended on its ability to *earn* customer loyalty. Europabank's CEO felt confident that the employees could become more market-oriented. Because he knew they would have to take more initiative and risk, he created small project groups to work out all the implementation details and get employees to buy into the new mission. He was pleased with the way the organization was responding.

The vice president for human resources was not so pleased. He worried that the buy-in wasn't genuine and that his boss was overly optimistic. Not wanting to be negative, however, he kept his misgivings to himself.

In order to assess what was really going on here, I needed to know more about the attitudes behind the CEO's behavior. I asked him for some written examples of how he would answer employee concerns about the spin-off. What would he say to allay their doubts and build their commitment? Here are two samples of what he wrote:

- "If the employees express fear about the new plan because the `old' company guaranteed employment, say: `The new organization will do its utmost to guarantee employment and better prospects for growth. I promise that.'"

- "If the employees express fear that they are not used to dealing with the market approach, say: `I promise you will get the education you need, and I will ensure that appropriate actions are rewarded.'"

When these very situations later arose and he made these very statements to employees, their reactions were positive. They felt that the CEO really cared about them.

But look at the confusion of messages and roles. If the CEO means to give these employees a sense of their own power over their own professional fate—and that was his stated intent—then why emphasize instead what *he* will do for *them?* Each time he said, "I promise you," the CEO undermined his own goal of creating internal commitment, intrinsic motivation, and genuine empowerment.

He might have begun to generate real buy-in by pointing out to employees that their wishes were unreasonable. They want management to deal with their fears and reassure them that everything will turn out for the best. They want management to take responsibility for a challenge that is theirs to face. In a market-driven business, the CEO cannot possibly give the guarantees these employees want. The employees see the CEO as caring when he promises to protect and reward them. Unfortunately, this kind of caring disempowers, and someday it will hurt both the employees and the company.

Once employees base their motivation on extrinsic factors—the CEO's promises—they are much less likely to take chances, question established policies and practices, or explore the territory that lies beyond the company vision as defined by management. They are much less likely to learn.

Externally committed employees believe that management manipulates them and see loyalty as allowing the manipulation to take place. They will give honest responses to a direct question or a typical employee survey because they will be glad to tell management what's wrong. They will see it as a loyal act. What they are *not* likely to do is examine the risky issues surrounding their dependence, their ambivalence, and their avoidance of personal responsibility. Employees will commit to TQM, for example, if they believe that their compensation is just and that their managers are fair and trustworthy. However, these conditions, like the commitment they produce, come from an outside source: management.

This is external commitment, and external commitment harnesses external motivation. The energy available for work derives from extrinsic factors like good pay, well-designed jobs, and management promises. Individuals whose commitment and motivation are external depend on their managers to give them the incentive to work.

I recently watched a videotape of the CEO of a large airline meeting with relatively upper-level managers. The CEO repeatedly emphasized the importance of individual empowerment at all levels of the organization. At one point in the tape, a young manager identified a problem that top managers at the home office had prevented him from resolving. The CEO thanked the man and then asked him to go directly to the senior vice president who ran the department in question and raise the issue again. In the meantime, he said, he would pave the way. By implication, he encouraged all the managers present to take the initiative and come to him if they encountered bureaucratic barriers.

I watched this video with a group of some 80 senior executives. All but one praised the CEO for empowering the young manager. The single dissenter wondered out loud about the quality of the empowerment, which struck him as entirely external, entirely dependent on the action of the CEO.

I agreed with that lonely voice. The CEO could have opened a window into genuine empowerment for the young manager by asking a few critical questions: What had the young man done to communicate his sense of disempowerment to those who blocked him? What fears would doing so have triggered? How could the organization redesign itself to give young managers the freedom and safety to take such initiatives? For that matter, the CEO could have asked these same questions of his senior vice presidents.

By failing to explore the deeper issues—and by failing to encourage his managers to do the same—all the CEO did was promise to lend the young manager some high-level executive power and authority the next time he had a problem. In other words, the CEO built external commitment and gave his manager access to it. What he did not do was encourage the young man to build permanent empowerment for himself on the basis of his own insights, abilities, and prerogatives.

Companies that hope to reap the rewards of a committed, empowered workforce have to learn to stop kidding themselves. External commitment, positive thinking at any price, employees protected from the consequences and even the knowledge of cause and effect—this mind-set may produce superficial honesty and single-loop learning, but it will never yield the kind of learning that might actually help a company change. The reason is quite simply that for companies to change, employees must take an active role not only in describing the faults of others but also in drawing out the truth about their *own* behavior and motivation. In my experience, moreover, employees dig deeper and harder into the truth when the task of scrutinizing the organization includes taking a good look at their own roles, responsibilities, and potential contributions to corrective action.

The problem is not that employees run away from this kind of organizational self-examination. The problem is that no one asks it of them. Managers seem to attach no importance to employees' feelings, defenses, and inner conflicts. Moreover, leaders focus so earnestly on "positive" values—employee satisfaction, upbeat attitude, high morale—that it would strike them as destructive to make demands on employee self-awareness.

But this emphasis on being positive is plainly counterproductive. First, it overlooks the critical role that dissatisfaction, low morale, and negative attitudes can play—often *should* play—in giving an accurate picture of organizational reality, especially with regard to threatening or sensitive issues. (For example, if employees are helping to eliminate their own jobs, why should we expect or encourage them to display high morale or disguise their mixed feelings?) Second, it condescendingly assumes that employees can only function in a cheerful world, even if the cheer is false. We make no such assumption about senior executives. We expect leaders to stand up and take their punches like adults, and we recognize that their best performance is often linked to shaky morale, job insecurity, high levels of frustration, and a vigilant focus on negatives. But leaders have a tendency to treat everyone below the top, including many of their managers, like members of a more fragile race, who can be productive only if they are contented.

Now, there is nothing wrong with contented people, if contentment is the only goal. My research suggests it is possible to achieve quite respectable productivity with middling commitment and morale. The key is a system of external compensation and job security that employees consider fair. In such a system, superficial answers to critical questions produce adequate results, and no one demands more.

But the criteria for effectiveness and responsibility have risen sharply in recent years and will rise more sharply still in the decades to come. A generation ago, business wanted employees to do exactly what they were told, and company leadership bought their acquiescence with a system of purely extrinsic rewards. Extrinsic motivation had fairly narrow boundaries—defined by phrases like "That's not my job"—but it did produce acceptable results with a minimum of complication.

Today, facing competitive pressures an earlier generation could hardly have imagined, managers need employees who think constantly and creatively about the needs of the organization. They need employees with as much *intrinsic* motivation and as deep a sense of organizational stewardship as any company executive. To bring this about, corporate communications must demand more of everyone involved. Leaders and subordinates alike—those who ask and those who answer—must all begin struggling with a new level of self-awareness, candor, and responsibility.

5

The Employee-Customer-Profit Chain at Sears

Anthony J. Rucci, Steven P. Kirn, and
Richard T. Quinn

It is no longer news that over the past five years, Sears, Roebuck
and Company has radically changed the way it does business and dramatically improved its financial results. Much has been written about
the Sears turnaround, detailing the company's strategic shifts and its
transition from big losses to big profits. But the Sears transformation
was more than a change in marketing strategy. It was also a change in
the logic and culture of the business. In fact, the process of altering the
logic is what changed the culture.

Led (and pushed) by CEO Arthur Martinez, a group of more than
100 top-level Sears executives spent the better part of three years rebuilding the company around its customers. In the course of rethinking what Sears was and wanted to become, these managers developed
a business model of the company that tracked success from management behavior through employee attitudes to customer satisfaction
and financial performance. Along with its measurement system, this
employee-customer-profit model is rigorous enough to serve as an integral
piece of the management information system and as a tool that every
individual in the company can use for self-assessment and self-
improvement. Moreover, the work of creating the model and
the measures made such demands on the managers involved that it
changed the way they think and behave. That cultural change is now
spreading through the company.

The basic elements of an employee-customer-profit model are not
difficult to grasp. Any person with even a little experience in retailing

understands intuitively that there is a chain of cause and effect running from employee behavior to customer behavior to profits, and it's not hard to see that behavior depends primarily on attitude. Which is not to say that implementing an employee-customer-profit chain, or model, is easy. One big problem is measurement. Unlike revenues and profits, soft data are hard to define and collect, and few measures are softer than customer and employee attitudes, or "satisfaction." In many businesses, it is difficult to measure even relatively hard behaviors like customer retention, and the inevitable result is that many companies are unwilling to expend the time, energy, and resources to do it effectively. Not surprisingly, many companies do not have a realistic grasp of what their customers and employees actually think and do.

Sears does. By means of an ongoing process of data collection, analysis, modeling, and experimentation, we have developed and continue to refine what we call our Total Performance Indicators, or TPI—a set of measures that shows us how well we are doing with customers, employees, and investors. We understand the several layers of factors that drive employee attitudes, and we know how employee attitudes affect employee retention, how employee retention affects the drivers of customer satisfaction, how customer satisfaction affects financials, and a great deal more. We have also calculated the lag time between a change in any of those metrics and a corresponding change in financial performance, so that when we see a shift in, say, employee attitudes, we know not only *how* but also *when* it will affect results. Our TPI makes the employee-customer-profit chain operational because we manage the company on the basis of these indicators, with remarkably positive results. But the system is a good deal more complex—and a good deal harder to imitate—than this glimpse suggests.

Any retailer could copy the Sears measures—even our modeling techniques—and still fail to achieve an operational employee-customer-profit chain, because the mechanics of the system are not in themselves enough to make it work. It goes without saying that you must be able to measure and manage the drivers of employee and customer satisfaction, and we will explain how we do this at Sears. But two additional elements are indispensable. First, a company must build management alignment around the model and the measures—which, for all practical purposes, make up a single system. Because this system is to be the cornerstone of management decision making, it is critically important that every manager—especially those at the top of the company—understand the system and buy into it wholeheartedly. Second, it is essential to deploy the system properly in order to create a sense of ownership among sales associates and staff. Deployment is easy to shrug off. It looks like a simple communication challenge, but it is a good deal more. It is an issue of trust and of business and economic literacy. Unless employees grasp the purpose of the system, understand the economics of their company and industry, and have a clear picture of how their own work fits into the employee-customer-profit model, they will never succeed in making the whole thing work.

Making an employee-customer-profit chain operational is therefore a challenge in three parts: creating and refining the employee-customer-profit model and the measurement system that supports it; creating management alignment around the use of the model to run the company; and deploying the model so as to build business literacy and trust among employees. At Sears, there was no distinction between parts one and two. Managers themselves created the model and aligned themselves with it as they did so, since people automatically buy into systems they invent. Part three, deployment, followed. The three together were a radical response to a 10-year business downturn that threatened the survival of the Sears retail business—a 111-year-old American institution.

Turnaround

The year 1992 was the worst in the history of Sears. On sales of $52.3 billion, the company's net loss was $3.9 billion, almost $3 billion of which came from the merchandising group. Worse yet, 1992 was no anomaly but the culmination of bad trends, most of them directly related to the company's lack of focus. For a century, Sears had flourished on the strength of its adaptive ability to understand and serve U.S. consumers and their changing needs and wants. Beginning in the 1980s, however, Sears diversified into insurance, financial services, brokerage, and real estate, while other retailers, notably Wal-Mart, were focusing fiercely on the retail consumer and were capturing market share with remarkable speed. The Sears response was to sell or spin off all its nonretail businesses and return to its roots.

Arthur Martinez arrived in September 1992 to head up the merchandising group. (In August 1995, when Sears had divested everything but merchandising, he became chairman and CEO.) Martinez had been vice chairman and a director of Saks Fifth Avenue, as well as group chief executive for the retail division of BATUS, where he was responsible for Saks, Marshall Field, J.B. Ivey, and Breuners. But no retailer in history had ever succeeded in effecting a turn-around of the kind and scope that Sears required, perhaps even to survive. Martinez and his leadership team needed to make some quick decisions about product lines, store types and locations, strategies, asset allocations—even about the company's basic identity as a retailer. Two factors worked in Sears's favor. First, we would not have to invent a crisis to get the attention of employees, who were hungry for improved performance. Second, the company's heritage was an asset. Research showed, almost surprisingly, that through years of turmoil— and despite specific customer-satisfaction ratings that were very low— American families had maintained a positive, trusting image of Sears as a good, honest place to shop.

Within 100 days of his arrival, Martinez initiated a comprehensive turnaround plan. For decades, the underlying assumption had been that Sears was a man's store, but market data showed that an extremely high percentage of buying decisions were being made by women. Martinez refocused marketing on "the softer side of Sears" and introduced new private-label lines of apparel and cosmetics. He expanded and accelerated existing plans to move into off-mall specialty stores, including Sears hardware stores and HomeLife furniture stores. He slated 113 stores for closing, reducing the number of mall-based stores to about 800; those that remained were to be thoroughly renovated over five years at a cost of $4 billion. He also terminated the 101-year-old Sears catalog, which was losing more than $100 million a year. Store operations were reengineered, with a heavy emphasis on training, incentives, and the elimination of administrative and other nonselling tasks for sales personnel. Staffing was adjusted to put more of the best people in the stores during evenings and weekends, when the best customers were shopping. The company's entire service strategy was revamped to make it more responsive to busy women and their families. Sears began offering Sunday deliveries and a long list of new services, including repairs on any brand of appliance. Martinez decreed that Sears would accept all major credit cards instead of limiting itself to Discover and the Sears card.

The results were spectacular. In 1993, the company's merchandising group reported net income of $752 million, a sales increase of more than 9% in existing stores, and market share gains in apparel, appliances, and electronics. Sears as a whole had one of its most profitable years ever. The resurrection produced a total shareholder return for the year of 56%.

Transformation

Business turnarounds are remarkable events, but all too often they are only skin deep. They are exciting, certainly. Management introduces a new strategy, speaks with great conviction about empowerment and customer focus, and lavishes a great deal of attention on the workforce. But few rank-and-file employees ever really understand the point of all the activity or grasp their own role in it. Moreover, the turnaround means a lot of extra work and can tire everyone out. So once the energy and excitement—and the results—have peaked, many companies fall back in relief and reassume bad habits.

We were determined to keep this pattern from repeating itself at Sears. Once the company was making money again, there was a widespread, perceptible sense of "Glad that's behind us," and we realized that success could become our enemy. The task we faced was substantial: to transform the company, turn its short-term survival program into a platform for long-term excellence, and, in the process, engage the creative power of employees in the vital task of shaping the company's future. We knew that Sears had to listen to its customers and respond to their needs. We also understood that no plan we devised and imposed from above was ever going to work. If Sears was to undergo a transformation—if attitudes and behavior were to change and a new sense of urgency and purpose were to spread through the company—senior management as a whole would have to take the lead. As Martinez saw it, his job was to coax or compel his senior managers to come up with a plan.

In March 1993, he called the first of several off-site meetings in Phoenix, Arizona, for about 65 senior managers. (This group, known as the Phoenix Team, grew steadily until it included roughly 150 people—the entire senior echelon.) In an intensive two-and-a-half-day session, Martinez presented five new strategic priorities—core business growth, customer focus ("Make Sears a compelling place to shop" was the way he put it), cost reduction, responsiveness to local markets, and organizational and cultural renewal—and then led the discussions himself. You are the future leaders of Sears, he said in effect, and as you go, so goes the company. Back at Sears headquarters in Chicago, the Phoenix Team continued to meet one Saturday a month to discuss the priorities and work on implementation.

At the November meeting later that year, Martinez wanted to know how the five strategic priorities were progressing, and a general discussion followed. Everyone agreed that the priorities made sense to top-level managers, but the rest of the company thought it was all a lot of "M.B.A. stuff." "They nod their heads when you talk about customer focus," someone said, "but they don't know what they're supposed to be doing differently." And then one candid and courageous soul stood up and said, "To be completely honest about it, I don't know what *I'm* supposed to be doing differently." People shifted uneasily in their seats, and a few nodded in agreement. It was a startling moment. Here was the Phoenix Team, whose job it was to design a corporate transformation and generate renewal among 300,000 employees at more than 2,000 locations, and no one seemed to have a clear sense of what, exactly, that might require.

In most companies, in most situations, it is the eight or ten most senior executives (along with the strategic planning department and various consultants) who ask the big strategic questions: What business are we in? Whom do we serve? How do we compete? What is our value proposition? As a rule, the 100 to 200 people in the second management layer take the answers to those questions on faith. What gets lost as a result is cross-functional dialogue, questioning, cooperative planning, creativity, and ownership. At Sears, the 1992 turnaround strategy—as well as the five strategic priorities—were developed and deployed more or less according to the old top-down paradigm, with strong initial results but without the broad ownership and employee engagement that Martinez wanted. In 1992, there had been no real alternative—the company was teetering on the edge. And the turn-around strategy worked. Then, in 1993, Martinez had needed a set of priorities he could use to make a direct, almost personal bid for the hearts and minds of his senior managers. He had won their hearts, it appeared, but he still needed to give them an opportunity and a compelling reason to think outside the old Sears box and figure out for themselves what they should be doing differently.

What followed was more than a year of careful but intense pressure on those senior managers. There were plenty of ideas on the table. The problem was getting members of the Phoenix Team to explore the possibilities until they themselves could develop a plan for Sears that would work because it was their own creation.

We began by asking each member of the team to write a "news

story" about where Sears would be in five years and how it got there. At the Phoenix meeting in March of 1994, task forces were formed around four recurring themes in those stories: customers, employees, financial performance, and innovation. The new groups were asked to define *world-class status* in their areas, identify obstacles to achieving it, and establish metrics for measuring progress. The task forces met for two-and-a-half days, then presented their findings to the whole assembly. Martinez told them it was a good start. But since the company was going to bet its future on their initiatives, they would need to spend more time, gather more information, and make specific recommendations.

When the team got back to Chicago, a lot of people complained about the extra workload. They had no time to spend on task forces, they insisted, because they had to run the company. The message came back that they had to do both. They had to find the strategic answers and create an operational strategy. For several weeks, everyone struggled. As the deadline for recommendations approached, the sense of urgency grew. The task forces began meeting weekly, usually at 7 A.M. or earlier. (Months later, when many people wondered if the 7 o'clock grind had to go on forever, they needed to be reminded that no one ever told them they had to meet at that hour, or every week, or at all. Urgency and involvement had scheduled all those early-morning meetings.)

The four task forces grew to five: customers, employees, financial performance, innovation, and values. The financial task force built a model of the drivers of total shareholder return over a 20-year period and drew inferences about what Sears would have to do to be in the top quartile of *Fortune* 500 companies. The innovation group did outside benchmarking, undertook a research project into the nature of change, and suggested an effort to generate one million ideas from employees. The values group gathered 80,000 employee surveys and identified six core values that Sears's people felt strongly about: honesty, integrity, respect for the individual, teamwork, trust, and customer focus. The old command-and-control culture was too parental and didn't value people enough. Performance should count more than effort.

The customer task force studied customer surveys going back several years and conducted 80 customer focus groups across the country, videotaping the sessions so that every member of the task force could watch. They asked the focus groups why they shopped at Sears, what they wanted, what they expected, what they disliked. Sears had always talked a great game on customer focus: "Satisfaction guaranteed or your money back" had been a Sears watchword for a hundred years, and "Take care of the customer, take care of the customer" was a kind of Sears mantra. Much of it was hollow, however, and it often seemed that no one at headquarters had been listening to customers. Across the country, the task force heard endless stories about how we failed to meet customers' expectations. Merchandise was out of stock, sales associates were hard to find, returns were time consuming, service was bad. The big surprise was that, in spite of it all, people basically liked Sears. One of our great assets was the American public's persistent wish to see the company succeed.

The employee task force conducted 26 employee focus groups and studied all the data on employee attitudes and behavior, including a 70-question opinion survey given to every employee every other year. What the group heard, again and again, was that employees took a great interest in the company's success. They were proud to be at Sears. "It's not a job," someone said. "It's my life's work."

While the task forces were busy gathering data, we set up an additional group to produce a vision and values statement. It had predictable difficulties. After talking to 80,000 employees, the group came up with a set of values that sounded like the Boy Scout oath. We were going to be the world's leading retailer, practice charity and kindness, end world hunger, and achieve peace in our time. All fine ambitions, but what did they have to do with retailing? We turned to outside professionals, and they came up with a vision statement that sounded like every other company's vision statement.

Then it struck us that we had been staring at it all along. Early in the process, Martinez had talked about making Sears a "compelling place to shop." We also wanted Sears to be a compelling place to work. And if we could achieve both of those goals, Sears would certainly become a compelling place to invest. So "Sears, a compelling place to work, to shop, and to invest" became not our vision, exactly, but a clear statement of what we wanted to be known for, internally and externally. We called it the "three compellings" and later just the three C's. We combined it with three shared values that we came to call the three P's: "passion for the customer, our people add value, and performance leadership." Some people in the company thought all of this was far too simplistic, but to most of us, simplicity was its strength. The three C's and the three P's were simple, yet they amounted to a wonderfully concise version of the entire employee-customer-profit chain, from motivated employees to satisfied customers to pleased investors. No one would have to carry around a little printed card to remember what Sears was all about.

Measurement

Times of crisis like the ones Sears had gone through make corporate transformation necessary and, ironically, somewhat easier. People know that change is required because they can easily remember when pieces of the sky were raining on their heads. But change to what? Change managed how, especially in a large organization? And change perpetuated how, as a dynamic process rather than as a onetime event?

The task forces had spent months listening to customers and employees, studying best practices at other companies, thinking about what would constitute world-class performance at Sears, and establishing measures and objectives. As a result, they had at least a partial answer to the first question: Change to what? The customer task force had established four goals: to build customer loyalty, to make Sears a fun place to shop, to provide excellent customer service by hiring and holding on to the best employees, and to offer the right merchandise at the right prices. The employee task force came up with three: to build a workforce of involved and empowered employees, to encourage new ideas, and to create an environment in which employees could realize their personal goals and develop their skills and abilities. The financial task force had four goals: to increase operating margins, to improve asset management, to raise productivity, and to grow revenues.

While the separate task forces were formulating those objectives, the Phoenix Team as a whole was beginning to think in terms of a business model that would link employees, customers, and investors into a single logical entity. In fact, it was a short step from "compelling place to work, to shop, and to invest" to the same thought expressed as a formula for the company's success: *work* $\times$ *shop* = *invest*. This simple algorithm looked more like a slogan than an operational strategy, but there was more to it than met the eye. In the first place, the formula took into account our conviction that for Sears to succeed financially, we had to be a compelling place *both* to work *and* to shop—that is, *work* $\times$ *shop*, not *work* + *shop*. The right merchandise at the right prices would get us nowhere if our employees were poorly motivated. Second, it was a formula made up of leading, not lagging,

Exhibit 5-1   The Initial Model: From Objectives to Measures

The first step in creating an employee-customer-profit model was to devise a set of measures based on our objectives in our three categories: a compelling place to work, to shop, and to invest.

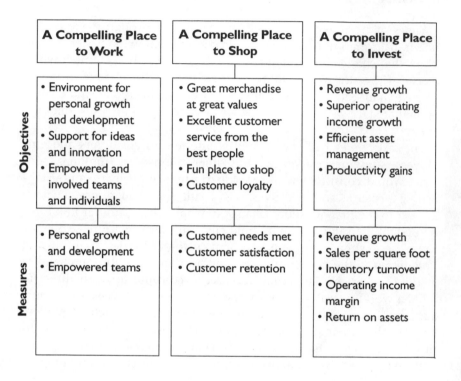

	A Compelling Place to Work	A Compelling Place to Shop	A Compelling Place to Invest
Objectives	• Environment for personal growth and development • Support for ideas and innovation • Empowered and involved teams and individuals	• Great merchandise at great values • Excellent customer service from the best people • Fun place to shop • Customer loyalty	• Revenue growth • Superior operating income growth • Efficient asset management • Productivity gains
Measures	• Personal growth and development • Empowered teams	• Customer needs met • Customer satisfaction • Customer retention	• Revenue growth • Sales per square foot • Inventory turnover • Operating income margin • Return on assets

indicators. It is now a truism that financial results are a rearview mirror, that they tell you only how you did in the last quarter and not how you will do in the next. But few if any companies have ever come up with dependable predictive metrics, and that's what we were after.

The objectives formulated by the task forces gave us a set of preliminary measures, on which the task forces had already begun to gather data. (See Exhibit 5-1.) We now formed a new team to convert those measures into an econometric model. The measurement team's task was to come up with a kind of balanced scorecard for the company—the Sears Total Performance Indicators, or TPI. But we wanted to go well beyond the usual balanced scorecard, commonly just a set of un-

Harvard Business School Press
A Division of Harvard Business School Publishing
Boston, Massachusetts 02163

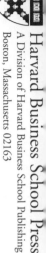

BUSINESS REPLY MAIL
FIRST CLASS MAIL   PERMIT NO. 2725   BOSTON, MA

POSTAGE WILL BE PAID BY ADDRESSEE:

HARVARD BUSINESS SCHOOL PUBLISHING
60 HARVARD WAY
BOX 230-5
BOSTON, MA 02163-9907

tested assumptions, and nail down the drivers of future financial performance with statistical rigor. We wanted to assemble the company's vast body of interview and research data—some of it from the task forces, much of it collected routinely over the course of years but never used strategically—then analyze it, draw connections across the data sets, and construct a model to show pathways of actual causation all the way from employee attitudes to profits. We wanted a set of nonfinancial measures that would be every bit as rigorous and auditable as financial ones. To make that happen, we had to take this first version of the employee-customer-profit model and elaborate and refine it until we had tested and proved the measures it was built on.

It was a task that struck many people as utopian, but even the skeptics understood that dependable information about causation would be invaluable if we could get it. Suppose, for example, that we wanted to spend some money to increase sales associates' knowledge of the products they sell. Would customers notice? Would the investment lead to increased customer retention, better word of mouth, higher revenues, greater market share? If so, how long would it take? Or, even more to the point, suppose that we wanted to measure the effects of an improvement in management skills. Because 70% of our employees work part-time, and part-time employees have a high turnover rate, we know that management skills are critically important. The model and the TPI could tell us *how* important those management skills actually were, measured in terms of employee attitudes and customer satisfaction. We wanted a chain of causation that would answer all those questions and more—a working model of the employee-customer-profit chain that would help us run the company.

For customers and employees, some of the metrics were brand-new. Personal growth and development was not something Sears had ever measured before, and neither was customer retention. We had to invent the measures and the new measurement techniques that went with them. Once we had defined our new measures, we spent the first two quarters of 1995 gathering metrics of every kind, old and new; in the third quarter, we gave our huge collection of survey and financial data to a firm of econometric statisticians for analysis. The methodology they use is called *causal pathway modeling*—as distinct from regression analysis, which examines data and observes correlations without establishing causation. The experts took our two quarters of data from 800 different stores, compared the results across time and place, and, using statistical techniques like cluster and factor analysis, found linkages and impacts in the data. A month later, they gave us their report, having found some strong and some weak connections, and some connections we had never expected or imagined. We made the appropriate adjustments in our model and went on collecting data for a new iteration at the end of the next quarter.

It was exciting stuff. We could see how employee attitudes drove not just customer service but also employee turnover and the likelihood that employees would recommend Sears and its merchandise to friends, family, and customers. We discovered that an employee's ability to see the connection between his or her work and the company's strategic objectives was a driver of positive behavior. We learned that asking customers whether Sears is a "fun place to shop" told us more than a long list of more specific questions would. We were also able to establish fairly precise statistical relationships. We began to see exactly how a change in training or business literacy affected revenues.

We also found that two dimensions of employee satisfaction—attitude toward the job and toward the company—had a greater effect on employee loyalty and behavior toward customers than all the other dimensions put together. We still use the 70-question employee survey to gather information about working conditions, satisfaction with pay and benefits, and so forth; but for econometric purposes, a mere 10 of those 70 questions captured the predictive relationship between employee satisfaction and customer satisfaction. Moreover, those 10 questions amounted to a report card on management, which reemphasized the importance of management skills in achieving company goals. (See Exhibit 5-2.)

Conversely, the statisticians could find no direct causal pathway from two of the measures we had put into our tentative model—*personal growth and development and empowered teams*—to any of our customer data. We believe that growth, empowerment, and teamwork matter, but clearly something about the way we measured them was flawed. However important they might be, the measures we had did not lie on a predictive pathway from employee attitudes to customer satisfaction to shareholder value. So in the next version of our employee-customer-profit model, we replaced those initial measures with the 10 questions about the job and the company.

In the 18 months from mid-1994 to the end of 1995, we produced a model, refined it three times, and created a TPI for the company as a whole, but the process of improvement continues. We conduct interviews and collect data continually, assemble our information quarterly, and recalculate the impacts in our model once a year to stay

Exhibit 5-2   A Compelling Place to Work

We discovered that responses to these 10 statements and questions on our 70-question employee survey had a higher impact on employee behavior (and, therefore, on customer satisfaction) than the measures we devised initially: personal growth and development and empowered teams.

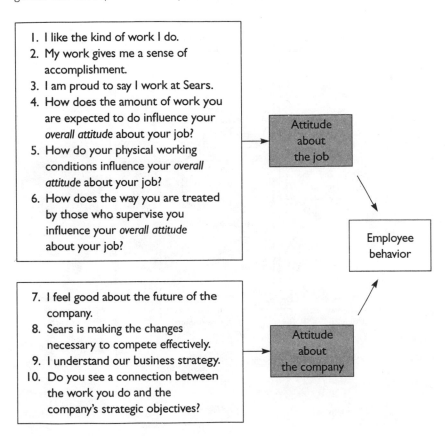

1. I like the kind of work I do.
2. My work gives me a sense of accomplishment.
3. I am proud to say I work at Sears.
4. How does the amount of work you are expected to do influence your *overall attitude* about your job?
5. How do your physical working conditions influence your *overall attitude* about your job?
6. How does the way you are treated by those who supervise you influence your *overall attitude* about your job?

Attitude about the job

Employee behavior

7. I feel good about the future of the company.
8. Sears is making the changes necessary to compete effectively.
9. I understand our business strategy.
10. Do you see a connection between the work you do and the company's strategic objectives?

Attitude about the company

abreast of the changing economy, changing demographics, and changing competitive circumstances.

The TPI is not a perfect system and never will be, despite our steady improvements. (See Exhibit 5-3.) It tells us less than we would like to know—and less, probably, than we need to know. The point is that we know vastly more than we once did, that all that information helps us run the company, and that some of it has given us a decided competitive edge. Take the example about the quality of management as a

Exhibit 5-3   *The Revised Model: The Employee-Customer-Profit Chain*

This is the model we use today. The rectangles represent survey information, the ovals, hard data. The measurements in gray are those we collect and distribute in the form of the Sears Total Performance Indicators.

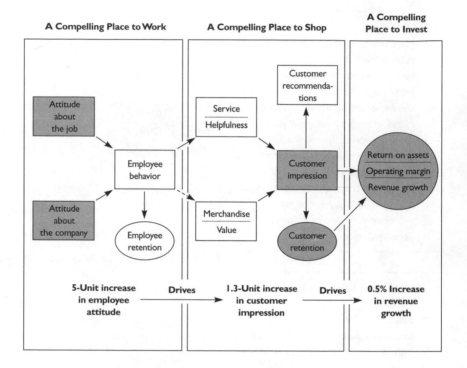

driver of employee attitudes. Our model shows that a 5 point improvement in employee attitudes will drive a 1.3 point improvement in customer satisfaction, which in turn will drive a 0.5% improvement in revenue growth. If we knew nothing about a local store except that employee attitudes had improved by 5 points on our survey scale, we could predict with confidence that if revenue growth in the district as a whole were 5%, revenue growth at this particular store would be 5.5%. These numbers are as rigorous as any others we work with at Sears. Every year, our accounting firm audits them as closely as it audits our financials.

Deployment

By mid-1995, as we began making the TPI operational, we had invested nearly two years in the transformation of senior management, a group of 100 to 200 people. We now had to build the same kind of ownership and engagement in the entire Sears workforce—a group of 300,000 people—in a much shorter period of time.

As we mentioned earlier, deploying the employee-customer-profit chain and the TPI throughout the company was more than a question of communication. In fact, only a few years earlier, the communication challenge had been the reverse. Before the turnaround, frontline employees sometimes seemed to be the only people in the company who understood that Sears was in trouble with its customers, and somehow they couldn't get the message through to management. Now that the financial turnaround had succeeded, what sales associates needed to be told was not just that the customer mattered but that *they* mattered, too—that the company could not survive without their active help and participation. We needed to take our statistical model in all its intellectual purity and bring it down to earth. We needed to change the perceptions and attitudes of our workforce, augment its grasp of how the business worked, and focus every individual's attention on his or her behavior in front of the customer.

To begin with, employees misunderstood what was expected of them, and that was a real barrier to effective change. Consider the experience of a top-level Sears executive who toured stores across the country and asked hundreds of employees, "What do you think is the primary thing you get paid to do here every day?" In more than half the cases, the answer was, "I get paid to protect the assets of the company." For two good reasons, that answer was a serious problem. In the first place, it is not an answer people would give you if you woke them out of a sound sleep at 2:30 in the morning. Someone had taught them that line. In the second place, it is the *wrong* answer. Sears is a retailer, not Fort Knox. The sort of answer we needed to hear was, "I get paid to satisfy the customer." And it needed to come from the heart.

Misunderstanding is also a barrier to trust. The same executive asked people a second question: "How much profit do you suppose Sears keeps on every dollar of revenue that goes through the register?" The median response was 45 cents. The real answer was 2 cents. How could we expect people to react well to a variety of necessary changes if they thought the company was rolling in wealth? We decided to address both misconceptions with a program we called "town hall meetings," which included learning maps, dialogue, and action plans.

Learning maps were not original with Sears—they were developed by a company called Root Learning of Perrysburg, Ohio—but combining them with town hall meetings was our own idea. The combination seemed ideally suited to our needs. Learning maps are easy to use and require no prior training or special skills, yet they draw people into the content, make substantial demands on their analytical reasoning, raise their economic literacy, and increase their understanding of how the company works. Town hall meetings expand that learning and convert it into action.

A learning map is a large picture of a town or a store or, in one instance, a river that leads small groups of participants through a business or historical process.

Every Sears employee from top management on down goes through the learning maps with a group of eight to ten colleagues. Then the group joins other groups for a town hall meeting and action-planning session, which the unit manager opens by saying, more or less, "In light of what you've learned and heard in studying the learning maps, what is one thing we could start doing in this store (service center, warehouse, or office) tomorrow to improve our competitive position? Or what could we stop doing? Or what could we simplify?" The only eligible suggestions are ones that can be implemented at the local level, which automatically excludes anything that company headquarters would have to approve. The goal is to reject as few ideas as possible and to act on the others at once, partly because so many of them are surprisingly good and partly because seeing the company take action on your own suggestion is a very positive experience.

We launched the town-hall-meeting process with the Phoenix Team, which now included 60 district managers, in April 1995. Later, the district managers held town hall meetings for their store managers, who then took charge of cascading the process down to the in-store associates. Every map is rolled out at a town hall meeting in the same manner—from the top of the company on down. The second map, "Voices of Our Customers," came along toward the end of 1995 and dealt with the way consumers see Sears and its principal competitors. Our third map, "The Sears Money Flow," appeared in early 1996 and gave employees a look at where revenues actually go and why it is that even today only about 3 cents of every dollar flows all the way through company operations to emerge on the other side as profit. Quite recently, we rolled out a new map called "Ownership," which leads people through the TPI and helps them see how measurement can enable them to do better and more rewarding work.

Town hall meetings are designed to be part of an ongoing engagement process with employees that goes well beyond learning maps. The goal of learning maps is economic and business literacy—but business literacy in the service of the larger goal of behavioral change. We want managers to change their behavior toward employees, to communicate the company's goals and vision more effectively, and to learn to make better customer-oriented decisions, because we cannot do well financially unless we do well in the eyes of the customer. We want frontline employees to change their behavior toward customers—to become more responsive, take more initiative, and provide better service. (To help them do so, we also give them greater decision-making authority. At Sears hardware stores, for example, sales associates can make refunds and adjustments of up to $25 in value without approval from their supervisors.) The learning maps were only a first step. Full-scale, meaningful, operational deployment of the employee-customer-profit model and the TPI involved three additional initiatives: a concerted effort to alter leadership behavior, changes in our reward and compensation systems, and a new initiative to bring the benefits of the TPI to departments and individual sales associates.

CHANGING LEADERSHIP BEHAVIOR

For managers in particular, a grasp of the TPI is indispensable because the TPI is so fundamental to corporate performance—and therefore to management—and therefore to the selection, promotion, and compensation of managers. We have talked a great deal about those 100 to 200 top-level managers because they are the people responsible for strategic implementation, operations, and resource allocation. But there is more to leadership than resource allocation, however strategic and insightful. We need leaders at every level of Sears who take responsibility not only for the company's business performance but also for the culture that keeps the new model alive and working.

In 1995, consequently, we set about creating a leadership model that would incorporate every aspect of the transformation: the employee-customer-profit chain, the TPI, the three C's, and the three P's—plus, of course, operational competence. Our first step in developing the model was to ask the team of 15 executives at the top of the

Exhibit 5-4   Leadership Skills

Every manager at Sears is hired, promoted, and appraised on the basis of these 12 criteria, grouped in relation to the three P's.

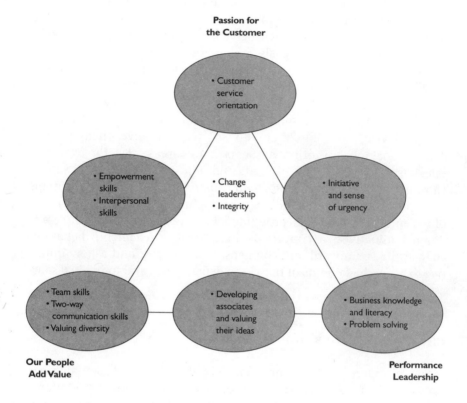

company to list the skills and qualities they looked for in appraising their own direct reports. We pared that list of 35 criteria down to 12, grouped around the three P's. (See Exhibit 5-4.) We announced that all of our 19,000 managers would get an annual performance appraisal by their boss and by small groups of their peers and subordinates. These 360-degree reviews, as they're called, rate managers on the 12 criteria. We use the 12 leadership skills as the basis for promotion, we use them in hiring future managers from college campuses, and we use them in training.

On January 1, 1995, we established Sears University, with a central campus in Chicago, seven regional centers around the country, a permanent staff of instructors, and a curriculum of course offerings in every subject we consider essential to the operation of the TPI and the employee-customer-profit model. All courses are also linked to one or more of the 12 leadership skills, which enables managers to identify the programs that will help them meet a specific development need.

Since opening our university, we have trained more than 40,000 Sears managers. We also operate a strategic-retail-management program, which 250 senior executives have attended in groups of about 30 at a time. The program was explicitly designed to create constructive discontent by requiring executives to do case studies of other retailers that have achieved world-class status on some critical dimension of retailing.

ALTERING REWARDS AND COMPENSATION

For the 200 managers at the top of the company, Sears took a truly revolutionary step in 1996 by basing all long-term incentives on the TPI. This means that for the first time in any corporation, as far as we know, long-term executive incentives are based on nonfinancial as well as financial performance—one-third on employee measures, one-third on customer measures, and one-third on traditional investor measures. The board of directors took a leap of faith in agreeing to this plan, which rests on the reliability of the TPI as a leading indicator.

Recognition of the importance of nonfinancial measures has made its way into the annual incentives of nearly all field managers as well. A significant portion of these managers' pay is at risk, based on targeted improvements in customer satisfaction. Moreover, in goal-sharing pilot programs at more than 45 locations, hourly associates are being given the opportunity to earn variable incentive pay that is almost always based on improved customer satisfaction.

CASCADING THE TPI

Ultimately, if the TPI methodology is to be fully effective, we must make it available at the local unit level. One current step in that direction is a new touch-tone telephone survey that we have now put in place. A random selection of customers receive a coupon worth $5 toward their next purchase if they will call an 800 number and answer

24 questions about their shopping experience. Some of the questions are tied to the performance of the company, store, and department; some relate to the behavior of the sales associate; and all are statistically significant with regard to customer satisfaction and retention. The data are aggregated nationwide, but we are beginning to make them available by district, store, department, and, soon, by individual sales associate as well. (The associate's employee number is on the transaction ticket, and the customer punches it in before punching in answers to the questions.) Our goal is to make it possible for managers and their sales associates to have constructive discussions about individual strengths and weaknesses *as seen by the customer*, and we are currently evaluating various approaches to the use of such information so that we can encourage and empower employees at the same time that we give them insight into how they are perceived.

From Employees to Customers to Profits

In one limited sense, the deployment of the Sears model and measures is virtually complete. We use the TPI at every level of the company, in every store and facility; and nearly every manager has some portion of his or her compensation at risk on the basis of nonfinancial measures. In a broader sense, of course, we still have a long way to go.

Deployment, for example, is an unending effort. Normal turnover rates in the retail industry require continual reorientation of new employees in both the three C's and the economic literacy maps. Even without turnover, communicating with 300,000 employees at thousands of locations is a challenge.

We have been working at this transformation for less than four years, and it seems to us that our track record so far is remarkable. But how much change can a company the size of Sears absorb in so short a time? And does the system work? Are we changing our employees' and our customers' perceptions of Sears?

To answer that question, let's look at some statistics. Independent surveys show that national retail customer satisfaction has fallen for several consecutive years, but in the course of the last 12 months, employee satisfaction on the Sears TPI has risen by 4%, and customer satisfaction by almost 4%. That may seem a trivial improvement. But if our model is correct—and its predictive record is extremely good—that 4% improvement in customer satisfaction translates into more than $200 million in additional revenues in the past 12 months.

At our current after-tax margin and price-earnings ratio, those extra revenues increase our market capitalization by nearly one-quarter of a billion dollars. Even more impressive from our point of view is what our model tells us: it is our managers and employees who, at the moment of truth in front of the customer, have achieved this prodigious feat of value creation.

PART

IV

Creating Intellectual Capital: Become an Employee Champion

1
Managing Professional Intellect: Making the Most of the Best

James Brian Quinn, Philip Anderson, and Sydney Finkelstein

In the postindustrial era, the success of a corporation lies more in its intellectual and systems capabilities than in its physical assets. The capacity to manage human intellect—and to convert it into useful products and services—is fast becoming the critical executive skill of the age. As a result, there has been a flurry of interest in intellectual capital, creativity, innovation, and the learning organization, but surprisingly little attention has been given to managing professional intellect.

This oversight is especially surprising because professional intellect creates most of the value in the new economy. Its benefits are immediately visible in the large service industries, such as software, health care, financial services, communications, and consulting. But in manufacturing industries as well, professionals generate the preponderance of value—through activities like research and development, process design, product design, logistics, marketing, or systems management. Despite the growing importance of professional intellect, few managers have systematic answers to even these basic questions: What is professional intellect? How can we develop it? How can we leverage it?

What Is Professional Intellect?

The true professional commands a body of knowledge—a discipline that must be updated constantly. The professional intellect of an organization operates on four levels, presented here in order of increasing importance:

Cognitive knowledge (or know-what) is the basic mastery of a discipline that professionals achieve through extensive training and certification. This knowledge is essential, but usually far from sufficient, for commercial success.

Advanced skills (know-how) translate "book learning" into effective execution. The ability to apply the rules of a discipline to complex real-world problems is the most widespread value-creating professional skill level.

Systems understanding (know-why) is deep knowledge of the web of cause-and-effect relationships underlying a discipline. It permits professionals to move beyond the execution of tasks to solve larger and more complex problems—and to create extraordinary value. Professionals with know-why can anticipate subtle interactions and unintended consequences. The ultimate expression of systems understanding is highly trained intuition—for example, the insight of a seasoned research director who knows instinctively which projects to fund and exactly when to do so.

Self-motivated creativity (care-why) consists of will, motivation, and adaptability for success. Highly motivated and creative groups often outperform groups with greater physical or financial resources. Without self-motivated creativity, intellectual leaders can lose their knowledge advantage through complacency. They may fail to adapt aggressively to changing external conditions and particularly to innovations that obsolesce their earlier skills—just as the techniques of molecular design are superseding chemical screening in pharmaceuticals today. That is why the highest level of intellect is now so vital. Organizations that nurture care-why in their people can simultaneously thrive in the face of today's rapid changes and renew their cognitive knowledge, advanced skills, and systems understanding in order to compete in the next wave of advances.

Intellect clearly resides in the brains of professionals. The first three levels can also exist in the organization's systems, databases, or operating technologies, whereas the fourth is often found in its culture. The value of intellect increases markedly as one moves up the intellectual scale from cognitive knowledge to self-motivated creativity. Yet most enterprises focus virtually all their training attention on developing basic (rather than advanced) skills and little or none on systems or creative skills.

Most of a typical professional's activity is directed at perfection, not creativity. Customers primarily want professional knowledge delivered reliably and with the most advanced skill available. Although there is an occasional call for creativity, most of the work done by accounting units, hospitals, software companies, or financial service providers requires the repeated use of highly developed skills on relatively similar, though complex, problems. People rarely want surgeons, accountants, pilots, maintenance personnel, or nuclear plant operators to be very creative. Managers clearly must prepare their professionals for the few emergencies or other special circumstances that require creativity, but they should focus the bulk of their attention on delivering consistent, high-quality intellectual output.

Because professionals have specialized knowledge and have been trained as an elite, they often tend to regard their judgment in other realms as sacrosanct as well. Professionals generally hesitate to subordinate themselves to others or to support organizational goals not completely congruous with their special viewpoint. That is why most professional firms operate as partnerships and not as hierarchies, and why it is difficult for them to adopt a unified strategy.

Members of every profession tend to look to their peers to determine codes of behavior and acceptable standards of performance. They often refuse to accept evaluations by those outside their discipline. Many doctors, for example, resist the attempts of HMOs and insurance companies to tell them how to practice medicine. Such a posture is the source of many professional organizations' problems. Professionals tend to surround themselves with people who have similar backgrounds and values. Unless deliberately fractured, these discipline-based cocoons quickly become inward-looking bureaucracies that are resistant to change and detached from customers. Consider the many software or basic research organizations that become isolated inside larger organizations, creating conflicts with other professional groups such as marketing or manufacturing departments.

Developing Professional Intellect

At the heart of the most effective professional organizations we have observed are a handful of best practices for managing intellect that resemble successful coaching more than anything else.

Recruit the best. The leverage of intellect is so great that a few topflight professionals can create a successful organization or make a lesser one flourish. Marvin Bower essentially created McKinsey &

Company; Robert Noyce and Gordon E. Moore spawned Intel; William H. Gates and Paul Allen built Microsoft; Herbert W. Boyer and Robert A. Swanson made Genentech; and Albert Einstein put Princeton's Institute for Advanced Study on the map. But even such organizations must find and attract extraordinary talent.

It is no accident that the leading management consultants devote enormous resources to recruiting and that they heavily screen the top graduates of the leading business schools. Microsoft interviews hundreds of highly recommended people for each key software designer it hires, and its grueling selection process tests not only cognitive knowledge but also the capacity to think about new problems under high pressure. The Four Seasons Hotels often interviews 50 candidates to make one hire. Venture capital firms, recognizing talent and commitment as the most critical elements for their success, spend as much time selecting and pursuing top people as they do making quantitative analyses of projects.

Because the most qualified professionals want to work with the best in their field, leading organizations can attract better talent than their lesser competitors. The best commercial programmers, for example, seek out and stay with Microsoft largely because they believe Microsoft will determine where the industry will move in the future and because they can share the excitement and rewards of being at that frontier. But second-tier organizations are not destined always to lag behind. Managers who understand the importance of the right kind of talent can pull a jujitsu reversal on industry leaders by acquiring such talent. When CEO Marshall N. Carter led State Street Bank's entry into the rapidly emerging custodials business, he hired world-class data processing managers to seed his new organization. Today State Street handles $1.7 trillion in custodial accounts, and virtually all its senior managers have data processing rather than traditional banking backgrounds.

Force intensive early development. Professional know-how is developed most rapidly through repeated exposure to the complexity of real problems. Thus for most professionals, the learning curve depends heavily on interactions with customers. Accordingly, the best companies systematically put new professionals in contact with customers, where they work under the watchful eye of an experienced coach. Microsoft, for example, assigns new software developers to small teams of three to seven people. Under the guidance of mentors, the developers participate in the design of complex new software systems at the frontier of users' needs.

The legendary 80-hour weeks and all-nighters that give investment bankers and software developers their bragging rights serve a more serious developmental purpose: They enable the best talent to move up a learning curve that is steeper than anyone else's. On-the-job training, mentoring, and peer pressure can force professionals to the top of their knowledge ziggurat. Although burnout can be a problem if people are pushed too far, many studies show that intensity and repetition are critical to developing advanced skills in fields as diverse as the law and piloting aircraft.

People who go through these intensive experiences become noticeably more capable and valuable—compared with their counterparts in less intensively managed organizations—within six months to a year. If they are properly coached, they also develop a greater in-depth feel for systems interactions (know-why) and identify more with the company and its goals (care-why). The most successful organizations ensure such growth through constantly heightened (preferably customer-driven) complexity, thoroughly planned mentoring, substantial rewards for performance, and strong incentives to understand, systematize, and advance the discipline. The great intellectual organizations all seem to develop deeply ingrained cultures that emphasize these values. Most others do not.

Constantly increase professional challenges. Intellect grows most when professionals buy into a serious challenge. Leaders of the best organizations tend to be demanding, visionary, and intolerant of halfhearted efforts. They often set almost impossible "stretch goals"— as did Hewlett-Packard's William R. Hewlett (improve performance by 50%), Intel's Gordon Moore (double the number of components per chip each year), and Motorola's Robert W. Galvin (achieve six sigma quality). Some professionals may drop out in response to such demands. Others will substitute their own even higher standards. The best organizations constantly push their professionals beyond the comfort of their book knowledge, simulation models, and controlled laboratories. They relentlessly drive associates to deal with the more complex intellectual realms of live customers, real operating systems, and highly differentiated external environments and cultural differences. Mediocre organizations do not.

Evaluate and weed. Professionals like to be evaluated, to compete, to know they have excelled against their peers. But they want to be evaluated objectively and by people at the top of their field. Hence, heavy internal competition and frequent performance appraisal and feedback are common in outstanding organizations. As a result, there is a progressive winnowing of talent. For example, at Andersen Consulting, only 10% of the carefully selected professional recruits move on to partnerships—a process that takes 9 to 12 years. Microsoft tries to force out the lowest-performing 5% of its highly screened talent each year. Great organizations are unabashed meritocracies; great organizations that fail are often those that forget the importance of objective praise and selective weeding.

Leveraging Professional Intellect

Conventional wisdom has long held that there are few opportunities for leverage in professional activities. A pilot can handle only one aircraft at a time; a chef can cook only so many different dishes at once; a researcher can conduct only so many unique experiments; a doctor can diagnose only one patient's illness at a time. In such situations, adding professionals at the very least multiplies costs at the same rate as benefits. In the past, growth most often brought diseconomies of scale as the bureaucracies coordinating, monitoring, or supporting the professionals expanded faster than the professional base. Universities, hospitals, research firms, accounting groups, and consultancies all seemed to pay the price.

For years, there were only two ways in which many organizations could create leverage: by pushing their people through more intensive training or work schedules than their competitors or by increasing the number of "associates" supporting each professional. The latter practice even became the accepted meaning of the term *leverage* in the fields of law, accounting, and consulting.

But new technologies and management approaches are changing the traditional economics of managing professional intellect. Organizations as diverse as Merrill Lynch, Andersen Worldwide, and NovaCare have found effective ways to link new software tools, incentive systems, and organizational designs in order to leverage professional intellect to much higher levels. Although each organization has developed solutions tailored to the specific needs of its business, there are a handful of common underlying principles.

Boost professionals' problem-solving abilities by capturing knowledge in systems and software. The core intellectual competence of many financial organizations—such as Merrill Lynch and State Street Bank—lies in the human experts and the systems software that collect and analyze the data that are relevant to investment decisions. A few financial specialists working at headquarters leverage their own high-level analytical skills through close interactions with other specialists and "rocket scientist" modelers, and through access to massive amounts of data about transactions. Proprietary software models and databases leverage the intellect of those professionals, allowing them to analyze markets, securities, and economic trends in ways that otherwise would be beyond their reach. Software systems then distribute the resulting investment recommendations to brokers at retail outlets who create further value by customizing the center's advice in order to meet the needs of individual clients. If one thinks about this organization as a center connected to customers at multiple points of contact, or nodes, leverage equals the value of the knowledge multiplied by the number of nodes using it. Value creation is enhanced if experimentation at the center increases know-why and incentive structures stimulate care-why.

Merrill Lynch's retail brokerage business follows the basic structure outlined above. Roughly 18,000 Merrill Lynch brokers operate out of more than 500 geographically dispersed offices to create custom investment solutions for clients. The typical retail broker is not a highly skilled financial professional with years of advanced training. Yet the firm's brokers serve millions of clients worldwide with sophisticated investment advice and detailed, up-to-date information on thousands of complex financial instruments. Information systems make this extraordinary leverage possible.

Electronic systems capture Merrill Lynch's aggregate experience curve, quickly enabling less-trained people to achieve performance levels ordinarily associated with much more experienced personnel. The firm's computer network ensures that the retail brokers' cognitive knowledge is current and accurate. Merrill Lynch's information technologies allow the center to capture and distribute to the brokerage offices information about transactions, trading rules, yields, securities features, availability, tax considerations, and new offerings. Proprietary software, available on-line, serves as an instant training vehicle. It ensures that all brokers adhere to current regulations, make no arithmetic or clerical errors, and can provide customers with the latest market information. Capturing and distributing the firm's knowledge base through software allows Merrill Lynch to leverage the professional intellect at its core.

Information technology allows a large modern brokerage to be both efficient and flexible. At the center, it can achieve the full information power and economies of scale available only to a major enterprise. Yet local brokers can manage their own small units and accounts as independently as if they alone provided the service on a local basis. Their reward system is that of local entrepreneurs. The center functions primarily as an information source, a communications coordinator, or a reference desk for unusual inquiries. Field personnel connect with the center to obtain information to improve their performance, rather than to ask for instructions or specific guidance. At the same time, the center can electronically monitor local operations for quality and consistency. Most operating rules are programmed into the system and changed automatically by software. Electronic systems replace human command-and-control procedures. They also can eliminate most of the routine in jobs, free up employees for more personalized or skilled work, and allow tasks to be more decentralized, challenging, and rewarding.

Overcome professionals' reluctance to share information. Information sharing is critical because intellectual assets, unlike physical assets, increase in value with use. Properly stimulated, knowledge and intellect grow exponentially when shared. All learning and experience curves have this characteristic. A basic tenet of communication theory states that a network's potential benefits grow exponentially as the nodes it can successfully interconnect expand numerically. It is not difficult to see how this growth occurs. If two people exchange knowledge with each other, both gain information and experience linear growth. But if both then share their new knowledge with others— each of whom feeds back questions, amplifications, and modifications —the benefits become exponential. Companies that learn from outsiders—especially from customers, suppliers, and specialists such as advanced design or software firms—can reap even greater benefits. The strategic consequences of exploiting this exponential growth are profound. Once a company gains a knowledge-based competitive edge, it becomes ever easier for it to maintain its lead and ever harder for its competitors to catch up.

Overcoming professionals' natural reluctance to share their most precious asset, knowledge, presents some common and difficult challenges. Competition among professionals often inhibits sharing, and assigning credit for intellectual contributions is difficult. When professionals are asked to collaborate as equals in problem solving, slow response is common as specialists try to refine their particular solutions to perfection. Because professionals' knowledge is their power base, strong inducements to share are necessary.

Even then, the tendency of each profession to regard itself as an elite with special cultural values may get in the way of cross-disciplinary sharing. Many professionals have little respect for those outside their field, even when all parties are supposedly seeking the same goal. Often, in manufacturing companies, researchers disdain product designers, who disdain engineers. In health care, basic researchers disdain physicians (because "they don't understand causation"). Physicians disdain both researchers (who "don't understand practical variations among real patients") and nurses (who "don't understand the discipline"). Nurses disdain both doctors and researchers (who "lack true compassion"). And all three groups disdain administrators (who are "nonproductive bureaucrats").

To facilitate sharing, Andersen Worldwide has developed an electronic system linking its 82,000 people operating in 360 offices in 76 countries. Known as ANet, the T1 and frame-relay network connects more than 85% of Andersen's professionals through data, voice, and video interlinks. ANet allows Andersen specialists—by posting problems on electronic bulletin boards and following up with visual and data contacts—to self-organize instantly around a customer's problem anywhere in the world. ANet thus taps into otherwise dormant capabilities and expands the energies and solution sets available to customers. Problem-solving capacity is further enhanced through centrally collected and carefully indexed subject, customer-reference, and resource files accessible directly through ANet or from CD-ROMs distributed to all offices.

Initially, Andersen spent large sums on hardware, travel, and professional training to encourage people not only to follow up on network exchanges but also to meet personally to discuss important problems—with disappointing results. Major changes in incentives and culture were needed to make the system work. Most important, participation in ANet began to be considered in all promotion and compensation reviews. To stimulate a cultural shift toward wider use of ANet, senior partners deliberately posed questions on employees' E-mail files each morning "to be answered by 10." Until those cultural changes were in place, ANet was less than successful despite its technological elegance.

Organize around intellect. In the past, most companies aimed to enhance returns from investments in physical assets: property, plant, and equipment. Command-and-control structures made sense when management's primary task was to leverage such physical assets. For example, the productivity of a manufacturing facility is determined largely by senior managers' decisions about capital equipment, adherence to standardized practices, the breadth of the product line, and capacity utilization. With intellectual assets, on the other hand, individual professionals typically provide customized solutions to an endless stream of new problems.

Inverting Organizations

Many successful enterprises we have studied have abandoned hierarchical structures, organizing themselves in patterns specifically tailored to the particular way their professional intellect creates value. Such reorganization often involves breaking away from traditional thinking about the role of the center as a directing force.

Consider NovaCare, the largest provider of rehabilitation care and one of the fastest-growing health-care companies in the United States. Its critical professional intellect resides in its more than 5,000 occupational, speech, and physical therapists. As professionals, they work alone to customize their expertise for individual patients at 2,090 locations in 40 states. To be of greatest value, they must be highly trained and constantly updated on the best practices in their fields.

By organizing around the work of its therapists, NovaCare achieves considerable leverage. To focus their time on serving patients' needs, the organization frees the therapists from administrative and business responsibilities by, for example, arranging and managing their contracts with care facilities, scheduling and reporting on treatments they give, handling their accounting and credit activities, providing them with training updates, and increasing their earnings through the company's marketing capabilities.

NovaCare's software system, NovaNet, captures and enhances much of the organization's systems knowledge, such as the rules with which therapists must comply and the information they need about customers, schedules, and billing; it highlights for executives those trends or problem areas most pertinent to future operations. NovaNet collects information from all therapists about, for example, their costs and services, techniques that have worked well, and changing care patterns in different regions. This information is vital for recruiting, training, motivating, and updating therapists.

To facilitate the collection and analysis of knowledge, NovaCare records its therapeutic care activities in ten-minute blocks. This detailed information creates a database that can be used by a diverse group of stakeholders: caregivers, hospitals, clinics, payers, government agencies, executives, and outside financial and regulatory bodies. NovaCare utilizes extensive peer and customer reviews in evaluating its therapists' work and (based on the time units captured in NovaNet) rewards them on the amount and quality of the care they deliver.

NovaCare's professionals are highly self-sufficient; they have tremendous autonomy on questions involving patient care. Therapists can give orders to all intermediate line organizations. The company's regional and functional specialists in accounting, marketing, purchasing, and logistics exist primarily to support the therapists. Even CEO John H. Foster refers to the therapists as "my bosses." The leverage of NovaCare's organizational structure is "distributive"—that is, the support organization efficiently distributes logistics, analysis, and administrative support to the professionals. But it does not give them orders.

NovaCare has thus inverted the traditional organization. The former line hierarchy becomes a support structure, intervening only in extreme emergencies—as might the CEO of a hospital or the chief pilot of an airline. The function of former line managers changes: Instead of giving orders, they are now removing barriers, expediting resources, conducting studies, and acting as consultants. They support and help articulate the new culture. In effect, line managers evolve into staff people. (See Exhibit 1-1.)

Inverted organizations like NovaCare make sense when individual experts embody most of the organization's knowledge, when they do not have to interact with one another to solve problems, and when they customize their knowledge at the point of contact with customers. The software behind inverted systems must serve two somewhat conflicting goals: rules enforcement and professional empowerment. First, because professionals often resist regimentation, the software forces NovaCare's therapists to provide information in a consistent format, to comply with corporate rules and external regulations, and to originate the information necessary to monitor quality, costs, and trends for the organization's overall operation. Second, the software captures and distributes to professionals all the knowledge the company has built up over time so they can do their jobs better or more efficiently. That knowledge includes information about customers, professional databases, analytical models, successful solutions to problems, and access to specialized sources of knowledge.

Inverted organizations pose some unique managerial challenges. The apparent loss of formal authority can be traumatic for former line managers. And field people who are granted formal power may tend to act more and more like specialists with strictly "professional" out-

Exhibit 1-1   In Inverted Organizations, Field Experts Become Bosses

The center provides support services that leverage the professionals in the field. Inverted organizations are appropriate when individual professionals have enough expertise to be self-sufficient and can act independently to meet specific customer needs. Many health-care providers, technical troubleshooting units, and universities are inverted organizations.

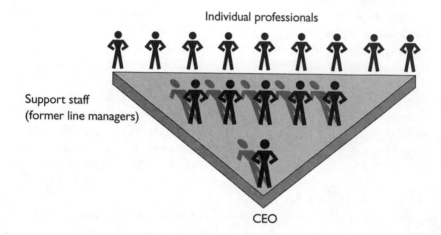

Individual professionals

Support staff
(former line managers)

CEO

looks and to resist any set of organizational rules or business norms. Given those tendencies and without a disciplining software, field people often don't stay current with details about their organization's own complex internal systems. And their empowerment without adequate information and controls embedded in the company's technology systems can be dangerous. A classic example is the rapid decline of People Express, which consciously inverted its organization and enjoyed highly empowered and motivated point people but lacked the systems or the computer infrastructures to enable them to adapt as the organization grew.

If such organizations fail, it is usually because—despite much rhetoric about inversion—their senior managers did not support the concept with thoroughly overhauled performance-measurement and reward systems. Inverted systems rarely work until field people largely determine their "support people's" wages, promotions, and organizational progress. Former line people are reluctant to take this last crucial step. In our studies of more than 100 major structural changes in

60 large service organizations, less than 20% of the organizations had changed their performance-measurement systems significantly, and only about 5% had changed their reward systems (*Information Technology in the Service Society*, National Academy Press, 1993). Without such changes, the complications were predictable: People continued to perform according to the traditional measures.

Creating Intellectual Webs

In NovaCare's business, the professional therapists who create value are largely self-sufficient individual contributors. The inverted organization, coupled with the right software and incentives, allows NovaCare to enhance its therapists' productivity while giving them the operating autonomy they need. In other businesses, professional intellect is called on to create value by solving problems that exceed the capabilities of any solo practitioner. When problems become much more complex or less well defined, no one person or organization may know exactly what their full dimensions are, where key issues will ultimately reside, or who may have potential new solutions.

To tackle such problems—and to leverage their own intellectual assets to the maximum—a number of companies are using a form of self-organizing network that we call a *spider's web*. We use this term to avoid confusion with other, more traditional networklike forms more akin to holding companies or matrix organizations. Typically, a spider's web brings people together quickly to solve a particular problem and then disbands just as quickly once the job is done. The power of such interconnections is so great that even with a modest number of collaborating independent professionals (8 to 10), a spider's web can leverage knowledge capabilities by hundreds of times. (See Exhibit 1-2.)

Consider Merrill Lynch's mergers and acquisitions group. At the firm's center, specialists work primarily with others in their own disciplines—for example, acquisitions, high-yield financings, or equity markets. But when a large financing opportunity emerges, the project becomes an intellectual focal point and a team of specialists from different locations forms to pursue each individual deal. Such projects are so complex that, as one executive says, "no one can be a know-everything banker. You can't have only specialists doing their own thing, and the client is not interested in dealing with multiple specialists." The key problem is focusing Merrill Lynch's rich but dispersed talents on a single customer's problem for a short time. Client-

*Exhibit 1-2   In Spider's Webs, a Few Experts Team Up to
Meet a Specific Challenge*

*Spider's webs form to accomplish a particular project and disband when the project
is completed. They are appropriate when knowledge is dispersed among many specialists, who must provide a coordinated solution to a complex customer problem.
Many consulting firms, investment banks, research consortia, and medical diagnostic
teams make use of spider's webs.*

Client-relationship   Specialists
managers

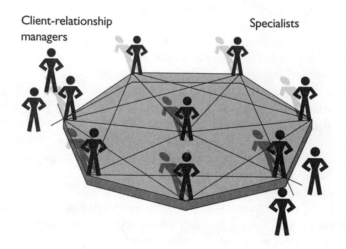

relationship managers, who best understand the customer's integrated
needs, usually coordinate these teams, but they don't have direct, hierarchical control over team members.

Despite the current popularity of virtual organizations and of networks, few companies understand when and how to use networked
forms to leverage professional intellect. As the Merrill Lynch example shows, networks can flexibly combine high specialization in many
different disciplines with multiple geographic contact points and a
sharp focus on a single problem or customer set. But without the
firm's specifically tailored promotion and compensation evaluation
processes, the system probably would not work.

At Merrill Lynch, individuals work with many different colleagues
on a variety of projects over the course of a year. All of them submit a
confidential evaluation on everyone with whom they have worked
closely. People are willing to share knowledge and cooperate because
their compensation is attached to this mosaic of peer relationships,

and compensation is a major motivating factor in this business. There are enough close personal team contacts to allow a truly multifaceted picture of an individual's performance. According to one vice president of the mergers and acquisitions group, "In addition to profits generated, people are evaluated on how well they throw themselves into various projects, work with different groups to meet priorities, and meet clients' needs. The culture penalizes those who fail to be team players or to meet clients' needs. Under these rules, spider's webs have worked well in our relationship world. In our transactional world, however, we generally win by having the best specialists for that transaction."

Because each spider's web is unique in its purpose, patterns, and organizational power relationships, there is no single "best way" to manage all of them. For many projects, there may not be a single authority center. Often if the goal, problem, or solution is sufficiently clear, decisions may occur through informal processes if the parties agree. When the various centers of excellence need to operate in a highly coordinated fashion, they may delegate temporary authority to a project leader—as when widely dispersed researchers present a contract proposal. In other cases, the organization may designate one person as the lead in order to force decisions or to make final commitments—as when an insurance or investment banking consortium faces a deadline.

How groups communicate and what they voluntarily communicate are as important as the advanced knowledge each center of excellence may have. For virtually all purposes, however, encouraging shared interests, common values, and mutually satisfying solutions is essential for leveraging knowledge in these structures. Research suggests that to accomplish this goal, network managers should force members to overlap on different teams in order to increase continuity of contact, joint learning, and informal information sharing; purposely keep hierarchical relations ill defined; constantly update and reinforce project goals; avoid overly elaborate rules for allocating profits to individual nodes; develop continuous mechanisms for updating information about the external environment (for example, tax code changes, customer needs, or scientific results); involve both clients and peers in performance evaluations; and provide node members with both individual and team rewards for participation. Such consciously structured management interactions can mitigate the most common failures and frustrations.

The other key leverage factor in most spider's webs is technology.

Electronics allow many more highly diverse, geographically dispersed, intellectually specialized talents to be brought to bear on a single project than ever before. Because public telecommunications networks allow interconnection almost anywhere, the key to effective network systems generally lies in software that provides a common language and database for communications, captures critical factual data about external environments, helps players find knowledge sources (usually through electronic menus, Web browsers like Netscape, or bulletin boards), and allows interactive sharing and problem solving. Each node will of course have its own specialized analytical software. But networking, groupware, and interactive software—along with a culture of and incentives for sharing—are the keys to success in these systems.

Much can be done to leverage professional intellect through extraordinary recruitment, training, and motivational measures. But, increasingly, managing human intellect alone is not enough. More radical organizational structures, supported by specifically designed software systems, are essential to capture, focus, and leverage capabilities to the fullest. Such systems have become the glue that both joins together highly dispersed service-delivery centers and leverages the critical knowledge bases, intellectual skills, and accumulated experience in professional organizations. They also bond professionals to the organization by providing them with databases, analytical models, and communication power that they cannot find elsewhere. These tools enable professionals to extend their performance beyond their personal limits, allowing them to achieve more inside the organization than they could on their own.

No organizational form is a panacea. In fact, many different forms often coexist successfully in the same company. Properly used, each helps a company attract, harness, leverage, and deploy intellect for a quite different purpose. Consequently, each requires a carefully developed set of cultural norms supported by software and by performance-measurement and reward systems tailored to the organization's specific purposes.

2
Toward a Career-Resilient Workforce

Robert H. Waterman Jr., Judith A. Waterman,
and Betsy A. Collard

People mourn its passing: the longtime covenant between employee and employer. We remember fondly the days when IBM could offer lifetime employment. And even if we didn't work for the likes of IBM, most of us understood that respectable companies would offer at least a measure of job security in exchange for adequate performance and some exhibition of loyalty. No longer. While a few prominent companies argue that the old covenant still exists, most people—and most companies—now hardened by downsizings, delayerings, right-sizings, layoffs, and restructurings, have concluded that the old covenant is null.

But what will take its place? Some management thinkers are arguing that instead of the traditional focus on *employment*, the focus should now be on *employability*. In other words, we should forget about clinging desperately to one job, one company, or one career path. What matters now is having the competitive skills required to find work when we need it, wherever we can find it.

Is that it? A workforce of loners roaming corporate halls, factories, and E-mail systems? What responsibility, if any, does a company now have to employees? Ought management be concerned only about staying lean to keep up with competition and not about acting mean? Should management be satisfied with employees whose only loyalty is to their own careers? How can an enterprise build capabilities, forge empowered teams, develop a deep understanding of its customers, and—most important—create a sense of community or common purpose unless it has a relationship with its employees based on mutual trust and caring? And how can an enterprise build such a relationship unless it commits something to employees and employees commit something to it?

The answer is by entering into a new covenant under which the employer and the employee share responsibility for maintaining— even enhancing—the individual's employability inside *and outside* the company. Under the old covenant, employees entrusted major decisions affecting their careers to a parental organization. Often, the result was a dependent employee and a relatively static workforce with a set of static skills. Under the new covenant, employers give individuals the opportunity to develop greatly enhanced employability in exchange for better productivity and some degree of commitment to company purpose and community for as long as the employee works there. It is the employee's responsibility to manage his or her own career. It is the company's responsibility to provide employees with the tools, the open environment, and the opportunities for assessing and developing their skills. And it is the responsibility of managers at all levels to show that they care about their employees whether or not they stay with the company. The result is a group of self-reliant workers—or a *career-resilient workforce*—and a company that can thrive in an era in which the skills needed to remain competitive are changing at a dizzying pace.

By a career-resilient workforce, we mean a group of employees who not only are dedicated to the idea of continuous learning but also stand ready to reinvent themselves to keep pace with change; who take responsibility for their own career management; and, last but not least, who are committed to the company's success. For each individual, this means staying knowledgeable about market trends and understanding the skills and behaviors the company will need down the road. It means being aware of one's own skills—of one's strengths and weaknesses—and having a plan for enhancing one's performance and long-term employability. It means having the willingness and ability to respond quickly and flexibly to changing business needs. And it means moving on when a win-win relationship is no longer possible.

A workforce that is constantly benchmarking and updating its skills is one that not only responds to change but anticipates it. Competitiveness—keeping close to customers, staying on top of technology and market trends, and striving to be ever more flexible—becomes everyone's responsibility, not that of just a handful of executives. All employees become involved in shaping the company's strategy, in shifting the company's collective eyes from navels to market forces. By looking out for themselves, employees look out for the company.

Sound far-fetched? Some companies are already moving in this direction. Not surprisingly, many of them are located in Silicon Valley, where the struggle to cope with the ever-faster pace of change has long been a way of life. These pioneers include Apple Computer; Sun Microsystems, the workstation manufacturer; Raychem Corporation, a manufacturer of specialized industrial products; and 3Com Corporation, a maker of computer-networking products. These companies are in various stages of implementing programs to create a career-resilient workforce. While their approaches may differ, they share a common aim: to give employees the power to assess, hone, redirect, and expand their skills so that they stay competitive in the job market. In return, they expect employees to make a bigger contribution to the company. "Companies must shift from using and then harvesting employees to constantly renewing employees," says Robert J. Saldich, president and CEO of Raychem and an ardent proponent of the new covenant.

This approach requires a sea change in attitudes and values. First, the traditional definition of loyalty must go. Companies can no longer take the view that talented employees who jump ship are betraying them. Nor can individuals take the view that they've been betrayed when a company no longer needs their skills. On the other hand, employees must feel like valued, trusted, and respected members of the corporate community while they are a part of it.

Second, the usual view of a career path must change. In the old days, it pretty much meant sticking with one company and rising in one specialty area. These days, both companies and employees are healthier if employees have multiple skills, if they can move easily across functional boundaries, if they are comfortable switching back and forth between regular duties and special projects, and if they feel comfortable moving on when the right fit within one company can no longer be found.

Third, all employees—not just bosses—must be much more aware that the purpose of the organization is to provide goods and services that customers value, and that if the organization does not do that, nobody in it will have a job. The corollary is that the organization has room only for people who contribute to creating such goods and services.

Fourth, a new relationship must be established between the organization and its employees. The traditional parent-child relationship must give way to an adult-adult relationship, and this applies to the organization's way of dealing with all employees, not just those on the fast track. Assignments that provide an opportunity to grow and to acquire new skills should be available to everyone.

Over the long run, companies have a lot to gain from encouraging career resilience. But there is also an immediate reason to adopt this approach: employees are beginning to demand it, say corporate leaders. People are angry these days when they find that they lack the skills needed to get another job. People are angry when their employers break the old covenant and offer nothing to take its place.

Awareness of that anger, plus an obsession with creating a "nimble organization" and a fervent belief in treating employees as respect-worthy adults, prompted Sun to establish its career-resilience program in 1991. Like many Silicon Valley companies, Sun was in the midst of rethinking its businesses, reorganizing its manufacturing operations, and reexamining the makeup of its workforce. The result was little change in the overall number of employees but a big change in the composition of the workforce. While Sun added hundreds of sales representatives, it "redeployed" hundreds of manufacturing employees. That meant that their jobs were being phased out and they had to find other jobs in the company, if they could, or accept a severance package, which was what most had to do.

"We became convinced that we had a responsibility to put employees back in control of their lives," says Marianne F. Jackson, who was a human resources director at Sun when she came up with the idea for the career-resilience program. Jackson, who is now at another high-tech company, believes that organizations that replace the old covenant with one based on career resilience will have a dramatic edge. We do too. They will have an edge in attracting and retaining the best people. And they will have an edge in the struggle to develop the capabilities needed to compete tomorrow.

Today the handful of pioneering companies with career-resilience programs are still feeling their way forward, learning what works and what doesn't. But from the progress they've made so far, we can discern some basic ingredients all programs should include and some pitfalls to avoid.

The Basics of Career Resilience

One ingredient of a successful program is a system that helps employees regularly assess their skills, interests, values, and temperaments so that they can figure out the type of job for which they are best suited. Another is a system that enables employees to benchmark their skills on a regular basis. These systems help employees understand both themselves and the work to be done so well that, ideally, they routinely find their way into the right jobs and routinely update their skills. These systems help prod, awaken, and galvanize so that square pegs and round pegs find their way into the right holes. Imagine how productivity would soar if most people had jobs that turned them on!

By self-assessment, we mean a systematic process of taking stock of those attributes that influence one's effectiveness, success, and happiness. Unless individuals understand the environments that let them shine, the interests that ignite them, and the skills that help them excel, how can they choose a company or job where they can make their greatest contribution? Unless they understand how their personal style affects others, how can they function with maximum effectiveness? Knowing yourself is the first step toward becoming career resilient.

Take Frank Aragona of Raychem. Aragona was a high-level nonexempt employee in the customer-service department of a plant that manufactures heating cables. After eight years in the same functional area of the same plant, Aragona felt dead-ended. He had learned all he could and, he thought, risen as high as he could with Raychem. His choices seemed to be to leave or to stagnate.

Then Aragona began attending some lunchtime seminars at the company's new career center. Using the center's library and working with a career counselor on self-assessment, he confirmed a long-felt need for something new and different. He also realized something else: some of his career interests—for example, becoming a historian—were just plain unrealistic for him. "[The center] gave me a shot of reality and set things in perspective," he explains.

Armed with better knowledge of himself, Aragona became interested when a coworker told him of a position in the international-sales division. It would build on his skills in customer service but offer new challenges, and the international aspect appealed to the explorer in him. He interviewed for the job and got it. He also got a promotion and a raise. Both Aragona and Raychem came out winners.

Companies certainly can encourage employees to assess themselves and can help them by providing the necessary tools. For some, self-assessment can be as simple as digesting a career-development book like Richard Nelson Bolles's *What Color Is Your Parachute?* or articulating their strengths and the value they can bring to a job. But most people will profit from a more thorough process. This may include tests—or "assessment instruments," as career-development professionals call them—designed to reveal an individual's motivations and interests (for example, the Myers-Briggs Type Indicator® and the Strong Interest Inventory) and sessions with a counselor trained to interpret the results.

As we mentioned, the second step in the process of becoming career resilient is ensuring that one has competitive skills. Companies need to give employees the tools to benchmark their skills and experience with what the job market inside and outside the company is demanding.

We are not saying that a company should relinquish its right to judge what skills it needs in its workforce in order to be competitive, and what training that involves. What we are saying is that, *in addition,* all employees should have the right to demand the training and challenging work experiences they need to update their skills. They have a right to minimize the risk of winding up stuck in a dead-end or vulnerable job. In other words, employers and employees should be partners in the continuous process of benchmarking and updating skills.

The Company's Obligations

To enable employees to benchmark their skills, companies will have to be much more open with them than most have traditionally been. Management must maintain a continuing dialogue about the company's business direction and what is happening in its markets. How else can employees determine which skills the company will need down the road? How else can they decide whether they want to develop those skills—or prepare to leave? Managers have an obligation to give employees as much time as possible to prepare for the future. Sun's management has promised workers that when it comes to strategic decisions that affect jobs or careers (like outsourcing a function), "as soon as we've decided something, you'll know."

At 3Com, most departments hold weekly discussion sessions on the status of the business and its implications. Those sessions helped most of the 40 people in the MIS department who supported 3Com's computer network to make the transition smoothly when 3Com changed the network operating system in April from 3+Open to Netware and Lotus Notes. They had long known that such a change was in the offing, that it would require them to get new skills or leave, and that the company would give them the time and resources to obtain the new skills. "The large majority were excited about making the change and getting the new skills," says Debra Engel, a 3Com vice president whose responsibilities include MIS and human resources. "Only a few departed—those who didn't want to make the change or didn't feel they could."

A company must help people explore job opportunities, facilitate lifelong learning and job movement, and, if it comes to that, support no-fault exits. Raychem, for example, has created an insiders' network of more than 360 people throughout the organization who are willing to take the time to talk with any employee who wants to learn about the nature of their work and the requirements of their jobs. Their names and backgrounds are in a computerized database called I.I.I.N.siders (for Internal Information Interview Network). Apple lets people sample jobs by filling in for those taking the sabbatical that is available to all employees.

Most of the companies we studied make information on job openings inside and outside the organization available to all employees. In addition, they provide reference materials and training to help employees develop plans for professional growth and hone their résumé-writing and interviewing skills. They also bring in experts to speak about market trends. Such support, which can be made available at a "career center" or through a computer network connecting the company's operations, is essential. It not only helps employees find new jobs inside or, if need be, outside the organization but also enables them to benchmark their skills.

Companies and individuals often fail to realize that benchmarking without self-assessment may cause an employee to make the wrong choices. The experiences of an electrical engineer at a progressive high-tech company that lacked a bona fide career-resilience program demonstrate why. Through benchmarking, the engineer learned that the road to modest riches lay in project management. He took that road and was successful. But at the end of his typical 12-hour day as a project leader, he was completely stressed out. At home all he wanted to do was to curl up in a corner and read. "When I got home, I just didn't want to be with people," he says, adding that this situation certainly didn't help his marriage, which ended in divorce.

The problem was this: By nature he was something of a perfectionist who enjoyed working alone. Constantly having to work with others was simply not a good fit. He finally realized this after working as a project leader for six years and decided to go back to straight engineering. But he'd been away from it for so long that he needed to go back to school to catch up. His company fully supported his move; it even paid the tuition. The engineer is now much happier, and, at least in this instance, a company was able to keep a valued employee.

Besides facilitating self-assessment and bench-marking, a company must make it easy for employees to learn and to become flexible. Workers should have the right to obtain ongoing training. Managers must be receptive to lateral transfers and even to employees' taking a step back to broaden their experience or to be happier and more productive. Indeed, an employee should have the right to switch jobs within the company, provided there is a need and he or she readily qualifies to fill it. An employee's manager should not have the power to block such a move unilaterally.

If an employee is not qualified for a desired job, then the company and the employee should jointly try to make the necessary training available. In some instances, the employee might take an in-house course on company time. In others, the company might help to pay for courses at a college or vocational school that the employee takes during his or her personal time.

For most companies, supporting each employee's need for lifelong learning will entail a greater commitment of time and resources to education. Raychem's Saldich passionately believes that it's not enough for an organization's leaders to make more resources available; they must campaign to get employees to use them. "I started out saying to people throughout Raychem that it's now okay to spend more time, money, and energy on learning," Saldich says. "After a year of that, I realized that saying it's okay is not good enough. Our philosophy now is that learning is mandatory and that every one of our people should have a learning or development plan."

Leaders elsewhere seem to agree. Executives from Motorola, who estimate that the company reaps a return of $33 for each dollar it spends on education, think that at least 5% of each employee's time should be spent on training or education. In his book *The Age of Unreason,* Charles Handy says that 20% is reasonable for managers. The "correct" percentage isn't important. (How do you measure it accurately? What about the value of special assignments that are both training and real work?) The point is that continuous learning is imperative, and the organization must be seen by its employees as committed to their development.

But employees must be aware that a shift in the company's direction may mean that the company, for justifiable reasons, suddenly will no longer need their skills. Similarly, people who decide to leave the organization should be able to depart with their heads held high. "The new covenant is about empowering people so they have job choices when circumstances change," says 3Com's Engel. "That's a lot healthier than the traditional blame relationship." Last and far from least among the company's obligations is to provide for no-fault exits.

Whether a departure is voluntary or involuntary, the company must support the affected employee in managing his or her transition. Kenneth M. Alvares, vice president for human resources at Sun Microsystems, puts it this way: "Companies ought to be able to figure out a way to manage all aspects of an employee's career with class or dignity. We do a great job of recruiting people. We also ought to do an equally great job of helping them to manage their careers while they're here. And when people find out it's time to leave this organization, we ought to handle that process with as much class as we do the recruiting process." Alvares does not just mean providing employees with the resources to make and implement a decision to leave. He also means continuing to treat them as valuable people. A company might even emphasize to departing employees that they will be welcomed back should their return serve the company's and their interests in the future.

Controlling the Risks

Creating a career-resilient workforce in the manner we have described is obviously easier said than done. "How can a company realistically give employees much greater freedom to demand new jobs and training?" skeptical managers will undoubtedly ask. "Won't it result in chaos? Isn't there a big danger that it will undermine productivity rather than increase it? Isn't it absurd to think that a company can put the career interests of an individual employee ahead of, say, getting a key product under development to market? And the notion of an insiders' network that will enable people to explore new jobs or careers might sound dandy, but how can we expect already overworked people to spend endless hours talking about what they do with employees in search of themselves?"

All those risks are real. But the short answer is that tomorrow's managers may have no choice. In this age of mobility, companies face even greater dangers if they do not commit themselves to developing self-reliant workers. They risk losing talented people who decide that the drawbacks of staying at such a company outweigh the rewards. This is already a big problem, managers tell us.

Consider the following story, which is replayed every day at scores of Silicon Valley companies. A gifted software engineer is an important member of a team that is developing a major new release of a workstation company's operating system. The engineer, who has been at the company for eight years, has worked on three previous releases and feels stale. In hunting around for a new challenge that will allow her to expand her skills, she discovers an opening in the division that is working on a decoder that the company hopes will give it a foothold in the emerging interactive-TV market.

The head of the division says he'd be thrilled to have her. But the manager of the release project doesn't want to let her go. Her departure will only make it more difficult for the team to meet its ambitious deadline. While interactive TV may be the big market of the future, there won't be a future if the workstation business continues to lose ground, he tells her. A month later, the engineer quits to join a start-up that is developing software for interactive TV. When the company's president learns about her departure, he is dismayed. "I would have overridden the project manager," he says. "If only I had known."

There is another element of our model that we know can make executives nervous: sharing sensitive information with employees. For example, conventional wisdom holds that a company has much to lose and little to gain by telling employees as soon as it has decided to exit a business or shut down an operation. The assumption is that morale and productivity will suffer, people will abandon ship, and the performance of the operation will quickly deteriorate, hurting the company and reducing the operation's value to a potential buyer.

But executives at such companies as Sun, Apple, and 3Com don't think there is a choice. By not sharing such information, a company perpetuates the traditional parent-child relationship with employees, which is no longer tenable, they say. Companies that do share information say that employees have appreciated being treated as adults and have responded in kind. That is what happened with 3Com's buildings-management function, which the company outsourced last year.

In 1992, when 3Com decided to analyze whether it should outsource the function, the company immediately informed the unit's 35 employees. 3Com told them that the decision would take about nine months to make, invited their input, and promised to give them monthly updates. The company also said that if it did decide to go with outside vendors, the employees would have two weeks to decide whether to take two months' severance pay or a temporary position that would tide them over until they found another job inside or outside 3Com. Most of the employees stayed until the end and took the severance pay. But even the few who didn't stick it out kept 3Com informed of their plans so that the company had time to figure out how to manage without them. "It is no coincidence that we were very open with them and they were very open with us," Engel says.

Once organizations accept the inevitability of change, there are systems they can put in place to minimize the risks involved in adopting career-resilience programs. At 3Com, for example, when an employee deemed critical by his or her current manager requests a transfer to an available job, the transfer cannot be denied but the date of the transfer can be negotiated. "If managers resist," says Engel, "they're reminded, `You'd find an answer if that employee quit tomorrow.' There's always an answer."

Raychem and Apple have devised a way to prevent their information networks from consuming much of the time of valuable, overworked employees. They ask people throughout the company to volunteer to give informational interviews. When someone signs up, he or she agrees to do a certain number. Afterward, the person has the option of doing a certain number more or dropping out.

In fact, managers themselves have a lot to gain by participating in such networks. Informational networking enables them to get a look at a broader set of people than they otherwise would in the normal course of their work. As they form task forces or look for people to fill vacant slots, they have more potential candidates. And this process can help their organization achieve something that is increasingly hard to do in this era of churning workforces: build a sense of community.

Gaining Credibility

Unless employees are convinced that a career-resilience program truly is there to serve their interests, they simply won't participate in it. Establishing a career-management center helps a program gain credibility. Sun, Raychem, and Apple have set up such centers as havens where employees can go to work on self-assessment, receive counseling, and attend seminars on, say, how to conduct an effective job interview or how to network. They are places where employees can obtain career reference materials, check on internal and external job openings, contribute to discussions on business strategy, and, most important, learn how to think strategically about their own careers.

The center's location is very important. By making it highly visible and easily accessible, the company sends the message that it is not only acceptable but desirable for employees to use it. The opposite message may be sent by locating it off the beaten track. Raychem and Sun are considering opening satellite centers for employees at other operations who cannot easily use the companies' single centers. Another idea is mobile centers that can serve several sites.

Sun and Apple also use their centers for outplacement. But before doing so, companies should carefully consider the trade-offs, according to several executives. The advantages are that the skills and resources needed for career development and outplacement overlap, and that the dual role makes the center easier to justify financially.

The disadvantage is that, especially in the beginning, employees might infer that the career-resilience program is an outplacement program in disguise—and misinterpret the message when management encourages them to use the center. For that reason, Raychem does not use its center, which opened last September, for outplacement; its sole mission is to enhance career resilience.

To allay employees' initial fears, several companies urge managers to encourage their employees to use the center, but they make it clear that managers do not have the right to know if they have gone there, let alone what transpired. Also, to assure employees that the purpose of the program is to help them manage their careers and not to help their superiors manage them, these companies believe that the career-management process must be separate from the regular performance-appraisal process.

The human dimension is perhaps the most crucial element of any career-resilience program. It is hard to imagine a successful program without counselors and career-research specialists to add a personal touch. Without them, many employees will not be able to use the information effectively; many probably won't even bother to try. Sun, Raychem, and Apple seem to understand that. At their centers, as soon as people walk in, they encounter specialists whose job is to teach them how to use the facilities.

But employees have to believe that the counselor represents their interests. Confidentiality is an obvious concern for people thinking about changing jobs or employers. It is difficult but not impossible for a staff counselor to gain an employee's trust. For example, Carol Dunne, the counselor at Apple's Career Resource Center, has earned such a reputation. But as one manager who uses outside career counselors puts it, "Employees often believe that the human resources department represents management's interests, not theirs." Using outside career counselors can help convince employees that the program really is there to serve them.

There is another advantage to using outside counselors: it can be more cost-effective. Several pioneers in developing career-resilient workers have taken this course.

Sun, Apple, and Raychem have turned to the Career Action Center, a nonprofit organization in Palo Alto, California. Formed in the early 1970s to provide career advice to women in Silicon Valley, the center has become a major institution in the area, serving thousands of Silicon Valley workers. While Sun's, Apple's, and Raychem's career centers are headed by their own employees, the staffs include career-research specialists and counselors from the Career Action Center. The mix of insiders and outsiders makes a powerful combination: the insiders know the company's culture, networks, and operations, and the outsiders bring special expertise, objectivity, and cost flexibility.

Taking the idea of partnership a step further, several midsize Silicon Valley companies led by 3Com are studying the idea of forming a consortium to provide career-resilience services to all their employees. The other companies include Quantum, Aspect Telecommunications, Novell, Octel Communications, Silicon Graphics, Claris, and ESL. There are several reasons why this idea appeals to them. One is that the consortium could afford to provide more services than each company could on its own. A second is that the companies could learn from one another. Finally, an operation relatively immune to the politics and financial ups and downs of any one company might be better able to serve its customers: the employees. The flip side is that it might be harder to integrate such a shared center into each company's mainstream operations.

Some companies, most notably Apple, are using technology to make career-resilience programs widely available and part of the mainstream. Apple is placing large amounts of career information on its "electronic campus," the computer network that ties together its operations. By strolling the right digital paths on the campus, individuals can find a "resource and referral" section that includes lists of books, professional associations, conferences, courses, articles, and other information that Apple employees recommend to their coworkers.

The big advantage of an electronic network over a career center is, of course, accessibility. All employees in Apple's far-flung global operations will have equal access to career-related information. Moreover, computer systems are private, available at the convenience of the user, and easy to update. The danger is that companies and people will become so absorbed by the technology that they will lose sight of the importance of the human dimension. Computer networks may be a superior way to make data widely available. But for individuals trying to remain employable and for executives trying to keep the organization competitive, the patterns and analysis that give meaning to the data are the most valuable tools. And it usually takes personal interactions for them to emerge.

Support from the Top

It almost goes without saying that a career-resilience program won't even get off the ground without visible support from the top. Without the backing of top management, it is implausible to think that managers down the ranks will consistently share with employees their knowledge about strategy and market conditions so that employees can anticipate the company's needs and make career decisions. Nor is it plausible to assume that most managers will automatically buy into the notion that employees should be the eyes and ears of the company, that all employees can and should help shape strategy. There is still too much tradition to be overcome.

Among the companies we studied, Raychem stands out in terms of top management's visible commitment. At the opening ceremony for the career center, Harry O. Postlewait, the company's executive vice president, spoke, and he made sure the audience knew that the CEO, Bob Saldich, would have been there, too, had he not been at home in bed with the flu. Several senior executives, including Saldich, are in the database of people who volunteered to be interviewed by anyone in the company seeking career information.

Saldich and other senior Raychem executives seem to realize that to cultivate a sense of community in a company, management must show that it genuinely cares about its people—even those who have left. That is why Raychem's policy is to try to find places inside the company for those in dead-end jobs or in need of development, to use outplacement only as the last resort, and to tell talented people who leave that they will be welcomed back if possible. This type of caring approach is the only way an organization can get employees to believe that its fate is their responsibility, not just that of top management. It's a new basis for loyalty in today's transient world. Potentially it's a great competitive advantage.

But for a company to reap the full benefits of a career-resilience program, the program must be consistent with and supported by the other elements of the company's business and human resources strategies. There must be systems to support the approach—like a pay system that rewards flexibility, not position in the hierarchy, and flexible work arrangements so that employees have time to improve their skills.

Contrast Raychem with another company we know of that has attracted a lot of naturally self-reliant people. Its top management has yet to prove that it is genuinely committed to helping employees become career resilient, however. While the company generously supports education and training, many of its employees feel that top management doesn't really care whether they stay or leave. And top management gets poor grades on keeping employees informed about the company's business direction and enlisting them in shaping strategy. No wonder employees, when surveyed, cited career development as their main concern.

At some companies, the conviction that helping employees become career resilient should be a top priority still seems largely confined to the human resources department. That's a good start. But the responsibility for building a career-resilient workforce is too important to be relegated to any one department over the long run. That is why the early converts must include top management—so that the conversion process will continue down the ranks until everyone in the company is a believer. This is the approach that has been taken at Raychem. Its human resources department, the original champion, sees itself as a partner with operating management in the effort to create a companywide career-resilience program.

Of course, we realize that many operating managers are lamenting that their jobs are already impossible. On the one hand, the manager is supposed to be the coach, the coordinator, the conductor, and the team leader who supports, advises, and cheers on others so *they* can carry out the task. On the other hand, the manager is still the one held accountable for the final results. "How can you heap even more contradictions and uncertainty on us?" some have said in reaction to our ideas.

The answer is that this is an age of perhaps unprecedented

uncertainty. Those managers who excel at juggling all the contradictions and uncertainties—who figure out how to harness the potentially awesome power of today's mobile workforce—will be the ones whose organizations will prevail in the marketplace.

On a less lofty level, managers have much to gain personally for two reasons. First, the career-resilience approach gives them a way to deal with an increasingly common phenomenon: the employee who is extremely distressed about his or her job—because the job is vulnerable, because it is no longer challenging, or because it offers no advancement opportunities. Second, career resilience is for managers too! Understanding themselves will help them be more effective managers. And by understanding themselves and benchmarking their own skills, managers—like all workers—will be better equipped to manage their own careers.

More than ever, the manager is responsible for creating an environment in which all employees have opportunities to develop so they do not hit a dead end, so their skills remain competitive. This means three things: keeping employees fully informed about the direction of the business; helping each employee understand that the responsibility for ensuring that he or she has competitive skills is ultimately the employee's; and abiding by the employee's right to be a free agent.

The switch from career dependence to career resilience is not only imperative but also inevitable. The company that recognizes this sea change and rides the waves has a huge strategic advantage. Such a company can be swift without being ruthless. It can encourage people to grow, to change, and to learn, and in doing so it becomes better at those things itself. Career resilience replaces a covenant we can no longer keep with one that is in everyone's best interest.

3
Opening the Books

John Case

Senior managers are under continuing competitive pressure to boost their companies' performance, so they naturally keep experimenting with new organizational tools and techniques. Yet most management innovations, such as process reengineering and self-managing teams, have only limited effects on a company's business performance. One problem is that they focus on methods and results but not reasons. They help managers show employees what they must do to improve performance but not why they should care. Then, too, 15 years of new techniques and programs (with no letup in sight) have left a thick residue of cynicism. An initiative that might once have seemed promising to employees is now grist for Dilbert's cartoon mill.

For the last four years, I have been studying a group of companies—most but not all small or midsize—that take a more direct and effective approach to continuous performance improvement. The approach, which has come to be known as open-book management, rests on the simple but potent idea that companies do better when employees care not just about quality, efficiency, or any other single performance variable but about the same thing that senior managers are supposed to care about: the success of the business. Open-book management isn't so much a program as it is a coherent system—a system, moreover, that makes as much sense to people on the shop floor as to those in the executive suite. It builds in the *why* of improved performance from the beginning, so that employees and managers are alike in wanting to discover the *how*. Companies that have implemented open-book management—not an easy process—can more easily learn and employ new tools and techniques precisely because they have first learned how to get people at every level working toward and caring about the objective of business success.

The news about open-book management, which has heretofore found application mainly in smaller and younger companies, is that larger, established organizations are learning that they, too, can adopt and use the system to enhance their performance.

Radical Thinking

The idea at the heart of open-book management—that employees should actively concern themselves with a company's business objectives—has a short pedigree. Frederick W. Taylor, the father of scientific management, would have thought it idiotic. So would generations of traditionally minded executives, middle managers, union leaders, and frontline workers. Recently, though, the idea has gained currency. It underlies some innovative compensation systems, such as gain sharing and employee stock-ownership plans (or stock option plans). And it is implicit in so-called empowerment or employee-involvement programs. Yet such plans and programs are at best only half measures. Owning a few shares of stock does not magically enable employees to think and act like owners; they may want the company to succeed but have no idea how to help it do so. And although teams of workers are often empowered to manage their own work areas, nothing in conventional employee-involvement programs gives those teams a reason to care how the business unit as a whole is doing.

If employees are to act with the organization's business objectives in mind, senior managers must see that three conditions are met. Taken together, these requirements are the building blocks of an open-book system.

First, information previously shared only among those in charge must be seen—and understood—by everyone in the organization. That means all relevant information: not just sales and shipments, for example, but financial goals, budgets, income statements, and forecasts. (Hence the moniker "open book.") Financial information is a business's ultimate measuring stick; it explains the reasons for managerial actions and allows employees to gauge the real success of their own actions. How many companies have, say, reengineered a process only to reengineer it again when the hoped-for financial benefits didn't materialize? If employees aren't privy to the same data as management, they'll decide that management doesn't know what it wants. If they do have the same data, they'll understand as well as management why the initial reengineering didn't work.

Second, managers must hold employees responsible and accountable not just for scheduling their work or hitting quality targets but for making their unit's budget or profit goals. Executives and senior managers—but, in most companies, few lower-level employees—know that a business unit's performance reflects many elements, including sales, cost of goods, labor productivity, and budget variances. Managers responsible for those numbers learn to identify and watch key drivers, to forecast and reforecast, to analyze the budget for possible trade-offs and fallbacks, and to figure out ways they can get more or better work done in the same amount of time. In open-book companies, all employees learn those skills.

Third, in addition to paying employees for their time, the compensation system must reward them for the success of the business. That usually involves creating a sizable bonus plan, often supplemented by stock ownership. Unlike many variable-compensation systems, open-book bonuses are always tied to some easily understood measure (or measures) of business-unit performance, and progress toward the goal is publicly tracked. The system is thus wholly transparent: people see and understand the numbers that determine success, learn the part they play in making those numbers, and know in advance how they will be rewarded if the unit achieves its goals.

Companies can assemble the building blocks of open-book management in a variety of ways, as we'll see when we examine the implementation process. However they are arranged, though, open-book precepts change fundamental assumptions about how an organization works. In open-book companies, managers and employees are expected to contribute to the business's profitability by making (or bettering) their unit's numbers. Managers may still issue instructions—open-book management doesn't abolish hierarchies—but those instructions derive their authority from a logic that's understandable to all. ("We're going to have to redesign that process again because, look here, you can see that our costs didn't drop the way we hoped they would.")

Unlike typical initiatives, which focus on improvements in one narrow area, the new organizational logic can lead to a wide variety of positive changes. An engineering-services company that I studied embarked on open-book management and found that its turf-minded salespeople suddenly began cooperating with one another in pursuit of a better bottom line. A regional bank climbed to market leadership because its tellers were more attuned to the importance of "service with a smile" and to the possibilities of cross-selling. A paint-and-coatings manufacturer saw profits soar after employees, faced with a surge in demand, voluntarily proposed a temporary third shift and figured out how to staff it. Open-book management can incorporate conventional how-to initiatives whenever they make good business sense. A new safety-training program, for instance, is no longer just another management-imposed distraction when it bears an understandable relationship to workers' compensation costs and hence to the bottom line.

Open-book management, like almost every business innovation, has deep roots in companies that have been practicing it intuitively, without giving it a name. Wal-Mart Stores, for example, has always shared numbers with its associates, rewarded them with stock, and encouraged them to think and act as if they were running the store. The approach has begun to spread, however, because of two recent developments.

One is the emergence during the past few years of a role model—a company that explicitly and systematically practices open-book management and thus serves as a benchmark, teacher, and converter of skeptics. ("Hey, this stuff actually works!") As Motorola played this role for TQM, Missouri-based Springfield ReManufacturing Corporation plays it for open-book management. SRC, indeed, is the Johnny Appleseed of this approach. The tale of its Great Game of Business open-book system has been told often in the press—and in the speeches and the popular book by chief executive Jack Stack.[1] Of the 2,500 executives and business owners who have attended seminars on SRC's system, several hundred gather annually for a conference to compare their subsequent experiences.

Second, many highly successful entrepreneurial companies have organized themselves on open-book principles right from the beginning and apparently have gained substantial competitive advantages as a result. Wabash National Corporation, founded in 1985 and now the nation's leading truck-trailer manufacturer, asks employees to complete several hours of business training and holds regular meetings on the shop floor to review the company's financial performance. AES Corporation, a 15-year-old global power producer that was recently listed on the New York Stock Exchange, shares so much financial data with its 2,000 employees that it has declared them all insiders for stock-trading purposes. A particularly powerful example is Physician Sales & Service, a distributor of supplies to doctors' offices, which has climbed from start-up to industry leadership (and more than half a billion dollars in revenues) in only 14 years. Chief executive Patrick C. Kelly believes the company owes much of its success to open-book management. Employees at each of PSS's 65 branches discuss their unit's monthly profit-and-loss statement line by line. The company pays bonuses that are tied not only to profitability but to critical financial measures such as asset days, thereby encouraging employees to monitor those numbers. Employees own a sizable portion of PSS's stock, both as individuals and as members of an employee stock-ownership plan.[2]

Managers who have noticed these developments and find open-book management appealing have nevertheless been left with a fundamental question. They can imagine implementing such a system in a small company or business unit, where the line of sight between an employee's job and the organization's performance is clear and direct. They perhaps can envision creating a new business, like PSS, built on open-book principles from the very beginning. But they have trouble seeing how the philosophy could conceivably be implemented in a large, established corporation. Political and cultural obstacles aside, the line of sight from individual employees' jobs to the large organization's financial performance is obscure. The idea of teaching hundreds or even thousands of people to understand and contribute day in and day out to the company's bottom line can seem hopelessly unrealistic.

And yet several major corporations are now implementing open-book management in sizable divisions or business units. They have indeed encountered significant challenges, mostly stemming from the scale on which they operate, but they have also invented imaginative solutions. In the process, people in these companies have learned to think about business in a new way and have engaged themselves in literally redesigning the way their organizations operate. The experience of the Northeastern Division of R.R. Donnelley & Sons Company is more or less typical and illustrates the problems that managers in other large companies can expect to encounter if they opt for open-book management. The division's experience also illustrates how problems can be solved and what longer-term payoffs open-book management is likely to bring.

Putting It into Practice

R.R. Donnelley & Sons, with 38,000 employees, is the nation's largest commercial printer, and the Northeastern Division, based in Lancaster, Pennsylvania, and run by senior vice president John Hallgren, serves some of Donnelley's biggest customers. The 1,100-employee East Plant churns out millions of copies of *TV Guide, Reader's Digest,* and the *New York Times Magazine.* The 1,000-employee West Plant produces catalogs and telephone directories for customers such as Williams-Sonoma, Bell Atlantic, and Nynex. Donnelley's experiences during the past 15 years could serve as a case study of the changes and pressures that have rocked most big U.S. companies. Once, for example, it could sign a contract with Western Electric to produce yellow-pages directories for telephone companies all over the country. ("The price pressures weren't there," recalls one manager wistfully. "There was a sense of big serving big—and we were the biggest.") Today Donnelley must deal with many more customers, each more concerned about price than in the past, and must compete head-on with printers that have nearly as much high-quality capacity. The sales process, executives say, often turns into a bidding war.

As competitive pressures ratcheted upward, Donnelley pursued the same kind of workplace initiatives that many other companies did: quality circles, a Do It Right the First Time program, single-minute-exchange-of-dies training, and so forth. Those initiatives fell under the general rubric of what the company called High Employee Involvement, or HEI. In printing, as in many other industries today, continuous performance improvement depends mainly on the extent to which frontline employees pay close attention to and make smart decisions about matters such as setup times, print quality, and spoilage.

Donnelley executives believed that HEI programs would help employees learn to focus on those issues and make better decisions about them. On-site managers, however, were never entirely convinced of HEI's benefits. John Bernard, who runs the directory module, says, "We were asking employees to become higher performers, to make decisions that supervisors used to make. But we weren't giving them the tools they needed, like how much does a pound of paper cost, how much does a plate cost?" When Hallgren, Bernard, East Plant manufacturing vice president Geoff Benes, and human resources manager Steve Prosser learned about open-book management by visiting Springfield ReManufacturing Corporation, they were enthusiastic; it seemed to provide both the tools and the motivation that HEI programs lacked. In early 1995, the Northeastern Division formally embarked on a program to implement open-book management. The effort was led by a young manager named Don Robb, recently put in charge of organization development. Robb studied the concept, then hired an outside consulting team to help guide the process.

GETTING BUY-IN

With conventional initiatives, a company's decision to hire consultants is usually the critical step. The consultants hand out the reading materials, teach the classes, and work directly with managers and employees to implement the prescribed changes. With open-book management, consultants typically coach from the sidelines. Because it affects many different parts of a business, open-book management requires the ongoing support and involvement of senior managers. Because it is in many ways a cultural change—it teaches everybody in the organization new ways of thinking and acting—it also requires the ongoing involvement of middle managers and frontline employees. Robb was aware of Donnelley's many previous initiatives, and he knew that people throughout the organization would be skeptical of anything that resembled another change program. So he moved slowly. He talked with people all over the plant about open-book management and gave them reading materials. He invited a sizable group of managers and supervisors to an SRC seminar and arranged for them to stay an extra day. That day, he asked for and got a personal commitment to open-book management from each of them. On his return, he set up a sponsor team of senior managers to ensure resources and support, and a project team of managers and supervisors to plan the implementation. In August 1995, Donnelley kicked off open-book management with a splashy two-day workshop. After that workshop, some 50 people agreed to serve on teams charged with specific implementation tasks.

For nonmanagement employees, Robb decided against any Olympic-style opening ceremony. Instead, he asked one of the implementation teams to oversee a series of intensive, four-hour focus groups that ultimately involved close to 100 people, or nearly one of every ten hourly workers. Facilitators from human resources and other departments explained open-book management, then posed open-ended questions designed to elicit employees' hopes, fears, and concerns. Participants got a chance to offer their own opinions as to whether Donnelley should proceed with open-book management. Most said yes.

COMMUNICATING AND TEACHING KEY NUMBERS

While the groundwork for change is being laid, an open-book company must develop "scoreboards"—vehicles for regular communication of key numbers to the workforce. Business-unit scoreboards include an income statement and a balance sheet, along with any other numbers that are critical to the unit's long-term health. Departmental scoreboards may focus on key operational measures, such as units shipped or defect rates, but they, too, must include a financial component. Because the goal is to enable people to take action in anticipation of future events, scoreboards usually include forecasts of months to come as well as actuals for past months. The scoreboards themselves may be electronic or they may be big bulletin boards or paper handouts. Sony Display Device San Diego, for example, utilizes a protected World Wide Web site (an intranet) to communicate key performance indicators and full profit-and-loss financials to 200 employees on one of its production lines.

At Donnelley, coming up with a unitwide scoreboard proved relatively easy. The corporation as a whole had recently developed a new income statement and balance sheet combined into an economic-value-added (EVA) bottom line. The scoreboard team—one of Robb's implementation task forces—took the statement, modified it slightly for ease of understanding, and added columns for a two-month forecast. The scoreboard is distributed every month over the company's E-mail system. Individual departments, meanwhile, developed scoreboards of their own, tracking numbers such as press efficiencies and revenue generated versus costs.

An open-book scoreboard is based on the shared understanding that a plant's or business unit's numbers are compiled from performance and financial data from each department or operating unit. The departmental scoreboards thus help employees understand the connection between their own efforts and the business unit's results. Amoco Canada Petroleum Company, based in Calgary, Alberta, launched open-book management at about the same time that Donnelley did and is taking steps to teach its 2,300 employees that connection. A pump-maintenance technician, for example, learns that the cost of operating his truck shows up in his facility's vehicle-cost line, which is

Exhibit 3-1   Employees See How Their Decisions Affect Company Income

Sales revenue

-Cost of goods sold
___
Gross margin

-Operating expenses
___
Operating earnings before depreciation

-Depreciation expense
___
Operating earnings

-Interest expense
___
Earnings before income tax

-Income tax expense
___
Net income

aggregated into the operations line on the business unit's income statement. (See Exhibit 3-1.) If a facility sets a goal of lowering vehicle costs, progress toward the goal is tracked on the income statement as well as on an operational chart. Employees learn not just that cost savings are important—any manager could convey that message—but *why* they're important. They also learn that cost savings can't be considered in isolation but only in conjunction with production volumes and revenues.

Open-book companies, of course, have no monopoly on keeping scoreboards.[3] But they do face a peculiar challenge in that they expect everyone in the organization to understand the scoreboard's numbers. Wabash National, the trailer manufacturer, pays a local college professor to teach employees the fundamentals of business, and it offers a wage incentive for attendance. At Donnelley, the team charged with business literacy training rejected formal classes as too boring and inflexible, and instead decided on a two-step process of individual computer-based learning. Computerized instruction dovetailed nicely with an ongoing initiative in the company to teach computer skills—and to provide enough PCs so that every employee would have easy access to one. Also, Donnelley's press operators were already familiar with computer-based learning: a program simulating the operation of the company's giant presses is used for training.

First, Donnelley acquired an interactive-computer-software program called the Yo-Yo Company; it walks employees through the creation of a highly simplified manufacturing business, prompting them to fill out income statements and balance sheets as they go. Next, team representatives worked with David Lough, the lead consultant, to develop a customized business-simulation computer game. The game they created, dubbed Celestial Cheese, allows players to manage a fanciful but highly realistic business—a capital-intensive, multiprocess, service-oriented company operating in an environment remarkably like the printing industry's. Each game takes several hours to complete and requires the player to make a wide variety of strategic and financial decisions over an imaginary ten-year period. The goal—no surprise—is to maximize EVA.

Developing and then rolling out this training program consumed a substantial amount of time during Donnelley's first year of open-book management. Managers and supervisors tested early versions of the software to spot bugs and other problems. The implementation team then identified employees who were computer literate and likely to enjoy playing business-simulation games, and distributed copies to them. This year, the team is rolling the games out to all employees and encouraging them to play at home and during breaks and downtime at the plants. The goal is to give employees a working understanding of the fundamentals of the printing business and hence of the numbers on the plant's monthly scoreboard.

DEVELOPING ACCOUNTABILITY

The hallmark of open-book management isn't just seeing and understanding financial and other numbers. It's taking joint responsibility for making them move in the right direction and thus for helping the company meet its objectives. Like any system of responsibility and accountability, open-book management needs a structure, a fact often missed in press accounts of open-book companies. Casual observers of SRC, for instance, seem to conclude that just knowing the numbers magically enables employees to think and act like senior managers.

In fact, SRC has a well-developed open-book structure of responsibility and accountability, which Donnelley and several other companies have found they can scale up for their larger organizations. SRC's annual planning process begins with strategic priorities (set by senior executives and the board) and sales forecasts (set by the sales staff in consultation with management). Then SRC involves employees at every level in translating the sales forecasts for their respective business units into projected income statements, materials requirements, departmental budgets, and so forth. Individual workers might be assigned to research and estimate electricity costs for the projected level of operation, for example. Departments and work units are expected to discuss—and to make sure everyone understands—the numbers that define the units' role in the plan. During the year, they all meet at least every two weeks to assess their performance against the plan and to forecast the immediate future. They report those results to the corporate staff, who hold similar meetings (often attended by frontline workers and supervisors) to compile, assess, and forecast companywide figures. The process allows each unit as a group to focus on unexplained variances in results. It also encourages people throughout the organization to anticipate and plan for what's going to happen, rather than simply react to what has already occurred.

Donnelley launched that process of collective monitoring and forecasting in early 1996. (Donnelley calls the meetings huddles, in keeping with the sports-related language that seems to characterize open-book management.) Every month, departments from Donnelley's preliminary center to its bindery compile results and make projections, drawing on whatever resources they may need from other parts of the company (sales and accounting information, for example). At the monthly plantwide huddle, representatives from each department build a projected income statement for the current month and two months ahead. Don Robb punches the numbers into a laptop computer as they're called out; the group discusses any significant variances or uncertainties.

The goal of Donnelley's huddles is twofold. One is to engage more people in developing forecasts, thus improving accuracy. The other is to spread accountability for developing and hitting budget targets. Spreading accountability from single managers to groups of employees may be the biggest challenge of open-book management. It usually begins with department-level meetings, which must develop and monitor numbers that come from the ground up. Then employees begin to experiment with ways of affecting the numbers, which may also encourage them to develop better metrics, so that they can get a handle on the most important drivers. Donnelley is in the early stages of that process. People working in the offset-printing module, for example, meet to plan their upcoming work and to discuss possible cost factors, such as overtime, that may affect their unit's performance. Alan Roufa, administrative manager for the East Plant, plans to develop a method for employees to track and forecast costs for each piece of equipment in their departments.

REWARDING EMPLOYEES FOR BUSINESS SUCCESS

Traditional bonus plans are typically designed by compensation consultants, communicated to employees through a handout, and forgotten about until it's time for the checks to arrive. An open-book bonus, by contrast, is pegged to numbers that employees see regularly, that they understand, and that they can affect. The bonus plan is thus an indispensable part of the management system because it answers the inevitable question What's in this for me? As I write, Donnelley's Northeastern Division is in the process of developing an open-book variable-compensation plan. Volunteer teams are identifying key operational drivers for each business unit and are planning a system of quarterly payouts based on targets for those drivers and for a business unit's overall EVA. The new system is slated to be in place in early 1997.

Open-book bonus systems vary widely. SRC budgets for a bonus of 13% of hourly employees' compensation and 18% of managers' compensation, to be paid only if the company hits predetermined income-statement and balance-sheet targets (which vary from year to year). All employees can add another 3% to 15% of pay through 401(k) matching and stock-participation programs. Amoco Canada's Variable Incentive Plan pays out up to 16% of earnings. In 1996, the division's Chicago-based U.S. parent first had to achieve certain financial objectives and the division itself had to attain a return of at least 8.5% on the capital it employed; the size of the bonus then depended on a combination of targets for net earnings and for replacement of reserves. Amoco Canada's business-education team, a group of volunteers much like Donnelley's, uses posters, handouts, and E-mail updates to communicate the numbers every month to the division's 2,300 employees.

The "beat the budget" bonus system at Hexacomb Corporation is a particularly clear example of an open-book system and its effects. Each of the company's seven plants develops a yearly budget in consultation with management. Plant managers discuss budget items at length with employees; scoreboards spread throughout the plants track performance against budget; and plantwide meetings review each month's financials in detail. The bonus plan is simplicity itself: any profits generated by the seven plants beyond the budgeted amount are split fifty-fifty, half going to the company and half into a bonus pool. Employees can collect the bonus, however, only if their own plant beats its budget.

Jim Siegel, manager of the Hexacomb plant in Trenton, Illinois, describes the system:

> Everybody learns how they contribute to the numbers. They learn that if they keep scrap low, if they don't have any rejects, the materials-costs line is going to be lower. We go through returns and allowances every month so that they understand that number, too. And labor: they know that the more hours they work, the higher labor is.
>
> It affects how people work. If you don't expand the product right, you put more pounds [of paper honeycomb material, the plant's product] in the truckload than you need to, and the customer doesn't pay any more for that. So what did that do? It added a certain amount on the materials line and cost us a certain amount on the operating-income line. We also play what-if games. What if you produced three more truckloads a week on regular time because you run your panel line one foot per minute faster? Assuming you had excellent quality and got the regular yield, the labor line doesn't change. You see what happens to the percentage. And you see that it doesn't get the 12% hit from factory overhead. Believe me, it has an effect.

Thanks in part to the new understanding, average productivity at Hexacomb has improved 13% per year for three successive years, and most employees have earned regular, often sizable, bonuses.

GENERATING—AND MAINTAINING—EXCITEMENT

Every manager has seen change initiatives that were introduced with great fanfare slide into obscurity as old priorities reasserted themselves. One reason that open-book management has not succumbed to this pattern at Donnelley's Northeastern Division is that it has the full support of senior managers. A second reason is that implementing open-book management is Don Robb's full-time job—and Robb, an energetic and ambitious young manager, has seen to it that many people throughout the organization are participating in implementation teams or otherwise working on the new management system.

A third reason is that Donnelley has borrowed a powerful technique practiced by other open-book companies: playing games. A game, as these organizations use the term, is simply an initiative focusing on immediate improvement in a given area. Companies call it a game because it has a starting point, a set of rules, a goal, and a reward for winning. Every game focuses on financial results. In effect, a game is open-book management in microcosm. Employees learn that what they do on the job every day affects some number that ultimately affects the financial performance of the business.

Donnelley's gravure pressroom, for example, played a game from March through May of 1996. The goal was to increase press efficiency—a measure of throughput that incorporates quality—by 3% over 1995's performance. Hitting the goal would save the company some $26,000 in costs. Jim Burrows, the department's production supervisor, explains how playing the game changed the way people approached their work:

> Let's say that the schedule allowed eight hours for make-ready on a job. In the past, the press crews felt that as long as they were done in eight hours, they had done a good job. Now they began thinking about ways to do it faster—by bringing out the cylinders ahead of time, for example. People also came to understand the importance of press speed. If they run the press at 25,000 impressions per hour, maybe they can get the job done on schedule. If they figure out how to bump that up to 30,000 impressions per hour, they can cut hours off the job. That creates extra capacity for us, and it allows us to get started on the next job that much sooner.

The game's scoreboard was an Excel spreadsheet that tracked press efficiency and multiplied time savings by a dollar rate established for each of the department's six presses. Because the goal was to beat the previous year by 3%, anything less than a 3% improvement in a given period counted as a loss, whereas anything better counted as a gain. All the workers on the press crews knew exactly where they were in relation to the game's goal at the end of any shift and what they had to accomplish at the start of the next one.

At the end of three months, the department had beaten the goal, and every employee got a bonus of about $75. That modest figure underscores two points about games. One is that it isn't the payoff that counts—it's the game itself. The satisfaction comes primarily from figuring out how to win and then winning. The other, however, is that game playing is dependent on the entire context of open-book management, which teaches employees to understand and care about the business as a whole. How many times could a conventional company ask its employees to take on an additional challenge for a mere $75 plus the satisfaction of winning? In open-book companies, by contrast, people understand that games are mostly a fun and interesting way to learn the business—and that the real payoff will come as the whole business unit improves its performance. Since that first game, indeed, the gravure pressroom has played two more, each with a higher target, and has won both times.

Knowing *Why* Matters

In their book *Lean Thinking: Banish Waste and Create Wealth in Your Corporation* (Simon & Schuster, 1996), James P. Womack and Daniel T. Jones make an important point about open-book management's connection to more conventional change initiatives.

> Readers familiar with the "open-book management" movement in the United States will recall that financial transparency and immediate feedback on results, in the form of monetary bonuses for employees, are its central elements. Thus there is a broad consistency between our approach [which focuses on methods of eliminating *muda,* or waste, from the value stream] and theirs. However, a major question emerges for open-book managers as finances are made transparent and employees are rewarded for performance. How can performance be improved? Sweat and longer hours are not the answer but will be employed if no one knows how to work smarter.

That statement is correct: sweat and longer hours are no substitute for the astute use of technology, for training in modern methods of quality assurance, or for the kind of waste-eliminating techniques that Womack and Jones describe. These are the tools and programs that teach companies and their employees *how* to improve performance. Open-book management provides the *why;* it teaches the connection between specific performance improvements and the company's business objectives. A financial incentive—often missing from conventional how-to programs—is a critically important part of this linkage, even though it is rarely more than a small fraction of an employee's compensation. It says, in effect, "There's a reason for all this extra effort that you're putting in, and that reason is the financial success of the business you work for. As the business produces wealth, that wealth will be shared with you." Such a message goes a long way toward overcoming the cynicism that greets so many change initiatives.

Because open-book management is a system rather than a how-to program, it is not a quick fix. Implementation is a long and cumbersome process, particularly in a large company, and the effect of the new way of thinking on the bottom line may not be apparent for some time. As it happens, Donnelley's East Plant, which is farthest along in open-book management, has performed exceptionally well over the past year, so it has attracted the attention of other Donnelley units around the country. But senior managers are appropriately cautious about attributing too much of that success to open-book management. Rather, they point to small benefits, such as departmental cost savings, gains in press efficiency, and improved forecasting accuracy. That is wise. The power of open-book management lies not in the short term but in the long term, in its ability to change how people think and act, day in and day out. Business success always depends on a wide variety of factors. But this is a constant: whether a company's employees care if it does well, know how to help it do better, and have a reason for learning new skills and attempting new tasks. The people who work for open-book companies give their employers a powerful competitive edge in that department.

Notes

1. Jack Stack, *The Great Game of Business* (New York: Currency/Doubleday, 1992).
2. "Physician Sales & Service, Inc.: June 1992 (A)," Case 395-066 (Boston: Harvard Business School, 1992).
3. See, for example, Robert S. Kaplan and David P. Norton, *The Balanced Scorecard* (Boston: Harvard Business School Press, 1996).

4

Putting Your Company's Whole Brain to Work

Dorothy Leonard and Susaan Straus

Innovate or fall behind: the competitive imperative for virtually all businesses today is that simple. Achieving it is hard, however, because innovation takes place when different ideas, perceptions, and ways of processing and judging information collide. That, in turn, often requires collaboration among various players who see the world in inherently different ways. As a result, the conflict that should take place constructively among ideas all too often ends up taking place unproductively among people who do not innately understand one another. Disputes become personal, and the creative process breaks down.

Generally, managers have two responses to this phenomenon. On the one hand, managers who dislike conflict—or value only their own approach—actively avoid the clash of ideas. They hire and reward people of a particular stripe, usually people like themselves. Their organizations fall victim to what we call the *comfortable clone syndrome:* coworkers share similar interests and training; everyone thinks alike. Because all ideas pass through similar cognitive screens, only familiar ones survive. For example, a new-business development group formed entirely of employees with the same disciplinary background and set of experiences will assess every idea with an unvarying set of assumptions and analytical tools. Such a group will struggle to innovate, often in vain.

On the other hand, managers who value employees with a variety of thinking styles frequently don't understand how to manage them. They act as if locking a group of diverse individuals in the same room will necessarily result in a creative solution to a problem. They over-look the fact that people with different styles often don't understand or respect one another, and that such differences can fuel personal dis-agreements. The "detail guy" dismisses the "vision thing"; the "con-cept man" deplores endless analysis; and the individualist considers the demands of a team an utter waste of time. They simply can't work together without help.

The manager successful at fostering innovation figures out how to get different approaches to grate against one another in a productive process we call *creative abrasion*. Such a manager understands that dif-ferent people have different thinking styles: analytical or intuitive, conceptual or experiential, social or independent, logical or values driven. She deliberately designs a full spectrum of approaches and perspectives into her organization—whether that organization is a team, a work group, or an entire company—and she understands that cognitively diverse people must respect the thinking styles of others. She sets ground rules for working together to discipline the creative process. Above all, the manager who wants to encourage innovation in her organization needs to examine what she does to promote or in-hibit creative abrasion.

We have worked with a number of organizations over the years and have observed many managers who know how to make creative abra-sion work for them. In order to create new ideas and products, such managers actively manage the process of bringing together a variety of people who think and act in potentially conflicting ways.

How We Think

What we call *cognitive differences* are varying approaches to perceiv-ing and assimilating data, making decisions, solving problems, and re-lating to other people. These approaches are *preferences* (not to be con-fused with skills or abilities). For instance, you may prefer to approach problems intuitively but in fact may be better trained to approach them analytically. Preferences are not rigid: most people can draw on a mixture of approaches and do not live their lives within narrow cog-nitive boundaries. We often stretch outside the borders of our pre-ferred operating modes if the conditions are right and the stakes are high enough. That said, we all tend to have one or two preferred hab-its of thought that influence our decision-making styles and our inter-actions with others—for good or for ill.

The most widely recognized cognitive distinction is between left-brained and right-brained ways of thinking. This categorization is more powerful metaphorically than it is accurate physiologically; not all the functions commonly associated with the left brain are located on the left side of the cortex and not all so-called right-brained functions are located on the right. Still, the simple description does usefully capture radically different ways of thinking. An analytical, logical, and sequential approach to problem framing and solving (left-brained thinking) clearly differs from an intuitive, values-based, and nonlinear one (right-brained thinking).

Cognitive preferences also reveal themselves in work styles and decision-making activities. Take collaboration as opposed to independence. Some people prefer to work together on solving problems, whereas others prefer to gather, absorb, and process information by themselves. Each type does its best work under different conditions. Or consider thinking as opposed to feeling. Some people evaluate evidence and make decisions through a structured, logical process, whereas others rely on their values and emotions to guide them to the appropriate action.

The list goes on. Abstract thinkers, for instance, assimilate information from a variety of sources, such as books, reports, videos, and conversations. They prefer learning *about* something rather than experiencing it directly. Experiential people, in contrast, get information from interacting directly with people and things. Some people demand quick decisions no matter the issue, whereas others prefer to generate a lot of options no matter the urgency. One type focuses on details, whereas the other looks for the big picture: the relationships and patterns that the data form.

Not surprisingly, people tend to choose professions that reward their own combination of preferences. Their work experience, in turn, reinforces the original preferences and deepens the associated skills. Therefore, one sees very different problem-solving approaches among accountants, entrepreneurs, social workers, and artists. Proof to an engineer, for example, resides in the numbers. But show a page of numerical data to a playwright, and, more persuaded by his intuition, he may well toss it aside. Of course, assessing people's likely approaches to problem solving only by their discipline can be as misleading as using gender or ethnicity as a guide. Within any profession, there are always people whose thinking styles are at odds with the dominant approach.

The best way for managers to assess the thinking styles of the people they are responsible for is to use an established diagnostic instrument as an assessment tool. A well-tested tool is both more objective and more thorough than the impressions of even the most sensitive and observant of managers. Dozens of diagnostic tools and descriptive analyses of human personality have been developed to identify categories of cognitive approaches to problem solving and communication. All the instruments agree on the following basic points:

- Preferences are neither inherently good nor inherently bad. They are assets or liabilities depending on the situation. For example, politicians or CEOs who prefer to think out loud in public create expectations that they sometimes cannot meet; but the person who requires quiet reflection before acting can be a liability in a crisis.
- Distinguishing preferences emerge early in our lives, and strongly held ones tend to remain relatively stable through the years. Thus, for example, those of us who crave certainty are unlikely ever to have an equal love of ambiguity and paradox.
- We can learn to expand our repertoire of behaviors, to act outside our preferred styles. But that is difficult—like writing with the opposite hand.
- Understanding others' preferences helps people communicate and collaborate.

Managers who use instruments with the credibility of the Myers-Briggs Type Indicator® (MBTI®) or the Herrmann Brain Dominance Instrument (HBDI) find that their employees accept the outcomes of the tests and use them to improve their processes and behaviors. (See "Identifying How We Think: The Myers-Briggs Type Indicator and the Herrmann Brain Dominance Instrument.")

Identifying How We Think: The Myers-Briggs Type Indicator and the Herrmann Brain Dominance Instrument

The Myers-Briggs Type Indicator (MBTI) is the most widely used personality-assessment instrument in the world. Designed by a mother-and-daughter team, Isabel Briggs Myers and her mother Katharine Cook Briggs, the MBTI is based on the work of Carl Jung. Myers and Briggs developed the instrument during World War II on the hypothesis that an

---

Myers-Briggs Type Indicator and MBTI are registered trademarks of Consulting Psychologists Press, Inc.

understanding of personality preferences might aid those civilians who were entering the workforce for the first time to find the right job for the war effort. The instrument conforms to standard testing conventions and, at last count in 1994, had been taken by more than two and a half million people around the world. The MBTI is widely used in business, psychology, and education, as well as in career counseling.

The MBTI uses four different pairs of attributes to create a matrix of 16 personality types:

- Extraversion Versus Introversion. The first pair looks at where people prefer to focus their attention. These E/I descriptors focus on the source of someone's mental energy: extraverts draw energy from other people; introverts draw energy from themselves. Each finds the other's preferred operating conditions enervating.

- Sensing Versus "Intuition." The second pair identifies how one absorbs information. "Sensors" (S) gather data through their five senses, whereas "iNtuitives" (N) rely on less direct perceptions, such as patterns, relationships, and hunches. For example, when asked to describe the same painting, a group of S's might comment on the brush strokes or the scar on the subject's left cheek, whereas a group of N's might imagine from the troubled look in the subject's eyes that he lived in difficult times or suffered from depression.

- Thinking Versus Feeling. The third pair indicates how one makes decisions once information is gathered. Feeling types (F) use their emotional intelligence to make decisions based on values—their internal sense of right and wrong. Thinking types (T) tend to make decisions based on logic and "objective" criteria—their assessment of truth and falsehood.

- Judging Versus Perceiving. The fourth pair describes how a person is oriented toward the outer world. Judging types (J) have a high need for closure. They reach conclusions quickly based on available data and move on. Perceiving types (P) prefer to keep their options open. They wait until they have gathered what they consider to be enough information to decide. J's crave certainty, and P's love ambiguity.

To read descriptions of the personality types identified in the MBTI, see the matrix on the following page.

Ned Herrmann created and developed the Herrmann Brain Dominance Instrument (HBDI) while he was a manager at General Electric. Starting his research with large groups within GE, he expanded it over 20 years through tens of thousands of surveys and has validated the data with prominent psychometric research institutions, including the Educational Testing Service.

The MBTI®			
Sensing Types (S)		**Intuitive Types (N)**	
Thinking (T)	Feeling (F)	Feeling (F)	Thinking (T)
Introverts (I) — Judging (J)			
ISTJ Serious, quiet, earn success by concentration and thoroughness. Practical, orderly, matter-of-fact, logical, realistic, and dependable. Take responsibility.	ISFJ Quiet, friendly, responsible, and conscientious. Work devotedly to meet their obligations. Thorough, painstaking, accurate. Loyal, considerate.	INFJ Succeed by perseverance, originality, and desire to do whatever is needed or wanted. Quietly forceful, conscientious, concerned for others. Respected for their firm principles.	INTJ Usually have original minds and great drive for their own ideas and purposes. Skeptical, critical, independent, determined, often stubborn.
Introverts (I) — Perceiving (P)			
ISTP Cool onlookers—quiet, reserved, and analytical. Usually interested in impersonal principles, how and why mechanical things work. Flashes of original humor.	ISFP Retiring, quietly friendly, sensitive, kind, modest about their abilities. Shun disagreements. Loyal followers. Often relaxed about getting things done.	INFP Care about learning, ideas, language, and independent projects of their own. Tend to undertake too much, then somehow get it done. Friendly, but often too absorbed.	INTP Quiet, reserved, impersonal. Enjoy theoretical or scientific subjects. Usually interested mainly in ideas, little liking for parties or small talk. Sharply defined interests.
Extraverts (E) — Perceiving (P)			
ESTP Matter-of-fact, do not worry or hurry, enjoy whatever comes along. May be a bit blunt or insensitive. Best with real things that can be taken apart or put together.	ESFP Outgoing, easygoing, accepting, friendly, make things fun for others by their enjoyment. Like sports and making things. Find remembering facts easier than mastering theories.	ENFP Warmly enthusiastic, high-spirited, ingenious, imaginative. Able to do almost anything that interests them. Quick with a solution and to help with a problem.	ENTP Quick, ingenious, good at many things. May argue either side of a question for fun. Resourceful in solving challenging problems, but may neglect routine assignments.
Extraverts (E) — Judging (J)			
ESTJ Practical, realistic, matter-of-fact, with a natural head for business or mechanics. Not interested in subjects they see no use for. Like to organize and run activities.	ESFJ Warm-hearted, talkative, popular, conscientious, born cooperators. Need harmony. Work best with encouragement. Little interest in abstract thinking or technical subjects.	ENFJ Responsive and responsible. Generally feel real concern for what others think or want. Sociable, popular. Sensitive to praise and criticism.	ENTJ Hearty, frank, decisive, leaders. Usually good at anything that requires reasoning and intelligent talk. May sometimes be more positive than their experience in an area warrants.

The HBDI measures a person's preference both for right-brained or left-brained thinking and for conceptual or experiential thinking. These preferences often correspond to specific professions. Engineers, for example, consistently describe themselves as analytical, mathematical, and logical, placing them on the left end of the continuum. Artists, in contrast, describe themselves as emotional, spatial, and aesthetic, placing them on the right end of the continuum.

The following charts show how the different preferences combine into four distinct quadrants and how one can use the chart to analyze teams with different cognitive preferences:

Composite One: *The Homogeneous Team*

The chart above shows that everyone in the group approaches problems and challenges with the same emphasis on correctness. As engineers, the members of the team know how to do things correctly. Although the quality of their work is excellent, the members are difficult to work with. They have their own ways of doing things, and they reject variations from set standards. As a corporate function, the team has long enjoyed a captive audience in the company. Recently, members found themselves in trouble when the company restructured and other functions in the organization were allowed to outsource engineering.

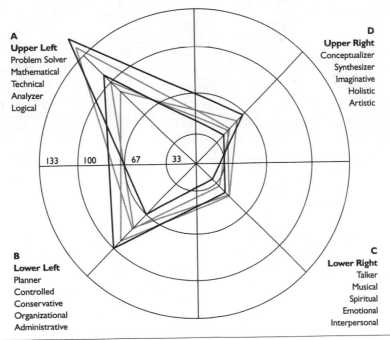

A
Upper Left
Problem Solver
Mathematical
Technical
Analyzer
Logical

D
Upper Right
Conceptualizer
Synthesizer
Imaginative
Holistic
Artistic

133   100   67   33

B
Lower Left
Planner
Controlled
Conservative
Organizational
Administrative

C
Lower Right
Talker
Musical
Spiritual
Emotional
Interpersonal

Composite Two: The Heterogeneous Team

The Management Services Group includes managers from information technology, the mail room, and the cafeteria. Although members share such goals as an orientation toward quality, they encounter a wide range of business problems. The manager's dominant thinking style is in the lower right quadrant: a natural facilitator, she develops people, listens empathetically, and fosters a spirit of respect among her reports. Her leadership unified what had been a fragmented, inefficient collection of functions. Members regard one another as resources, enjoy the group's diversity, and take great pride in their work.

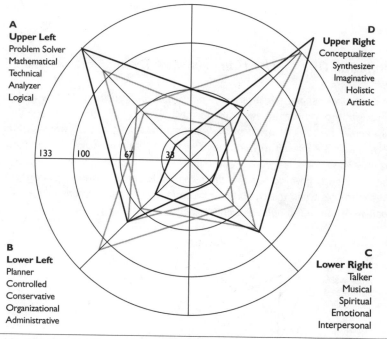

A
Upper Left
Problem Solver
Mathematical
Technical
Analyzer
Logical

D
Upper Right
Conceptualizer
Synthesizer
Imaginative
Holistic
Artistic

133   100   67   33

B
Lower Left
Planner
Controlled
Conservative
Organizational
Administrative

C
Lower Right
Talker
Musical
Spiritual
Emotional
Interpersonal

How We Act

All the assessment in the world means nothing unless new understanding brings different actions. Instruments such as the MBTI® and the HBDI will help you understand yourself and will help others understand themselves. The managerial challenge is to use the insights that these instruments offer to create new processes and encourage new behaviors that will help innovation efforts succeed.

UNDERSTAND YOURSELF

Start with yourself. When you identify your own style, you gain insight into the ways your preferences unconsciously shape your style of leadership and patterns of communication. You may be surprised to discover that your style can stifle the very creativity you seek from your employees. Consider the experiences of two managers of highly creative organizations. Each was at odds with his direct reports—but for very different reasons.

Jim Shaw, executive vice president of MTV Networks, is a left-brained guy in a right-brained organization. Said Shaw:

> I have always characterized the creative, right-brained, visionary-type people here as dreamers. What I've realized is that when a dreamer expressed a vision, my gut reaction was to say, `Well, if you want to do that, what you've got to do is A, then B, then you have to work out C, and because you've got no people and you've got no satellite up-link, you'll have to do D and E.' I've learned that saying that to a creative type is like throwing up on the dream. When I say that stuff too soon, the dreamer personalizes it as an attack. I've learned *not* to put all of the things that need to be done on the table initially. I can't just blurt it all out—it makes me look like a naysayer. What I've learned to do is to leak the information gradually, then the dreamer knows that I am meeting him halfway.

Jerry Hirshberg, president of Nissan Design International, ran into precisely the opposite problem. Hirshberg discovered that some of his employees craved the very kind of structure that he personally abhorred. Before this epiphany, he inundated them with information and expected creativity in return. In short, he tried to manage his employees the way *he* would have wanted to be managed. Hirshberg found, however, that a few individuals reacted to every suggestion with a "yes, but . . ." Initially, he interpreted such hesitancy as an anti-innovation bias. But he eventually realized that some of his employees preferred to have more time both to digest problems and to construct logical approaches to his intuitively derived ideas. Given a bit of extra time, they would return to the project with solid, helpful, and insightful plans for implementation. Ironically, it was their commitment to the success of the initiative that caused the employees to hesitate: they wanted the best possible result. Hirshberg recognized that their contributions were as critical as his own or those of any of the other "right-brainers" in the company.

Both Shaw and Hirshberg came to realize that their own cognitive preferences unconsciously shaped their leadership styles and communication patterns. In fact, their automatic reactions initially stifled the very creativity they sought from their employees. And note that it was just as important for the predominantly right-brained manager to recognize the contributions of the logicians as it was for the left-brained manager to acknowledge the organic approach of the visionaries. Except in theoretical models, creativity is not the exclusive province of one side or the other.

If you want an innovative organization, you need to hire, work with, and promote people who make you uncomfortable. You need to understand your own preferences so that you can complement your weaknesses and exploit your strengths. The biggest barrier to recognizing the contributions of people who are unlike you is your own ego. Suppose you are stalled on a difficult problem. To whom do you go for help? Usually to someone who is on the same wavelength or to someone whose opinion you respect. These people may give you soothing strokes, but they are unlikely to help spark a new idea. Suppose you were to take the problem instead to someone with whom you often find yourself at odds, someone who rarely validates your ideas or perspectives. It may take courage and tact to get constructive feedback, and the process may not be exactly pleasant. But that feedback will likely improve the quality of your solution. And when your adversary recovers from his amazement at your request, he may even get along with you better because the disagreement was clearly intellectual, not personal.

FORGET THE GOLDEN RULE

Don't treat people the way you want to be treated. Tailor communications to the receiver instead of the sender. In a cognitively diverse environment, a message sent is not necessarily a message received. Some people respond well to facts, figures, and statistics. Others prefer anecdotes. Still others digest graphic presentations most easily. Information must be delivered in the preferred "language" of the recipient if it is to be received at all.

For example, say you want to persuade an organization to adopt an open office layout. Arguments appealing to the analytical mind would rely on statistics from well-documented research conducted by objective experts that prove that open architecture enhances the effectiveness of communication. Arguments geared toward the action-oriented type would answer specific questions about implementation: How long will the office conversion take? Exactly what kind of furniture is needed? What are the implications for acoustics? Arguments aimed at people-oriented individuals would focus on such questions as, How does an open office affect relationships? How would this setup affect morale? and Are people happy in this sort of setup? Arguments crafted for people with a future-oriented perspective would include graphics as well as artists' renderings of the proposed environment. In short, regardless of how you personally would prefer to deliver the message, you will be more persuasive and better understood if you formulate messages to appeal to the particular thinking style of your listener.

CREATE "WHOLE-BRAINED" TEAMS

Either over time or by initial design, company or group cultures can become dominated by one particular cognitive style. IBM, in the days when it was known as "Big Blue," presented a uniform face to the world; Digital Equipment prided itself on its engineering culture. Such homogeneity makes for efficient functioning—and limited approaches to problems or opportunities. Companies with strong cultures can indeed be very creative, but within predictable boundaries: say, clever marketing or imaginative engineering. When the market demands that such companies innovate in different ways, they have to learn new responses. Doing so requires adopting a variety of approaches to solving a problem—using not just the right brain or the left brain but the *whole* brain.

Consider the all-too-common error made by John, a rising star in a large, diversified instrument company: he forfeited an important career opportunity because he failed to see the need for a whole-brained team. Appointed manager of a new-product development group, John had a charter to bring in radically innovative ideas for products and services for launch in three to six years. "Surprise me," the CEO said.

Given a free hand in hiring, John lured in three of the brightest M.B.A.'s he could find. They immediately went to work conducting industry analyses and sorting through existing product possibilities, applying their recently acquired skills in financial analysis. To complete the team, John turned to the pile of résumés on his desk sent to him by human resources. All the applicants had especially strong quantitative skills, and a couple were engineers. John was pleased. Surely a group of such intelligent, well-trained, rigorous thinkers would be able to come up with some radical innovations for the company. Ignoring advice to hire some right-brained people to stimulate different ideas, he continued to populate his group with left-brained wizards. After 18 months, the team had rejected all the proposed new projects in the pipeline on the basis of well-argued and impressively documented financial and technical risk analysis. But the team's members had not come up with a single new idea. The CEO was neither surprised nor pleased, and the group was disbanded just short of its second anniversary.

In contrast, Bob, a successful entrepreneur embarking on his latest venture, resisted the strong temptation to tolerate only like-minded people. He knew from his prior ventures that his highly analytical style alienated some of his most creative people. Despite his unusual degree of self-awareness, Bob came within a hair's breadth of firing a strong and experienced manager: Wally, his director of human resources. According to Bob, after several months on board, Wally appeared to be "a quart and a half low." Why? Because he was inattentive in budget meetings and focused on what Bob perceived as trivia—day care, flextime, and benefits. Before taking action, however, Bob decided to look at the management team through the lens of thinking styles. He soon realized that Wally was exactly the kind of person he needed to help him grow his small company. Wally contributed a key element that was otherwise missing in the management team: a sensitivity to human needs that helped the company foresee and forestall problems with employees. So Bob learned to meet Wally halfway. Describing his success in learning to work with Wally, he told us, "You would have been proud of me. I started our meetings with five minutes of dogs, kids, and station wagons." Although the concern Wally demonstrated for the workers in the company did not eliminate union issues completely, it did minimize antagonism toward management and made disputes easier to resolve.

The list of whole-brained teams that continue to innovate successfully is long. At Xerox PARC, social scientists work alongside computer scientists. For instance, computer scientist Pavel Curtis, who is creating a virtual world in which people will meet and mingle, is working with an anthropologist who understands how communities form. As a result, Curtis's cyber-space meeting places have more human touches and are more welcoming than they would have been had they been designed only by scientists. Another example is the PARC PAIR (PARC Artist In Residence) program, which links computer scientists with artists so that each may influence the other's perceptions and representations of the world. At Interval Research, a California think tank dedicated to multimedia technologies, Director David Liddle invites leaders from various disciplines to visit for short "sabbaticals." The purpose is to stimulate a cross-fertilization of ideas and approaches to solving problems. The resulting exchanges have helped Interval Research create and spin off several highly innovative start-ups. And Jerry Hirshberg applies the whole-brain principle to hiring practices at Nissan Design by bringing designers into his organization in virtual pairs. That is, when he hires a designer who glories in the freedom of pure color and rhythm, he will next hire a very rational, Bauhaus-trained designer who favors analysis and focuses on function.

Complete homogeneity in an organization's cognitive approach can be very efficient. But as managers at Xerox PARC, Interval Research, and Nissan Design have learned, no matter how brilliant the group of individuals, their contributions to innovative problem solving are enhanced by coming up against totally different perspectives.

LOOK FOR THE UGLY DUCKLING

Suppose you don't have the luxury of hiring new people yet find your organization mired in a swamp of stale thinking patterns. Consider the experience of the CEO of the U.S. subsidiary of a tightly controlled and conservative European chemical company. Even though the company's business strategy had never worked well in the United States, headquarters pushed the CEO to do more of the same. He knew he needed to figure out a fresh approach because the U.S. company was struggling to compete in a rapidly changing marketplace. But his direct reports were as uniformly left-brained as his superiors in Europe and were disinclined to work with him to figure out new solutions.

Rather than give up, the CEO tested thinking preferences further down in the organization. He found the cognitive disparity that he needed in managers one layer below his direct reports—a small but dynamic set of individuals whose countercultural thinking patterns had constrained their advancement. In this company, people with right-brained preferences were seen as helpful but were not considered top management material. They were never promoted above a certain level.

The CEO changed that. He elevated three managers with right-brained proclivities to the roles of senior vice president and division head—lofty positions occupied until then exclusively by leftbrained individuals. The new executives were strong supporters of the CEO's intentions to innovate and worked with him to develop new approaches to the business. They understood that their communication strategy with headquarters would be critical to their success. They deliberately packaged their new ideas in a way that appealed to the cognitive framework of their European owner. Instead of lecturing about the need to change and try new ideas as they had in the past, the Americans presented their ideas as ways of solving problems. They supported their positions with well-researched quantitative data and with calculated anticipated cost savings and ROI—and described how similar approaches had succeeded elsewhere. They detailed the specific steps they would follow to succeed. Within two years, the U.S. subsidiary embarked on a major organizational redesign effort that included such radical notions as permitting outside competition for internal services. The quality of internal services soared—as did the number of innovations generated by the company in the United States.

MANAGE THE CREATIVE PROCESS

Abrasion is not creative unless managers make it so. Members of whole-brained teams don't naturally understand one another, and they can easily come to dislike one another. Successful managers of richly diverse groups spend time from the outset getting members to acknowledge their differences—often through a joint exploration of the results of a diagnostic analysis—and devise guidelines for working together before attempting to act on the problem at hand. Managers who find it awkward or difficult to lead their groups in identifying cognitive styles or in establishing guidelines can usually enlist the aid of someone who is trained in facilitation.

People often feel a bit foolish creating rules about how they will work together. Surely, the thinking goes, we are all adults and have years of experience in dealing with group dynamics. That, of course, is the problem. Everyone has practiced dysfunctional behavior for years. We learn to value politeness over truth at our mothers' knees. (Who hasn't mastered the art of the white lie by age 16?) We often discount an argument if it has an element of emotion or passion. We opt out if we feel ignored—people with unappreciated thinking styles learn to sit against the wall during meetings (the organizational back-of-the-bus). And we usually don't even notice those behaviors because they are so routine.

But the cost of allowing such behaviors to overtake a group is too high. Bob Meyers, senior vice president of interactive media at NBC, uses a sports analogy to make the point: "On a football team, for example, you have to use all kinds of people. Like the little, skinny guy who can only kick the ball. He may not even look as if he belongs on the team. This guy can't stand up to the refrigerator types that play in other positions. But as long as he does his job, he doesn't need to be big. He can just do what he does best. The catch is that the team needs to recognize what the little skinny guy can do—or they lose the benefit of his talent."

Managing the process of creative abrasion means making sure that everyone is at the front of the bus and talking. Some simple but powerful techniques can be helpful. First, clarify why you are working together by keeping the common goal in front of the group at all times. "If the goal is a real-world one with shared accountability and timetables attached," one manager observed, "then everyone understands the relevance of honoring one another's differences."

Second, make your operating guidelines explicit. Effective guidelines are always simple, clear, and concise. For example, one group set up the following principles about handling disagreements: "Anyone can disagree about anything with anyone, but no one can disagree without stating the reason" and "When someone states an objection, everyone else should listen to it, try to understand it, treat it as legitimate, and counter with their reasons if they don't agree with it." Some principles are as simple as "discuss taboo subjects," "verify assumptions," and "arrive on time with your homework done."

Third, set up an agenda ahead of time that explicitly provides enough time for both *divergent* discussion to uncover imaginative alternatives and *convergent* discussion to select an option and plan its implementation. Innovation requires both types of discussion, but people who excel at different types can, as one manager observed, "drive each other nuts." Another manager said, "If you ask people comfortable with ambiguity whether they prefer A or B, they will ask, 'How about C?'" Meanwhile, the people who crave closure will be squirming in their seats at the seemingly pointless discussion. Moreover, if one approach dominates, the unbalanced group process can risk producing an unacceptable or unfeasible new product, service, or change. Clearly allocating time to the two different types of discussion will contain the frustrations of both the decisive types, who are constantly looking at their watches wanting the decision to be made now, and the ambiguous types, who want to be sure that all possible avenues for creativity have been explored. Otherwise, the decisive members generally will pound the others into silence by invoking time pressures and scheduling. They will grab the first viable option rather than the best one. Or if the less decisive dominate, the group may never reach a conclusion. Innovation requires both divergent and convergent thinking, both brainstorming and action plans.

DEPERSONALIZE CONFLICT

Diverse cognitive preferences can cause tremendous tensions in any group, yet innovation requires the cross-fertilization of ideas. And because many new products are systems rather than stand-alone pieces, many business projects cannot proceed without the cooperation of people who receive different messages from the same words and make different observations about the same incidents. The single most valuable contribution that understanding different thinking and communication styles brings to the process of innovation is taking the sting out of intellectual disagreements that turn personal.

Consider the experience of the product manager of a radically new product for a medical supplies company. Facing a strict deadline of just 14 months to design and deliver a new surgical instrument, the manager's team needed to pull together fast. Design felt misled by marketing, however, and manufacturing couldn't understand design's delay in choosing between two mechanical hinges. The disagreements turned personal, starting with "you always . . ." and ending with "irresponsible ignorance." Two months into the project, the manager began to wonder whether he should disband the team and start over again. But he knew that his boss, the vice president of marketing, would not agree to extend the deadline. "I was desperate," he recalled. "I decided to make one last attempt at getting them to work together."

The manager decided to experiment with an off-site gathering of his staff, including sessions diagnosing cognitive preferences. When they returned to work, the team members used the new language they had learned to label their differences in opinion and style. "At first, using the terms was kind of a joke," the manager recalled. "They'd say things like, `Well, of course I want the schedule right now. I'm a J!' Yet you could tell that people were really seeing one another in a different light, and they weren't getting angry." The team made its deadline;

perhaps even more important, several members voluntarily joined forces to work on the next iteration of the product. This willingness to work together generated more value for the company than just "warm fuzzies." Critical technical knowledge was preserved in one small, colocated group—knowledge that would have been scattered had project members dispersed to different product lines. Moreover, keeping part of the team together resulted in a rapid development time for the derivative product.

People who do not understand cognitive preferences tend to personalize conflict or avoid it—or both. The realization that another person's approach is not wrongheaded and stubborn, but merely predictably different, diffuses anger. For example, at Viacom, a planning session involving two managers had ground to a halt. One manager simply wouldn't buy into the idea that the other was presenting. Suddenly, the presenter slapped his head and said, "Oooohhh! I get it! You're left-brained! Give me half an hour to switch gears, and I'll be right back. Let me try this one more time." The left-brained manager laughingly agreed—he understood the paradigm—and the meeting resumed with the presenter armed with quantitative data and a much more cohesive and logical presentation. Establishing that kind of effective two-way communication led to a common understanding of the issues at hand and, ultimately, a solution.

Understanding that someone views a problem differently does not mean you will agree. But an important element in understanding thinking styles is recognizing that no one style is inherently better than another. Each style brings a uniquely valuable perspective to the process of innovation, just as each style has some negatives associated with it. Stereotypes of the cold-hearted logician, the absent-minded, creative scientist, and the bleeding-heart liberal have some basis in reality. If people even partially internalize the inherent value of different perspectives, they will take disagreements less personally and will be better able to argue and reach a compromise or a consensus with less animosity. They will be open to the possibility that an alien view of the world might actually enhance their own. They will be better equipped to listen for the "a-ha" that occurs at the intersection of different planes of thought.

Caveat Emptor

Personality analysis of the type we describe is no more than a helpful tool, and it has many limitations. The diagnostic instruments measure only one aspect of personality: preferences in thinking styles and communication. They do not measure ability or intelligence, and they do not predict performance. Neither the MBTI® nor the HBDI measure other qualities that are critical to successful innovation such as courage, curiosity, integrity, empathy, or drive.

Preferences tend to be relatively stable, but life experiences can affect them. For example, repeated application of the MBTI® over a period of years has revealed a tendency for people to drift from a thinking style toward a feeling style when they have children. For the most part, however, studies done with both the MBTI® and the HBDI suggest that people retain their dominant preferences throughout a variety of work and social circumstances.

One critical warning label should be attached to any of these diagnostic instruments: only trained individuals should administer them. Not only can results be incorrectly interpreted (for instance, what are intended to be neutral descriptions of preferences might be labeled "right" or "wrong" behavior), but they can also be misused to invade people's privacy or to stereotype them. Of course, it is a human tendency to simplify in order to comprehend complexities; we stereotype people all the time on the basis of their language, dress, and behavior. Because these diagnostics have the weight of considerable psychological research behind them, however, they can be dangerous when misused. Without structured, reliable diagnoses, judgments are likely to be superficial and flawed. And without a substantial investment of time and resources, managers can't expect abrasion to be creative.

One of the paradoxes of modern management is that, in the midst of technical and social change so pervasive and rapid that it seems out of pace with the rhythms of nature, human personality has not altered throughout recorded history. People have always had distinct preferences in their approaches to problem solving. Why then is it only now becoming so necessary for managers to understand those differences? Because today's complex products demand integrating the expertise of individuals who do not innately understand one another. Today's pace of change demands that these individuals quickly develop the ability to work together. If abrasion is not managed into creativity, it will constrict the constructive impulses of individuals and organizations alike. Rightly harnessed, the energy released by the intersection of different thought processes will propel innovation.

Executive Summaries

A New Mandate for Human Resources

Dave Ulrich

Should we do away with HR? In recent years, a number of people who study and write about business—along with many who run businesses—have been debating that question. The debate arises out of serious and widespread doubts about HR's contribution to organizational performance.

Dave Ulrich acknowledges that HR, as it is configured today in many companies, is indeed ineffective, incompetent, and costly. But he contends that it has never been more necessary. The solution, he believes, is to create an entirely new role for the field that focuses it not on traditional HR activities, such as staffing and compensation, but on business results that enrich the company's value to customers, investors, and employees.

Ulrich elaborates on four broad tasks for HR that would allow it to help deliver organizational excellence. First, HR should become a partner in strategy execution. Second, it should become an expert in the way work is organized and executed. Third, it should become a champion for employees. And fourth, it should become an agent of continual change. Fulfilling this agenda would mean that every one of HR's activities would in some concrete way help a company better serve its customers or otherwise increase shareholder value.

Can HR transform itself on its own? Certainly not—in fact, the primary responsibility for transforming the role of HR, Ulrich says, belongs to the CEO and to every line manager who works with the HR staff. Competitive success is a function of organizational excellence, and senior managers must hold HR accountable for delivering it.

The Core Competence of the Corporation

C.K. Prahalad and Gary Hamel

In the early 1980s, GTE was positioned to become a major player in the information technology industry. NEC was much smaller and had no experience as an operating telecommunications company. Today NEC is among the top five companies in telecommunications, semiconductors, and mainframes. GTE has become essentially a telephone company with a position in defense and lighting products.

What happened? NEC built and nurtured a group of core competencies. GTE, on the other hand, couldn't agree on which competencies to base its strategy. It organized itself around strategic business units, which by nature underinvest in core competencies, imprison resources, and bind innovation.

A company's competitiveness derives from its core competencies and core products (the tangible results of core competencies). Core competence is the collective learning in the organization, especially the capacity to coordinate diverse production skills and integrate streams of technologies. It is also a commitment to working across organizational boundaries.

Organizing around core competencies requires a radical change in corporate organization. The first step requires identifying core competencies, which meet these three requirements: they provide potential access to a wide variety of markets, make a contribution to the customer benefits of the product, and are difficult for competitors to imitate.

The next step is to redesign the architecture of the company and provide an impetus for learning from alliances and a focus for internal development. Management should ask: How long could we preserve our competitiveness if we did not control this core competence? How central is this core competence to customer benefits? What opportunities would be foreclosed if we lost this competence?

Competing on Capabilities: The New Rules of Corporate Strategy

George Stalk Jr., Philip Evans, and Lawrence E. Shulman

In the 1980s, companies discovered time as a new source of competitive advantage. In the 1990s, they will discover that time is only one piece of a more far-reaching transformation in the logic of competition. Using examples from Wal-Mart and other highly successful companies, Stalk, Evans, and Shulman of the Boston Consulting Group provide managers with a guide to the new world of "capabilities-based competition."

In today's dynamic business environment, strategy too must become dynamic. Competition is a "war of movement" in which success depends on anticipation of market trends and quick response to changing customer needs. In such an environment, the essence of strategy is *not* the structure of a company's products and markets but the dynamics of its behavior. To succeed, a company must weave its key business processes into hard-to-imitate strategic capabilities that distinguish it from its competitors in the eyes of customers.

A capability is a set of business processes strategically understood—for example, Wal-Mart's expertise in inventory replenishment, Honda's skill at dealer management, or Banc One's ability to "out-local the national banks and out-national the local banks." Such capabilities are collective and cross-functional—a small part of many people's jobs, not a large part of a few. Finally, competing on capabilities requires strategic investments in support systems that span traditional SBUs and functions and go far beyond what traditional cost-benefit metrics can justify.

A CEO's success in building and managing a company's capabilities will be the chief test of management skill in the 1990s. The prize: companies that combine scale and flexibility to outperform the competition.

What Is Strategy?

Michael E. Porter

Today's dynamic markets and technologies have called into question the sustainability of competitive advantage. Under pressure to improve productivity, quality, and speed, managers have embraced tools such as TQM, benchmarking, and reengineering. Dramatic operational improvements have resulted, but rarely have these gains translated into sustainable profitability. And gradually, the tools have taken the place of strategy.

In his five-part article, Michael Porter explores how that shift has led to the rise of mutually destructive competitive battles that damage the profitability of many companies. As managers push to improve on all fronts, they move further away from viable competitive positions.

Porter argues that operational effectiveness, although necessary to superior performance, is not sufficient, because its techniques are easy to imitate. In contrast, the essence of strategy is choosing a unique and valuable position rooted in systems of activities that are much more difficult to match.

Porter thus traces the economic basis of competitive advantage down to the level of the specific activities a company performs. Using cases such as Ikea and Vanguard, he shows how making trade-offs among activities is critical to the sustainability of a strategy.

Whereas managers often focus on individual components of success such as core competencies or critical resources, Porter shows how managing *fit* across all of a company's activities enhances both competitive advantage and sustainability. While stressing the role of leadership in making and enforcing clear strategic choices, Porter also offers advice on how companies can reconnect with strategies that have become blurred over time.

Changing the Role of Top Management: Beyond Strategy to Purpose

Christopher A. Bartlett and Sumantra Ghoshal

Structure follows strategy. And systems support structure. In the high-growth environment of post-World War II, a whole management doctrine rose up around these two aphorisms. But today the business environment has changed. Overcapacity is the norm, markets are global, lines separating businesses are fuzzy, and, with equal access to technology, early-market-entry advantages are minimal. A change in management doctrine is needed to match this new landscape.

After five years researching 20 leading European, U.S., and Japanese companies, the authors concluded that the role of top management must change. Using these companies as examples, they prescribe the necessary transformation. First, senior managers must change their own priorities and ways of thinking. Beyond designing corporate strategy, they must shape a shared institutional purpose. They must expand their focus from devising formal structures to developing organizational processes. And more than just managing systems, they must develop people.

Top management's role in the companies researched already reflects the changes the authors prescribe. Consequently, 3M has managed to retain an innovative capability and an entrepreneurial spirit despite its $14 billion bulk. ABB transformed two "also-ran" companies into the leading competitors in the global power-equipment industry at a time when world markets were in recession. And big, complex companies like AT&T,

Royal Dutch/Shell, Intel, Andersen Consulting, Kao, and Corning are doing well despite what some people predicted as the inevitable decline of large corporations.

Building Your Company's Vision

James C. Collins and Jerry I. Porras

Companies that enjoy enduring success have a core purpose and core values that remain fixed while their strategies and practices endlessly adapt to a changing world. The rare ability to balance continuity and change—requiring a consciously practiced discipline—is closely linked to the ability to develop a vision. Vision provides guidance about what to preserve and what to change. A new prescriptive framework adds clarity and rigor to the vague and fuzzy vision concepts at large today.

The framework has two principal parts: *core ideology* and *envisioned future*. Core ideology combines an organization's core values and core purpose. It's the glue that holds a company together as it grows and changes. Core values are an organization's essential and enduring tenets—the values it would hold even if they became a competitive disadvantage; core purpose is the organization's fundamental reason for being.

The second component of the vision framework is the envisioned future. First, a company must identify bold stretch goals; then it should articulate vivid descriptions of what it will mean to achieve them. Henry Ford set the goal of democratizing the automobile, then told the world, "When I'm through . . . everyone will have one. The horse will have disappeared from our highways"—an imaginative stretch for the time.

Unfortunately, the usual vision statement is fuzzy and inspires only boredom. But managers who master a discovery process to identify core ideology can link their vision statements to the fundamental dynamic that motivates truly visionary companies—that is, the dynamic of preserving the core and stimulating progress.

Changing the Way We Change

Richard Tanner Pascale, Mark Millemann, and Linda Gioja

More and more companies struggle with growing competition by introducing improvements into every aspect of performance. But the treadmill keeps moving faster, the companies keep working harder, and results improve slowly or not at all.

The problem here is not the improvement programs. The problem is that the whole burden of change typically rests on so few people. Companies achieve real agility only when every function and process—when every *person*—is able and eager to rise to every challenge. This type and degree of fundamental change, commonly called *revitalization* or *transformation*, is what many companies seek but rarely achieve because they have never before identified the factors that produce sustained transformational change.

The authors identify three interventions that will restore companies to vital agility and then keep them in good health: incorporating employees fully into the principal business challenges facing the company; leading the organization in a different way in order to sharpen and maintain incorporation and constructive stress; and instilling mental disciplines that will make people behave differently and then help them sustain their new behavior.

The authors discovered these basic sources of revitalization by tracking the change efforts of Sears, Roebuck & Company, Royal Dutch Shell, and the United States Army. The organizations used these interventions to alter the way their people experienced their own power and identity, as well as the way they dealt with conflict and learning. As at Sears, Shell, and the U.S. Army, any major shift in those four elements will create a landmark shift in any organization's operating state or culture.

Breaking the Functional Mind-Set in Process Organizations

Ann Majchrzak and Qianwei Wang

Thousands of businesses have reengineered work to focus employees on processes that clearly provide value to customers. They have done away with their functional silos and created process-complete departments, each able to perform all the cross-functional tasks required to meet customers' needs. Although many of those efforts have paid off in the form of lower costs, shorter cycle times, and greater customer satisfaction, many others have resulted in disappointment.

What went wrong? In some companies, managers may have underestimated the actions necessary to transform the way employees work with one another. Many of them may have assumed that simply switching to process-complete departments would forge people instantly into a team.

The authors argue that this assumption is wrong. In a study of U.S. electronics manufacturers, they found that process-complete departments had faster cycle times than functional departments *only* when their managers had used one or more of four ways to cultivate collective responsibility: structuring jobs with overlapping responsibilities, basing rewards on unit performance, laying out the work area so that people can see one another's work, and designing procedures so that employees with different jobs are better able to collaborate.

The particular method or number of methods employed did not seem to matter. What did was whether a company had adopted *any* of them. And it mattered considerably: process-complete departments that had embraced one or more of the methods had significantly faster cycle times than those that hadn't.

Fix the Process, Not the Problem

Harold Sirkin and George Stalk Jr.

In 1983, a paper company was on the verge of filing Chapter 11 for a subsidiary, a mill acquired two years earlier that was losing more than $1 million a month. One year later, the paper mill was just about breaking even. Today it is a highly profitable operation.

What happened? Everyone at the mill became a problem solver. Both managers and mill workers learned to take the initiative not just for identifying problems but also for developing better ways to fix problems and improve products. The key to the mill's success: a multiyear learning process in which employees developed four progressively more sophisticated problem-solving loops:

- Fix-as-fail—solving problems after they occur.
- Prevention—keeping problems from occurring.
- Root causes—discovering what is truly causing a problem.
- Anticipation—solving problems before they occur and finding innovative solutions to customers' problems.

Drawing on the paper mill's experience, the authors illustrate the four loops and suggest ways managers can help this organizational learning process move ahead. Paradoxically, a key to becoming a faster, smoother running operation is to start slow and avoid the temptation to jump to root-cause problem solving before you truly understand what your problems are or have freed up the resources to go after them.

Good Communication That Blocks Learning

Chris Argyris

The new but now familiar techniques of corporate communication—focus groups, surveys, management-by-walking-around—can block organizational learning even as they help solve certain kinds of problems. These techniques *do* help gather simple, single-loop information. But they also promote defensive reasoning by encouraging employees to believe that their proper role is to criticize management while the proper role of management is to take action and fix whatever is wrong.

Worse yet, they discourage double-loop learning, which is the process of asking questions not only about objective facts but also about the reasons and motives behind those facts. Double-loop learning encourages people to examine their own behavior, take personal responsibility for their own action and inaction, and surface the kind of potentially threatening or embarrassing information that can produce real change.

The problem is not that employees run away from this kind of organizational self-examination, the problem is that no one asks it of them. Managers focus so earnestly on "positive" values—employee satisfaction, upbeat attitude, high morale—that it would strike them as destructive to make demands on employee self-awareness. Yet employees dig deeper and harder into the truth when the task of scrutinizing the organization includes looking at their own roles, responsibilities, and potential contributions to corrective action.

The criteria for effectiveness have risen sharply in recent years. Today managers need employees who think constantly and creatively about the needs of the organization, employees with as much intrinsic motivation and as deep a sense of organizational stewardship as any company executive.

The Employee-Customer-Profit Chain at Sears

Anthony J. Rucci, Steven P. Kirn, and Richard T. Quinn

It is no longer news that over the past five years, Sears, Roebuck and Company has radically changed the way it does business and dramatically improved its financial results. But the Sears transformation was more than a change in marketing strategy. It was also a change in the logic and culture of the business.

Led by CEO Arthur Martinez, a group of more than 100 top-level Sears executives spent three years rebuilding the company around its customers. In rethinking what Sears was and what it wanted to become, these managers developed a business model of the company—the employee-customer-profit model—and an accompanying measurement system that tracks success from management behavior through employee attitudes to customer satisfaction and financial performance.

The basic elements of the model are not difficult to grasp. In retailing, there is a chain of cause and effect running from employees' behavior to customers' behavior to profits, and it is not hard to see that behavior depends primarily on attitude. Still, implementing the model is not easy. One problem is measuring such soft data as customer and employee "satisfaction." Not surprisingly, many companies do not have a realistic grasp of what their customers and employees actually think and do. By means of an ongoing process of data collection, analysis, modeling, and experimentation, Sears does. Moreover, the work of creating the model and the measures has made such demands on managers that it has changed the way they think and behave. And now that cultural change is spreading throughout the company.

Managing Professional Intellect: Making the Most of the Best

James Brian Quinn, Philip Anderson, and Sydney Finkelstein

A corporation's success today lies more in its intellectual and systems capabilities than in its physical assets. Managing human intellect—and converting it into useful products and services—is fast becoming the critical executive skill of the age. It is therefore surprising that so little attention has been given to that endeavor.

This oversight is especially surprising because professional intellect creates most of the value in the new economy, in service and manufacturing industries alike. But few managers have systematic answers to even these basic questions: What is professional intellect? How can we develop it? How can we leverage it?

According to James Brian Quinn and his coauthors, an organization's professional intellect operates on four levels: cognitive knowledge, advanced skills, systems understanding, and self-motivated creativity. They argue that organizations that nurture self-motivated creativity are more likely to thrive in the face of today's rapid changes.

The authors offer best practices for developing professional intellect: recruiting the best people, forcing development and increasing challenges, and evaluating and weeding. And they illustrate how organizations as diverse as Merrill Lynch and NovaCare have leveraged professional intellect by linking new software tools, incentive systems, and organizational designs. The authors contend that organizations can tailor themselves to the particular way their professional intellect creates value by inverting the traditional hierarchical structure and by creating self-organizing networks.

Toward a Career-Resilient Workforce

Robert H. Waterman Jr., Judith A. Waterman, and Betsy A. Collard

Virtually everyone agrees that the old covenant between employer and employee—under which companies offered at least a measure of job security in exchange for adequate performance and some exhibition of loyalty—is dead. Some management thinkers argue that instead of the traditional focus on *employment,* the focus should now be on *employability.* That means having the competitive skills required to find work, when you need it, wherever you can find it. But that notion does not spell out what responsibilities companies now have to employees and vice versa.

In this article, the authors say the answer is a new covenant under which the employee and the employer share responsibility for maintaining—even enhancing—the individual's employability both inside *and outside* the company. It is the company's responsibility to provide employees with the tools, the open environment, and the opportunities for assessing and developing their skills. It is the employee's responsibility to manage his or her own career and to show some commitment to the company's purpose and community for as long as he or she works there. The result is a group of self-reliant workers—or a *career-resilient* workforce—and a company that can thrive in an era in which the skills needed to remain competitive are constantly changing.

Some companies, such as Apple Computer, Sun Microsystems, Raychem, and 3Com, are already moving in this direction. And from their progress so far, the authors can discern basic ingredients all programs should include and pitfalls to avoid.

The company that embraces career resilience will have a huge strategic advantage. By encouraging people to grow, to change, and to learn, it will do those things better itself.

Opening the Books

John Case

For years, small companies have experimented with forms of open-book management. Open-book systems have smoothed change efforts by giving workers the *why* instead of just the *how* of initiatives; they have enabled employees to think like owners.

Now divisions of large organizations such as R.R. Donnelley & Sons and Amoco Canada are finding that opening the books can work for them, too. It isn't easy, and companies must adapt the principles to their own situations. AES Corporation, for example, found that it had to declare all its employees "insiders" when it went public.

One of the reasons for large companies' interest in open-book management is the success of a role-model company, Missouri-based Springfield ReManufacturing. Leaders of divisions of large companies have been able to visit and ask questions. Other early adopters are also showing competitive advantages. Among them are Wabash National, now the nation's leading truck and tractor manufacturer, and Physician Sales & Service, a distributor of supplies to doctors' offices.

Open-book principles are the same whether a company is large or small: every employee must receive all relevant financial information and be taught to understand it; managers must hold employees accountable for making their unit's goals; and the compensation system must reward everyone for the overall success of the business.

Hexacomb Corporation is one large organization that has done well. Workers at the company's seven plants are inspired by a system of splitting profits over budget fifty-fifty: half goes to the company and half to the bonus pool. Such companies are learning the benefits of having everyone working to push the numbers in the right direction.

Putting Your Company's Whole Brain to Work

Dorothy Leonard and Susaan Straus

Innovate or fall behind: the competitive imperative for virtually all businesses today is that simple. Responding to that command is difficult, however, because innovation takes place when different ideas, perceptions, and ways of processing and judging information collide. And it often requires collaboration among players who see the world differently. As a result, the conflict that should take place constructively among ideas all too often ends up taking place unproductively among people. Disputes become personal, and the creative process breaks down.

The manager successful at fostering innovation figures out how to get different approaches to grate against one another in a productive process the authors call *creative abrasion*. The authors have worked with a number of organizations over the years and have observed many managers who know how to make creative abrasion work for them. Those managers understand that different people have different thinking styles: analytical or intuitive, conceptual or experiential, social or independent, logical or values driven, They deliberately design a full spectrum of approaches and perspectives into their organizations and understand that cognitively diverse people must respect other thinking styles. They set ground rules for working together to discipline the creative process. Above all, managers who want to encourage innovation need to examine what *they* do to promote or inhibit creative abrasion.

About the Contributors

Philip Anderson is an associate professor of business administration at the Amos Tuck School of Business at Dartmouth College. He is on the editorial boards of four academic journals, and is also the editor of the *Organization Science Electronic Letters,* the first department of a major academic business journal to be published via the Internet. He is co-author of *Managing Strategic Innovation and Change: A Collection of Readings* and *Inside the Kaisha: Demystifying Japanese Business Behavior* (HBS Press, 1997).

Chris Argyris is the James Bryant Conant Professor of Education and Organizational Behavior at Harvard University. He has consulted for numerous organizations, and has served as special consultant to the governments of England, France, Germany, Italy, and Sweden on problems of executive development and productivity. Professor Argyris is the author of 300 articles and 30 books, including *Knowledge for Action: A Guide to Overlooking Barriers to Organizational Change* and *On Organizational Learning.* In 1994, Professor Argyris was the recipient of the Academy of Management's Award for Lifetime Contributions to the Discipline of Management.

Christopher A. Bartlett holds the MBA Class of 1966 Chair of Business Administration at Harvard Business School. He is the author or coauthor of six books, including, with Sumantra Ghoshal, *The Individualized Corporation* and *Managing Across Borders: The Transnational Solution* (HBS Press, 1989), which has been translated into nine languages and adapted into a video program. His articles have appeared in journals such as the *Harvard Business Review, Sloan Management Review, California*

Management Review, McKinsey Quarterly, Strategic Management Journal, Academy of Management Review, and the *Journal of International Business Studies*.

John Case is a veteran observer and analyst of the business world, and a nationally known expert on the subject of open-book management. He is the author of five books and collaborator on two others, and has written for a variety of periodicals. He is currently president of Open-Book Management Inc. and editor-at-large for *Inc.* magazine.

Betsy A. Collard is the director of Strategic Development at the Career Action Center (CAC). Prior to joining CAC, she worked for the State of California as a career consultant and served as a dean at Stanford University and the University of California, Santa Cruz. With more than twenty years of experience in the career management field, Ms. Collard speaks, writes, and consults on a wide range of issues relating to career self-reliance and workforce resilience. She is the author of *The High-Tech Career Book* and the coauthor of the article "Career Resilience in Changing Workplace."

James C. Collins is the coauthor of *Built to Last: Successful Habits of Visionary Companies*. He operates a management research and teaching laboratory in Boulder, Colorado.

Philip Evans is a senior vice president in The Boston Consulting Group's (BCG) Boston office, and worldwide co-leader of BCG's Media Convergence practices, which focuses on the strategic implications of the economics of information. He writes on business strategy, and is the coauthor of "Strategy and the New Economics of Information" (*Harvard Business Review*), which was awarded a McKinsey Prize.

Sydney Finkelstein is an associate professor of business administration at the Amos Tuck School of Business at Dartmouth College, where he teaches courses on business policy and managing mergers and acquisitions. He is also faculty director for Custom Executive Education Programs at Tuck, and a member of the faculty at Duxx Graduate School of Business Leadership in Monterrey, Mexico. An expert on mergers and acquisitions, and on managing knowledge flows in organizations, Professor Finkelstein currently serves on the editorial review boards of the *Strategic Management Journal, Administrative Science Quarterly*, and *Organization Science*. He is a consulting editor for the *Journal of Management* and is the author of *Strategic Leadership: Top Executives and Their Effects on Organizations*.

Sumantra Ghoshal holds the Robert P. Bauman Chair in Strategic Leadership at the London Business School and serves as the director of the school's Strategic Leadership Research Programme. He has authored nine books including *The Differentiated Network: Organizing the Multinational for Value Creation* and, with Christopher A. Bartlett, *Managing Across Borders: The Transnational Solution* (HBS Press, 1989), which was translated into nine languages and adapted into a video program. His most recent book, *The Individualized Corporation*, won the 1997 Igor Ansoff Award.

Linda Gioja has worked for twelve years in the development of consulting practices related to accelerated cultural change and leadership in large organizations. As a principal with CSC Index, she consulted with the senior executives of companies such as Sears, Hughes Space and Communications, and Allstate. She recently left CSC Index to pursue the facilitation of collaboration among business executives, regulators, and environmentalists who are seeking to create innovative solutions to environmental problems. Ms. Goija, Richard Pascale, and Mark Millemann continue to explore the ideas expressed in the article "Changing the Way We Change" and are working on a book that explores organizations as complex adaptive systems.

Gary Hamel is the founder and chairman of Strategos, a company dedicated to helping its clients get to the future first. He is the Thomas S. Murphy Distinguished Research Fellow at the Harvard Business School, as well as a visiting professor of strategic and international management at the London Business School. Called "the world's reigning strategy guru" by the *Economist*, Mr. Hamel has originated such concepts as strategic intent, core competence, corporate imagination, strategic architecture, and industry foresight. With C.K. Prahalad, he authored *Competing for the Future* (HBS Press, 1994), hailed by numerous business journals as one of the decade's most influential business books, and wrote several articles for the *Harvard Business Review*.

Steven P. Kirn is the vice president of education and development for Sears, Roebuck and Co. In that role, he is responsible for managing a variety of programs aimed at enhancing Sears' intellectual capital and organizational transformation. Mr. Kirn was previously a principal in the firm of William M. Mercer, and held earlier positions in executive development and college teaching.

Dorothy Leonard is the William J. Abernathy Professor of Business Administration at the Harvard Business School, where she has taught in MBA and executive education programs since 1983. She researches and consults about new technology commercialization, new product development, and the transfer of knowledge across geographic, cultural, and cognitive boundaries. She has published more than two dozen articles based on field research in academic journals such as *Organization Science*. Her book *Wellsprings of Knowledge* (HBS Press, 1995) illustrates the managerial activities that sustain innovation and enhance strategic technological capabilities.

Ann Majchrzak is a professor of information systems in the Information and Operations Management Department of the Gordon S. Marshall School of Business, University of Southern California. She is a nationally prominent authority on the management and design of information-intensive technologies that jointly optimize organizational, individual, strategic, and technological needs and capabilities. In addition to being the author of numerous articles, Dr. Majchrzak's publications include *The Human Side of Factory Automation*, *Human Aspects of CAD*, and *Methods for Policy Research*.

Mark Millemann is the founder of Millemann & Associates, a management consulting firm based in Portland, Oregon. He also acts as a senior advisor to CSC Index with an emphasis on transformational change and building an agile organization. He has extensive experience as a consultant to CEOs and executive teams of major global corporations, including Sears, Hughes Space and Communications, BP Oil, Borg Warner Automotive, and Illinois Power Company. He is a recognized thought leader, whose thinking is grounded in practical case work with clients. In addition to his active client work, he is a regular lecturer at executive conferences. His recent publications focus on leading sustainable transformational change.

Richard Tanner Pascale is an associate fellow of Oxford University and a visiting scholar of the Santa Fe Institute. He was a member of the faculty at the Stanford Graduate School of Business for twenty years. He is a leading business consultant worldwide, a best-selling author and a respected scholar. Dr. Pascale is the coauthor of *The Art of Japanese Management*, a New York Times best-seller, and author of *Managing on the Edge*. His seminal *Harvard Business Review* article, "Zen and the Art of Management," won a McKinsey Award. He has worked closely with two dozen CEOs and top management teams of *Fortune* 500 firms engaged in organizational transformation.

Jerry I. Porras is the Lane Professor of Organizational Behavior and Change at the Stanford Graduate School of Business. He is the director of Stanford's executive program in leading and managing change and teaches MBA courses in visionary companies, leadership, organization development, and interpersonal dynamics. Dr. Porras is the author of *Stream Analysis: A Powerful New Way to Diagnose and Manage Organizational Change,* and coauthor of *Built to Last: Successful Habits of Visionary Companies,* which has been translated into thirteen languages. He has served on the editorial boards of the *Academy of Management Journal, Academy of Management Review, Journal of Applied Behavioral Science, Business Review,* and the *Journal of Organizational Change Management.*

Michael E. Porter is the C. Roland Christensen Professor of Business Administration at the Harvard Business School and a leading authority on competitive strategy. He has served as a counselor on competitive strategy to many leading U.S. and international companies and speaks widely on issues of international competitiveness to business and government audiences throughout the world. Professor Porter is the author of fourteen books including *Competitive Advantage: Creating and Sustaining Superior Performance,* which won the Academy of Management's 1985 George R. Terry Book Award, as well as *The Competitive Advantage of Nations.* Actively involved in economic policy initiatives, his most recent work focuses on the development of America's inner cities.

C.K. Prahalad is the Harvey C. Fruehauf Professor of Business Administration at the University of Michigan Business School. His research focuses on the role and value added of top management in large diversified, multinational corporations and he has consulted with numerous firms worldwide. Mr. Prahalad is the coauthor with Gary Hamel of *Competing for the Future,* named the Best-Selling Business Book of the Year in 1994 by *Business Week* and currently translated into fourteen languages. He is also the author of many award-winning articles, such as "Strategic Intent" and "The Core Competence of the Corporation," which won McKinsey Prizes in 1989 and 1990 respectively.

James Brian Quinn is the William and Josephine Buchanan Professor of Management, Emeritus, at the Amos Tuck School at Dartmouth. He is a recognized authority in the fields of strategic planning, the management of technological change, entrepreneurial innovation, and the impact of technology in the service sector. Professor Quinn has published extensively on both corporate and national policy issues involving strategic planning, research and development management, management of entrepreneurial organizations, and the impact of technology in services. His book *Intelligent Enterprise* won both the American Publisher's Association Award as Book of the Year in Business and Scholarship, and the American Academy of Management's Book of the Year Award for Outstanding Contribution to Advancing Management Knowledge.

Richard T. Quinn, the president of The Quinn Consulting Group, Inc., was formerly the vice president of total performance indicators at Sears and is generally regarded as a key architect of the Sears transformation. As the vice president of total performance indicators, also known as the balanced scorecard, he was responsible for the development and implementation of a corporate strategic measurement system that statistically predicts the impact of several layers of leading employee and customer measurements on financial results. Quinn is a member of the Strategic Advisory Board for the Saratoga Institute and frequently works with human resource groups committed to leading change in their organizations. The Quinn Consulting Group, Inc. focuses on helping organizations that are interested in rapid and continual organizational transformation, particularly in service organizations.

Anthony J. Rucci is the executive vice president, administration, of Sears Roebuck and Co. He is the senior administrative officer at Sears with company-wide responsibility for law, human resources, quality labs, ethics, strategic sourcing, diversity, aviation, facilities management, and Sears University. Mr. Rucci has served on the board of directors of numerous professional organizations, been a member of the White House Fellows regional selection panels, and has been on the editorial boards of the *Journal of Applied Psychology, Human Resource Planning,* and *Human Resource Management.* In 1996, he was named to *HR Executive* magazine's honor roll of top human resource executives in the country, and was also elected as a fellow of the National Academy of Human Resources.

Lawrence E. Shulman is a senior vice president and director of The Boston Consulting Group in Chicago. He joined BCG in 1979, after earning his MBA at Harvard Business School, where he was a Baker Scholar.

Harold Sirkin is a senior vice president of The Boston Consulting Group (BCG) where he is a practice leader of BCG's information technology practice area. He is a founding member of BCG's operational effectiveness practice area and has authored several publications on operations and organization. Mr. Sirkin has worked with a wide range of clients on strategic issues, including global strategy, process reengineering, and customer service.

George Stalk Jr. is a senior vice president of The Boston Consulting Group (BCG) and focuses his professional practice on international and time-based competition. He speaks regularly to business and industry associations on time-based competition and other topics. Based in Toronto, he has served as a consultant to a variety of leading manufacturing, retailing, and technology- and consumer-oriented companies. Mr. Stalk is the coauthor of the critically acclaimed *Competing Across Time* and *Kaisha: The Japanese Corporation* and his articles have appeared in numerous business publications.

Susaan Straus is a management consultant and internationally recognized speaker who specializes in organizational change and management team effectiveness. Her research with thousands of managers and executives in *Fortune* 500 companies has focused on the effect of cognitive preference and on the abilities of leaders, managers, and teams as they face the challenges of the need to innovate in a rapidly changing workplace. An experienced conflict mediator and process facilitator, she leads Performance Resources, whose mission it is to elicit excellent performance in organizations committed to transformation and renewal.

Dave Ulrich is a professor of business administration at the University of Michigan where he is on the core faculty of the Michigan Executive Program, codirector of Michigan's Human Resource Executive Program, and Advanced Human Resource Executive Program. Mr. Ulrich is also a partner in Global Consulting Alliance. He is the author of numerous books including, most recently, *Human Resource Champions* (HBS Press, 1997).

Qianwei Wang is a Ph.D. candidate in the Department of Sociology at the University of Southern California. Her current research interests include quantitative methods, social organization, and health.

Judith A. Waterman is a U.S. Nationally Certified Career Counselor and the managing director of Career Management Group, which she founded in 1977. Her company works with individuals to promote both their professional development and their noncareer fulfillment. She is the author of several computer programs as well as many publications. Her more recent writing includes *Introduction to the FIRO-B*, a definitive interpretation to one of the more commonly used personnel development instruments. Besides her individual and corporate practices, Ms. Waterman is a founder and director of MindSteps, Inc., a company that designs, programs, tests, and sells software for an individual's use on a company's intranet.

Robert H. Waterman Jr. pursues a varied business career as author, corporate director, consultant, nonprofit trustee, and new venture manager. His books include *In Search of Excellence, The Renewal Factor, Adhocracy: The Power to Change,* and *What America Does Right.* In 1986, after twenty-one years at McKinsey & Company, Inc., where he was senior director, Mr. Waterman founded The Waterman Group, Inc., a firm that supports his research, writing, new venture, and consulting activities. Mr. Waterman has taught in the MBA program at IMD, a graduate business school in Lausanne, Switzerland, and is a founder and the chairman of the board of MindSteps, Inc., a company that develops and sells career resilience software for an individual's use on a company's intranet.

Index